PR Writer's toolbox:

Blueprints for Success
Second Edition

JOSEPH BASSO   RANDY HINES   SUZANNE FITZGERALD

Kendall Hunt
publishing company

Cover image © 2013 Thinkstock.
Cover design courtesy of Caitlin Ward.
Practical Tips and Toolbox clipart © Shutterstock, Inc.
Photo Credits:
  Courtesy of Claudia M. Cuddy
  © Gordon R. Wenzel
  Courtesy of Jonathan H. FitzGerald

Special thanks to Claudia M. Cuddy for her help with proofreading.

Kendall Hunt
publishing company

www.kendallhunt.com
Send all inquiries to:
4050 Westmark Drive
Dubuque, IA 52004-1840

Copyright © 2005 by Randy Hines and Joseph Basso
Copyright © 2014 by Joseph Basso, Randy Hines, and Suzanne FitzGerald

ISBN 978-1-4652-1322-8

Printed in the United States of America
10 9 8 7 6 5 4 3 2

Contents

Grammar Depot eBook Information   v

1

Strategic Writing   1

2

Print Media Writing   11

3

Business Writing: How to Write Letters, Email and Reports   35

4

Business Writing: How to Write Newsletters,
E-Newsletters and Intranet Entries   57

5

Social Media Writing   69

6

Electronic Media Writing   87

7

Persuasive Writing   101

8

Feature Writing   119

9

Advertising Copywriting   139

10

Speech Writing   159

11

Law for PR Writing   175

12

PR Campaign Writing   191

Index   203

Contents

Grammar Depot & Book Information v

1
Strategic Writing 1

2
Print Media Writing 11

3
Business Writing: How to Write Letters, Email and Reports 35

4
Business Writing: How to Write Newsletter,
E-Newsletters and Intranet Entries 57

5
Social Media Writing 65

6
Electronic Media Writing 87

7
Persuasive Writing 101

8
Feature Writing 113

9
Advertising Copywriting 133

10
Speech Writing 155

11
Law for PR Writing 175

12
PR Campaign Writing 191

Index 207

Grammar Depot eBook Information

JOSEPH BASSO   RANDY HINES   SUZANNE FITZGERALD

- ▶ Features the parts of speech and how to use them.
- ▶ Shows many examples of good grammar use.
- ▶ Reviews easy-to-access punctuation guide.
- ▶ Defines rules of grammatical structure.
- ▶ References common misused words and phrases.
- ▶ Features your access code (see inside front cover).

Chapter 1

Strategic Writing

"The pen is mightier than the sword."

Edward Bulwer-Lytton

When English playwright Edward Bulwer-Lytton coined his now famous line in 1839, he could only dream of a world where skilled wordsmiths would use instant communication channels to disseminate powerful and poignant information. These words, disseminated with lightning speed, would become the backbone of modern society, shaping our economic, political and social worlds. In today's information society, the ability to craft effective prose transcends most other skills professionals bring to the workforce. Now a majority of employees, especially those working in communication-specific professions, must have a mastery of the written word.

Unfortunately, countless studies show just the opposite. An overwhelming number of employers report their employees have difficulty in crafting readable, easy-to-understand messages. Yet scores of young professionals enter the workforce each year graduating from highly respected colleges and universities lacking the most strategic of all business tools—the ability to write. Simply put, today anyone working in business must be skilled at planning and designing a message.

To construct effective prose, writers must first master the use of the tools of the trade. These tools include a thorough understanding of the rules of grammar and punctuation, a willingness to plan and organize thoughts and ideas before starting the writing process, and a firm understanding of proper sentence and paragraph construction to avoid miscommunication and shoddy work.

However, business also recognizes that hiring highly skilled and technical workers does not always result in getting someone with polished writing skills. In fact, business reports just the opposite. While economic capital has increased in the areas of computing skills, the fundamental skills of writing have continued to diminish. Unfortunately, such unflattering assessments are also directed at the staff of communication departments. This creates an enormous burden on companies that rely on written communication skills to advance their business efforts.

Furthermore, persuasion rests at the foot of most business writing. Writers must use carefully crafted words to move audiences to action. To accomplish this, writers must understand attitude formation and how writers build public opinion.

Public opinion exists only after an issue or incident affects a number of people who hold similar attitudes. People must know an issue before they form any opinion about it. In general, people appear more certain about what they want rather than how they can get it. Therefore, public opinion formation begins when the writer can carefully design a message that resonates with the audience and points it toward a result.

A business plan begins with a single idea. However, presenting that idea and gaining acceptance generally begins with the written word. That process, though, begins with a thorough understanding of sentence construction.

Building effective prose requires a firm grasp of the fundamentals of the English language. Writers who fully understand proper word usage, punctuation and syntax have in their literary arsenal the firepower to effectively and efficiently communicate with the written word.

The process of writing intimidates many who bellow that they lack the fundamentals to properly communicate in writing. Somehow these people lose sight of the fact that good writers develop their skills from a commitment to hard work rather than some natural gift. Taking the writing process from a logical approach begins with first mastering basic skills of grammar, punctuation and sentence structure. These provide the essential tools in constructing clear, crisp and concise sentences.

If you lack basic writing skills, don't despair. Learning how to write begins with simple steps. Isolating your biggest weakness takes some soul searching and commitment. While the journey to the finish line of writing proficiency may seem bumpy, you can complete it with diligence and adherence to sound principles.

Former newspaper editor and writing professor Jack Gillespie fondly talked about giving your writing "bricks and mortar." Gillespie compared the writing process to a mason building a wall. A wall needs bricks, which represent the sentences in our paragraphs. These sentences provide our writing with unity. But the bricks need mortar—coherence that keeps it together. Writing that lacks unity and coherence also lacks clarity and, thus, confuses readers.

Unity means that each sentence in the paragraph belongs together. Professional writers stay focused and organized. They avoid making readers work too hard to get the meaning. But unity without coherence lacks rhythm and flow. Therefore, to make your writing cohesive you must include transitions that guide readers logically through the writing. Consider this example of a unified paragraph that lacks coherence.

Atlantic City, N.J., opened its first gaming hall in 1978. Resorts International opened on Memorial Day Weekend. Resorts opened to great success. Resorts earned more than $100 million in its first six months of operation. Caesars opened the Boardwalk Regency 10 months after Resorts opened. Atlantic City has 13 gaming halls today.

By simply adding transitions and repositioning some paragraph elements, the paragraph becomes more cohesive.

Atlantic City, N.J., opened its first gaming hall, Resorts International, on Memorial Day Weekend, 1978. The seaside gaming establishment earned more than $100 million in its first six months. However, it soon faced competition when Caesars opened the Boardwalk Regency 10 months later. Today, Atlantic City has 13 gaming halls.

Often words, usually nouns, repeated within sentences and paragraphs provide transition. A story about a football player may include key words such as *athlete* and *gridiron hero*. You may repeat *football player* a couple of times and then use *athlete* or *gridiron hero* as synonyms to provide transition.

Transitions will help you write a story that glides from start to finish. But they cannot create coherence if none exists. So don't just throw transitions in here and there and think you've done your job.

You must make sure the transitions you use make clear to readers the exact relations within and between sentences and paragraphs. Don't use anything that will sidetrack readers. Make every word and phrase flow naturally from what has gone before. You'll find a list of transition words and phrases by category in this chapter to help get you started.

Clarity in your writing signifies honesty. When you write with a clear purpose you create a bond with your audience. Now, you'll occasionally find a need for vague writing, for those occasions when you want to leave room for debate and creativity. But more often than not you should avoid third-degree writing.

Third-degree writing fails to honestly represent the writer's true meaning. If you wish to convey clarity you should use concrete words rather than vague terms. Consider this example.

Third Degree—A labor issue
Second Degree—A labor dispute
First Degree—A labor strike over wages

Simply, vague wording causes problems because it distorts understanding. To avoid misunderstanding and achieve clarity you need to write with a sense of purpose and to avoid ambiguous words and phrases.

As public relations practitioners, we must know how to write! Research indicates that hiring PR practitioners list writing as the number one desired skill in any level of new employee. The need to hire people with polished writing skills has transcended the knowledge base required for success in today's information economy. Such skills include the ability to quickly organize, construct and communicate information that both informs and persuades. It stands to reason that employers need workers with sophisticated writing skills since success in the information age depends largely on the ability to pen (or keyboard) effective prose. Therefore, clearly written, concise and crisp messages offer the most efficient way to gain success.

The process of effective writing begins with recognizing writing as a strategic process rather than a creative endeavor. You must be skilled at the dissemination of information in both a one-way communication model and a two-way communication model to successfully communicate in the workplace. The emergence of direct links via social media places organizations in contact with consumers or end users at a rate never before envisioned. In fact, the instant dialogue and rapid response of information expand the potential for business success. However, they also increase the likelihood that messages will fail because of sloppy errors and fuzzy language.

A message must succeed at five levels. First, the intended audience must *receive* the message. This involves research and audience identification. Second, the message must grab the audience's *attention*. Third, the audience must clearly *understand* the message. Fourth, the audience must *remember* the message. And, fifth, the audience must *act* on the message.

Media Writing

Every real story you read has some sort of logic and point to it. Why, then, would writing for the media be any different? Whether the author is writing a short story about people, or a technical document related to an area of work, many identical aspects exist.

1. Writers can often create a setting for the communication—what's happening and the circumstances surrounding the event.
2. Writers often get a chance to humanize their writing—focus on a major character or some fundamental point that creates interest.
3. Writers often get a chance to deal with a triggering event or occurrence that creates the need to communicate.
4. Writers get the opportunity to present ideas to solve a problem, address a conflict or offer an opportunity.
5. Writers often get an opportunity to draw a conclusion or present an ideal ending.
6. Writers often get an opportunity to peer into the future and set the table for future communication.

A rift that often exists between communicators and media outlets stems from the inability of many writers to identify "newsworthy" information. To recognize newsworthy information, we need to think like journalists. Thinking like a journalist means writing with a purpose and crafting simple and pure communication. Its intent is simple: forget the hype and offer factual information that attracts an audience because of its soundness and clarity. Thinking like a journalist follows these eight basic steps.

1. Identify the focus or main idea of the story from notes.
2. Write a brief summary of the main idea.
3. Separate the material relating to the main idea from secondary matter.
4. Organize the material in order of importance.
5. Begin to write and like ideas with transitions.
6. Read the story for accuracy, brevity, clarity.
7. Read the story for grammar, style and word usage.
8. Rewrite if necessary (and it usually is).

News story construction follows the inverted pyramid style. Simply, the inverted pyramid style puts the "most important information"—the lead—first. This is followed by the second, third, fourth, down to the least important information. The inverted pyramid provides that all readers get at least the main idea regardless of whether they read only the lead or the entire story.

Chapter 2 addresses print media writing including writing leads, news releases, media kits as well as using the AP Stylebook. You'll find examples of good and poor writing as well as formulas to follow to write your own pieces for the media. Likewise, Chapter 6 discusses electronic media writing including writing broadcast leads, Video News Releasess (VNR), feature and straight news stories as well as Public Service Announcements.

PRactical TIP

Active Voice as Opposed to Passive Voice

We define passive voice as any form of the verb "to be" followed by a verb's past participle. Forms of the verb to be in English are as follows:

Infinitive =	to be
Present =	am, is, are
Past =	was, were
Present Participle =	being
Past Participle =	been
Present Subjunctive =	be
Past Subjunctive =	were
Imperative =	be

Focusing on active voice construction strengthens writing and lends it boldness and force. It keeps the writing direct and focused. On the other hand, passive voice construction sometimes gives the impression that the "doer of the action" wants to avoid taking responsibility. In passive voice construction the true subject is relegated to the end of the sentence and therefore acted on rather than acting. This often weakens the statement.

We find an overabundance of passive voice in sentences where the writer wants to avoid responsibility for the action taken. The active voice offers a more straightforward relationship between the subject and the verb. In the active voice the verb drives the sentence and the subject receives its action. In the passive voice, the subject is no longer active, but, instead, the subject is acted upon by the verb.

The letter was mailed by Marilyn.
  The **letter** (subject) was being **mailed** (verb).
Marilyn mailed the letter.
  Marilyn → subject   letter → direct object
At each concert, at least one tune from a well-known opera was sung by the soprano.
  Tune → receiver of the action   was → action
  Soprano → doer of the action
At each concert, the soprano sang at least one tune from a well-known opera.
  Soprano → doer of the action   sang → action
  Tune → receiver of action

The passive voice does, however, have some use. Passive voice construction is particularly useful in two situations.

1. When it is more important to draw attention to the person or thing acted upon.
   The unsuspecting employee was fired by his boss yesterday.
2. When the actor in the situation is not important
   The dense fog can be observed in the early morning hours.

Simply, sentences in the active voice have energy and directness, both of which keep the reader engaged. Sentences in the active also use fewer words—and cutting unnecessary words always improves a piece of writing.

Business Writing

When writing for businesses or organizations, you must first know your audience; then feature clarity, economy and straightforwardness in all your products; and lastly, avoid negative writing and passive voice.

Chapters 3 and 4 address business writing and discuss how to write letters, email, reports, newsletters, e-newsletters and intranet entries. The chapters provide formats or structures for how to write each product as well as examples of direct mail letters, persuasive emails, effective e-newsletters, etc.

Social Media Writing

According to McDonald's, its head of social media is the customer. As "connected" consumers, we have the ability to self-select information and channels as well as act as our own gatekeeper. Social media gives us 24/7 access to channels to beam our messages out. Public relations writers need to embrace social media knowing that it will evolve, expand and energize the communication process among target markets and the business community. Chapter 5 addresses how to write Facebook posts, tweets and blogposts. It covers use of Pinterest, LinkedIn and Google+. The chapter features how-to checklists to make your social media writing effective.

Persuasive Writing

Chapter 7 discusses the many types of persuasive writing PR writers construct daily such as pitch letters, letters to the editor, op-ed pieces, position papers, brochures and direct mail letters. Again, you'll find examples of each persuasive writing type as well as suggested structures to use in designing them.

Feature Writing

Many PR writers scan for feature ideas about their clients they can pass along to media professionals. Features entertain readers, provide fodder for internal publications and websites and make ideal outlets for creative juices.

Chapter 8 provides tips for brainstorming, writing feature leads, overcoming writer's block, developing mat releases and sidebars.

Advertising Copywriting

Chapter 9 discusses the many types of public relations advertising practitioners will have to create. From advocacy ads to Public Service Announcements (PSA), you can view examples of ad types as well as checklists/suggestions of how to develop institutional, cooperative, cause-related marketing, house ads. The emphasis in Chapter 9 is on how to develop ad copy through use of many current advertisements.

Speech Writing

A speech allows an organization to articulate its values and goals. One estimate puts the number of presentations in the United States at 8 billion per year. Many PR writers ghostwrite their CEOs' speeches and public addresses. Chapter 10 addresses topics such as how to get more mileage from speeches, handling Q & A sessions to PowerPoint issues.

Law for PR Writing

Today's practitioners face litigation on many levels. Badly written documents can cause increased administration costs as well as a case against the company. The increased use of computer technology has placed a burden on organizations to control the production and dissemination of information. Chapter 11 covers inflammatory language, content neutral versus content specific speech, false and deceptive advertising as well as copyright and trademarks.

PR Campaign Writing

Perhaps the most comprehensive document PR writers draft—the public relations plan—distances a publicist from a strategic writer. Knowing how to draft a situation analysis and craft a plan to create the ideal state for a client marks a true PR counselor. The final chapter, Chapter 12, discusses the components of a plan as well as fleshes out how to write measureable, behavioral objectives, strategic approaches that contain messages and tactics that provide an indication of how to reach those objectives and strategies.

Summary

Successful public relations practitioners share one skill—the ability to write strategically. Most professionals cite the ability to write as the top skill needed in public relations practice. Yet, educators rue the writing skills of seniors bound for the workplace.

Public relations students from across the U.S. hope to receive jobs as a result of their public relations education. Most students want to have the skills and knowledge to make them employable. To that end, a nationwide survey indicates that public relations students want to improve their writing skills.

Because writing skills are paramount for anyone wishing to succeed in public relations, practitioners looking for interns or entry level candidates test students to determine their writing acumen. Organizations need public relations writers with the strategic skills of critical thinking, planning and crafting messages.

The following chapters will provide specific blueprints for constructing a variety of writing products necessary for success in public relations. These chapters will discuss a writing product, give concrete steps on how to write it and provide examples. We address not only media writing, but also internal, external and marketing writing. Look for how to write media advisories, advocacy ads, PSAs, brochures, VNRs, blogs, annual reports, position papers, leads, e-newsletters and more. To become a complete writer, read on and remember: practice makes perfect.

Chapter 2
Print Media Writing

"The most valuable of all talents is that of never using two words when one will do."

Thomas Jefferson

Public relations professionals constantly stress to students the importance of writing. In fact, most interviews for PR positions include a writing exercise, often a news release. Being a good writer used to be a given when public relations was taking off in the United States at the start of the 20th century.

A majority of practitioners—including modern PR founder Ivy Lee—would come directly from the newspaper industry for the profession's first 50 years or so. Their writing ability was not difficult to gauge. Today, however, many new hires might come from business, marketing or liberal arts, without having taken any appropriate news writing or PR writing courses. That's a major reason many companies today devise their own writing tests for public relations applicants. It's even true for public relations agencies around the globe. All three of the PR firms contacted Down Under in Sydney, for example, confirmed their giving a writing exam before considering anyone for employment. Former journalists are still in demand for the PR profession. That may be why the Vatican hired a Fox News reporter as its senior communications adviser in 2012.

Fraser P. Seitel, often-quoted veteran PR guru, has long endorsed the need for writing expertise within his profession. He emphasized that once again in his 2011 text, *The Practice of Public Relations:* "Even in the age of the Internet, writing remains the key to public relations: Public relations practitioners are professional communicators. And communication means writing."

Newspapers, along with magazines and other traditional media, have seen a drop in their circulation numbers, advertising revenue and staff members. Yet, print is far from writing its own obituary. According to the Newspaper Association of America, 113 million adult unique visitors were counted in its website traffic research for the first quarter of 2012. That's a 4.4 percent increase from the previous year for online reading. Among newspaper readers with more than $100,000 income, it's a 6 percent jump. Only a few of the 1,400 dailies are without Web editions. More and more of the 8,000 nondailies are heading toward online versions as well.

Magazines, likewise, have been resilient over the past century. More than 25 million copies of magazines are purchased weekly at newsstands alone in the United States. And that's not counting the subscription circulation or the high number of pass-along readers. The number of overall magazine readers has increased over the past five years, aided by online versions and app downloads of popular publications. More than nine out of 10 U.S. adults read at least one magazine—print or digital—monthly.

Despite such resiliency, a few so-called experts are even predicting the death of news releases for the traditional media. Others counter that good news releases will still get to their intended audiences, whether in print, online or via social media. Online and interactive media have continued to capture a sizeable quantity of readers and revenue. Citizen journalists now arrive on the scene with their smartphone cameras and social outlets to immediately inform the world about any event. The Weather Channel and CNN enlist the help of their viewers to send in photos and videos of weather developments and news events. CNN even gives awards to its citizen journalists. Many local television stations and newspapers are doing the same thing in their markets.

The newspaper industry has been fighting back and even started its own national public relations campaign about the importance of the press. A Vocus White Paper, "Maximizing the Value of Your News: From Twitter to Google," stressed that traditional media are still valid.

With everyone talking about the new world of social media tools, it is important to start with the basics and grow your PR strategy from there. Traditional methods for distributing your news have not been replaced but can be used in conjunction with these new tools to extend the reach and impact of your message.

Personally reaching out to targeted journalists has always been the cornerstone of public relations. Email is a powerful communications tool to reach individual journalists and deliver news straight to their inbox.

People simply like the permanency of print. And for thoroughly covering community news, numerous surveys confirm that neither national nor local broadcast outlets can compete with the local newspaper.

Billionaire investor Warren Buffet still has confidence in the newspaper industry. His company in 2012 purchased 63 Media General local papers, where there's "more of a feeling of community," Nebraska native Buffet told Howard Kurtz in *The Daily Beast* on June 4, 2012. "High school sports will pull them into the paper. They want to know about Nebraska football and care about every player on the team. That means a shot at getting young people in the habit of reading a newspaper."

Therefore, despite social media and other forms of new media on the horizon, PR folks cannot overlook traditional media when distributing news about their client or organization. The person attempting that task can't be one with strong thumbs but weak writing skills.

No corporation should attempt to send news releases to the media without having at least one quality writer on staff or on call. That sentence sounds so fundamentally valid, yet so many companies—including Fortune 500 ones—haven't a clue on producing valid news stories, let alone other written documents.

No matter what communication channel is chosen, as other chapters emphasize, quality production is still the goal for all communication efforts. Sharp public relations writers, in fact, can still place their outgoing efforts with newspapers and magazines. They could also wind up on display for the organization's web pages, social media sites, bloggers, journalists and consumers. Because many magazines and newspapers have trimmed their news staffs, they are even more dependent on the contributions of outside sources such as PR writers. To make matters worse, journalists are often asked to cover more ground than before, including both print and online versions. Local papers don't have the employees to thoroughly cover as many areas as before. Beat reporters have been downsized from zoned editions, along with traditional assignments as news, entertainment, business and sports. Based on a poll by Business Wire, the best time to send a release to reporters may be Tuesday mornings at 10. Journalists are typically in their offices with emptied inboxes.

To meet all the multiple outlet opportunities, today's cross-trained writers must be capable of producing copy for various formats. A majority of journalists are reading blogs daily, a topic discussed in Chapter 5, for example. This chapter focuses on print, yet most of its points will apply to the media convergent landscape as well as internal audiences (see Chapters 3 and 4). Expanded newspaper online editions, a rarity a few years ago, are now the norm. And the content has shifted from mere stories condensed from the print version to videos and slideshows, along with extra photos, audio and links.

Therefore, corporate communicators now write for several audiences: traditional media, social media and individuals (employees, consumers, opinion leaders, other authors). Their writing must be accurate and adhere to the consistency of Associated Press guidelines (as discussed later in this chapter). Along with reporters, unfortunately, many publications have also eliminated some editors from their newsrooms.

John McIntyre, assistant managing editor of the copy desk at the *Baltimore Sun*, emphasized how writing skills are even more crucial in today's media environment.

"Daily newspapers have been shedding editors, because editing is time consuming and expensive. So there are fewer opportunities to check something that's wrong. At newspapers there are things that go up on the Internet without anybody having double-checked them. If you are submitting something that you want published, you have to take the responsibility to make sure that it is factually accurate, because you can't count on somebody else doing it for you anymore."

Once a publication runs something from a writer that's full of inaccuracies, its editors will make a mental note to avoid submissions from that person—and perhaps that company—in the future. It has too many other releases in its inbox to have to put up with poor prose. There isn't enough time with the 24/7 news cycle to double check and rewrite lousy copy. If public relations writers lose credibility with the media, they should take up another career. Not only will they be ostracized, but also might their employer or PR firm.

However, media outlets aren't so desperate for copy they will run anything they receive from outside sources. Prior surveys have placed the rejection rate for releases around an astounding 90 percent. With shrinking news holes available in the media, it probably will stay in that range in the future. So how can company writers make the lucky 10 percent pile? That's the quick question that stumps even the Public Relations Society of America, despite its professional training programs. Its leaders, along with many other PR associations and professionals, say they deplore the poor quality of writing being produced today in corporate America.

However, a sharp editor could even take issue with most of the releases coming out of the PRSA headquarters in New York City. The same holds true for a majority of the national news release distribution services. Various lists of annoying gobbledygook words and phrases used too often by corporate writers are frequently published. Although they're intended to be a warning to avoid such words, the lists seem to repeat many items from year to year.

Holdovers typically include FYI, give 110 percent, think outside the box, at this point in time, change agent and paradigm shift.

Poor writing is noticed and condemned by those who view it, whether its readers are internal or external audiences. Criticism from within the profession can be harsh at times. Here's such evidence by writing consultant Steve Crescenzo's sarcastic condemnation of corporate news releases.

> *Here at C.R.A.P. (Corporate Rhetoric Awards Program) Central, we get a lot of press releases. Stacks and stacks of them. We get them in print, and we get them via email.*
>
> *After going through a stack of them recently, we can't believe that we have never given out a C.R.A.P. Award to one of the trained monkeys writing these releases. Some of the prose is so bad, it makes the average employee publication editor look like Will Shakespeare.*
>
> *Ninety percent of the press releases we see follow the same formula. . . . But the formula that most press release writers follow is pure C.R.A.P. It looks like this:*
>
> *Name of company + everything great about this company that nobody really cares about + bad verb + bad quote by a guy with too many titles.*
>
> ("Dumping C.R.A.P. on Reporters." www.crescenzocomm.com. Reprinted by permission of Steve Crescenzo.)

Formula writing, as Crescenzo points out, is one of the major downfalls in company news releases today. And it starts before the actual news story even begins. A typical submission will usually have three or four lines as a headline. Then the copy will start with the dateline (or city of origin), flush left, boldfaced and all capitalized, followed by the date. Back up the truck! Such writers have already identified themselves as dunces to the journalism profession without writing another word. (And PR practitioners still really wonder why reporters and editors don't like them?) They should simply look at the newspapers they target as a comparison.

- ▶ How long is the actual newspaper headline at the top of the story? One short line? Try to keep yours to that same length.
- ▶ Do they indent paragraphs? Yes, even the opening one with the dateline.
- ▶ Is the dateline boldfaced? Probably not. So don't do it.
- ▶ Is the dateline in all caps? Yes, according to the Associated Press, but only the city should be.
- ▶ Is the state necessary in the dateline? Not for major cities or those in the same state as the source of the release. If you need the state, use it the way AP says to write it. Don't abbreviate it the post office method, for example.

If a newspaper on the receiving end of most releases from an organization has its own unique style, adapt for that one particular paper and send the rest of your submissions the standard way.

News Release Disaster

The news release reprinted in **Figure 2-1** is a classic example of what we've been discussing. It's a fictitious revision from an actual national retailer, announcing a minor internal promotion. It goes on for four pages of extensive quotes, ignoring AP style, with wider print margins than shown below. The company name and contact information has been deliberately altered from the first page to save personal embarrassment. This opening page follows, enough for readers to decide whether this is a release they would want to use to represent their company. A majority of reporters would simply hit the delete key or toss paper versions in the recycle bin.

As you can see, these errors are mere preliminaries to the formula writing that follows in too many releases. This is before an examination has started on the actual copy. Most stories will start off with the company name, with superlatives about said organization, followed by a statement about something that's overhyped as being earth-shattering, groundbreaking and even *extremely* unique. This opening sentence could range from 30 to 50 words in many cases. (Pioneer's is an alarming 51, not counting the dateline material.)

As if this is not bad enough, the next often tops it. The CEO or some other egotistical executive demands that a lengthy, convoluted direct quotation be inserted in the lead as well, along with that fancy title. Pity the poor business communicator who is forced to deliver such drivel on a daily basis. Journalists, of course, will not be so sentimental. They will hit their delete key and make a note of the asinine author and the company that allows it. But what about the rest of the no-news release? Don't worry. It won't even be read in most cases, which is why the actual news (whenever it does occur) has to fit in the top of the story.

PIONEER CANDLE COMPANY
1776 Pioneer Road, Pioneer MA 01111

FOR IMMEDIATE RELEASE
Contact: Randy Hines
(800) PIONEER
hines@pioneer.com

The Pioneer Candle Company, Inc. Makes CEO Changes

Joseph N. Basso will Become President and CEO on November 1, 2013
Suzanne D. FitzGerald to Become Executive Chairwoman

Pioneer, MA—October 22, 2013—Pioneer Holding Corp. and its subsidiary The Pioneer Candle Company, Inc. ("Pioneer Candle" or the "Company") made the official announcement today that Joseph N. Basso, now serving as President and Chief Operating Officer of Pioneer Candle, will take on the role of President and Chief Executive Officer on November 1, 2013. Mr. Basso will take over the reins of Suzanne D. FitzGerald, who has agreed to stay on as both Chairwoman and Chief Executive Officer through the above-mentioned date and will thereafter become Executive Chairwoman of the Board of Pioneer Candle through November 1, 2014.

"This is a wonderful day in the life of our company that we can welcome Joseph Basso as our incoming CEO," said Suzanne FitzGerald, Chairwoman and CEO of Pioneer Candle. "Joseph brings a wonderful background to his position with us. His abilities speak for themselves. He has done a fantastic job in his current positions for Pioneer Candle over the past 10 years of employment at our corporate headquarters here in Massachusetts." (etc.)

FIGURE 2-1

Admittedly, these are harsh words, but much cleaner than the variety you would hear in actual newsrooms across North America when ubiquitous formula writing pops on their computer screens. What kinds of problems do most corporate writers routinely produce in a typical news story submission?

> ▶ Subjective adjectives about a company do not belong in a news release. PR writers should save them for those internal publications, but only when forced to use them at all.

▶ Hyperboles regarding the executives, news event or product may seem fitting to some within an organization. But for the rest of humanity, it may not matter that much; so keep the right perspective with the news peg. Avoid the hype.

▶ Technical words and jargon turn off readership. If a corporate communications staffer is a mere stenographer for the research and development division, few readers will have a clue what the story is about. It gets worse, of course, if news release copy has to be "lawyerized" before it's sent to the media. Short, simple words are always better than long, complicated ones. Stop being a typist for the geek squad and ask, "What does that mean?"

▶ If an executive is allowed free rein to give repetitive, redundant statements, a good writer needs to tighten those quotes before they appear in the news release. Two sentences of quoted matter are usually sufficient to provide the official company stance on an issue.

▶ How many words are in the typical release's first sentence? Many public relations writers haven't yet learned the ideal average sentence length is 17 words. (That prior one is 15 words long.) Comprehension decreases as word length increases.

▶ How many words are in the first paragraph? Good publications will often intersperse one- or two-sentence paragraphs. They do this for aesthetics, not because the specific topic has been thoroughly exhausted. Breaking up a long, gray copy block with shorter paragraphs makes the page more inviting for the typical reader's eyes. News article lines are much longer than the narrowed column width in newspapers and magazines. So six lines of type could become 10 or more in a publication's format. Just as in sentence lengths, however, a good writer will want to strive for variety.

▶ Many releases are targeted to please the wrong audience. Many executives with the lengthy quotes just want to see their names and fancy job titles in print. To them, that's more important than any newsworthy development that could have been expounded in a better news release. Perhaps they should have adhered to actor John Wayne's advice: "Talk low, talk slow, and don't talk too much."

So whom do PR pros write for? Many say their primary audience is the reading public. After all, they are the potential customers of the organization's products or services. They are the consumers who buy the publication or download the release when it finally appears. (Back to this thought in a minute.)

But an even more important audience is necessary to persuade first before company scribes can reach all those potential readers. That's the media gatekeeper—whether a managing editor, city editor, section editor or regular journalist. (As this book continues to point out, it could also include bloggers, Twitterites, webmasters and citizen journalists.) Sharp PR practitioners find out who covers their area. They can check the latest issue or look on its website for the person's name. National directories, although quite helpful, are expensive and can become outdated too soon. Even costly online versions are not guaranteed to be as timely as necessary to get the correct name and title.

Company public relations writers should get to know their journalists' likes and dislikes. What days and times are better to approach and when are frantic deadlines to avoid? What topics are on their backburners that PR workers might be able to help research? They should send personalized emails to those individuals. (Although up to 90 percent of journalists prefer receiving releases via email, public relations workers should always ask for their top choice.) They need to send material directly to that person, who may not even use the actual words from the release.

However, if they can convince the appropriate journalist that their news release contains timely, factual information of interest to the publication's audience, their job is successful. Additional links for photos, backgrounders or biographies are always appreciated. Many journalists prefer to write their own stories, to put their own fingerprint and style on a document. Some newspapers still have a policy not to reprint a news release. It's treated simply as a news tip. So PR contributions may simply be the facts and resources from which an article is drafted within the newsroom or a social media site.

PRactical TIP
Media Advisory Fills Gap

Because some journalists eschew using actual news releases—for personal or newspaper policy reasons—public relations writers can send instead media advisories. Just as road signs warn drivers, a media advisory cautions journalists about an upcoming event or changes in a previously announced occasion.

Writing an effective media advisory is a combination of objective writing—the kind that's been drilled into you—and subjective writing. The latter comes into play when you persuasively inform media representatives why they should spend the time and resources to cover your event.

Many PR pros feel a media advisory can be more effective than a typical news release. If the publication conducts its own interviews or the local broadcast station invests the time to bring its own camera crew along, you will get more extensive coverage than your 10-inch release. That's why the advisory often mentions, for example, that a speaker or celebrity is available for an exclusive interview immediately before or after an event.

Media advisories should pique interest in your planned speaker or activity. This short document (usually one page on news release letterhead) typically opens with a one-paragraph convincing reason why your news item deserves coverage. With short words and short sentences, it explains the event in fuller detail, hoping to entice coverage. In addition to an accurate list of the essential five W's and H, it's wise to include SW: so what. Why is this news important to this area? Localize your advisory as much as possible so the media gatekeepers will consider the coverage as being essential for their viewers or readers.

Advisories—sometimes called media alerts—are also issued as reminders to journalists previously contacted about an upcoming event. These are typically short lists of the essential details, often written in bullet format, similar to a fact sheet.

As with any communication to the media, direct it to the right individual. Often, because of the urgency of a media advisory, it is faxed or emailed to selected media. Be sure to provide additional contact information if a journalist decides to cover your event. Cell phone numbers and email addresses are essential, just as they are on news releases.

So once PR practitioners have met and conquered their first audience, the journalist who's now convinced the accurate and AP style news story deserves merit, who else do they write for? Certainly the public is a vital target for most writing efforts. They are the end users, ones who will apply their resources to buy, vote, travel and consume services. But a writer must understand who those readers are, especially true for blogs, magazines and other specialized publications. PR writers may wish to emphasize the brand for these readers, but not blatant persuasion at the expense of factual information. If releases are posted in an online newsroom, the reading audience can expand to include a variety of other journalists, bloggers and consumers. These additional audiences, in turn, could place the news onto multiple social media sites.

Release Regulations

A key consideration before starting to type news releases is their appearance. The major writing principles to follow for the release increase its chances of appearing in the media. However, its appearance and format can persuade a journalist to reject its use. Because of paper, postage and environmental interests, the now-rare snail-mailed release is often printed on both sides of the page, something shunned only 10 years ago. Such green behavior by itself will not get a message tossed aside.

Since the release should be as newspaper-looking as possible—by following Associated Press customs, for example—PR writers will want to follow similar guidelines:

 ▶ use a one-inch margin all around the white or light-colored paper.
 ▶ use organizational letterhead for just the first page, either the regular style or one designed solely for news releases.

- ▶ place the day's date near the top of the page.
- ▶ provide a contact's name, email and office phone number (including cell for after-hours calling).
- ▶ don't hyphenate words at the end of lines.
- ▶ don't break from one page to the next unless it's between paragraphs.
- ▶ put "more" at the bottom of page one and "end" or "###" or "30" on the last page. (These last two rules can be modified for email submissions, although writers still need an ending symbol.)

These should seem like common-sense adages no writer would ignore. But without a date, as some releases do arrive dateless, a journalist wouldn't know if the word "tomorrow" in the story refers to the next day or yesterday, depending on when it was written. (That's why AP shuns the word in the first place.)

Similarly, many reporters have wanted to obtain more particulars about a release, but no one is in the office when they get around to calling at 5:15 p.m. Sports department staffs at most morning newspapers, for example, work up until deadline in many cases, so they may not get to the office until late afternoon. If a PR person cannot be contacted after 5, it may doom an otherwise wonderfully written release. That's one reason why two names could be listed at the top as contacts. A journalist's decision to delay the use of a story because of the inability to confirm one key detail could spell disaster on time-sensitive copy.

Another format issue is open to occasional debate. This book encourages the use of a one-line, boldfaced headline just above the dateline. Others insist a short subhead below the main head can bring more details to the attention of a media gatekeeper and sneak in more keywords for search engines.

When you think about the reasons for newspaper headlines on stories—summary of main point, getting audience's attention—you can see their need for releases as well. After all, PR writers want to help the media gatekeeper by summarizing their copy. Their newsroom audience is usually just one person, but it's the key individual they have to fully inform (entice, entertain or persuade) for their organization's contribution to proceed throughout the chain, from newsroom desk, to design, to consumer delivery (either online or print). A few might argue that headlines are the sole task of the copydesk, but PR pros aren't writing a final version for the publication. They just want to capture the gatekeeper's attention.

It's best to imitate the journalism style of headline writing. With computer word searches zeroing in on nouns, rather than clever phrases, it's best if PR writers get straight to the meat of the story. Not all of these classic standards, of course, are followed by today's newspaper and news magazine copy desks. However, it's wise to mimic them anyway to help the release's headline have impact in fewer than 10 words. That means news release heads should use:

- ▶ short, simple words,
- ▶ no articles,
- ▶ few adverbs or adjectives,

▶ comma rather than the word "and,"
▶ present or future tense verb instead of past tense,
▶ active voice verb instead of passive voice,
▶ single quote mark (apostrophe) rather than double (to save space).

The headline is important (beyond search engine optimization) since it's one of the first things a reader sees in releases, pitches and other media relations pieces. If it's not effective, the headline may be the last thing that reader sees as well.

News Release Triumph

In contrast to your Pioneer Candle news release fiasco, **Figure 2-2** is an example of a typical story format you might be sending to the media with much better results. This one concerns high school summer workshops sponsored by a fictitious Indiana university. When double-spaced, it's shorter than two full pages. Contrast these short, informative quotes with the long ones produced by Pioneer Candle.

Start Off Right

As mentioned already, the dateline that begins the release under the headline is used to tell readers where the story originates. A better term for it might be cityline, since dates rarely appear in datelines of any publications. Instead, the date emerges near the top of the page, along with contact information. If it's a local article, no dateline is used in most dailies. In-state stories need the city, but no state mention. If a PR writer is sending an item out of state, the dateline includes both the city and state of the host organization, as seen in the Sandell University release above. Of course, about 30 major cities always stand alone in datelines and in copy without reference to their states. When you need a state's abbreviation, always use AP's version, not that of the postal service.

Writing Leads

Then comes the most important sentence in a news release. Many writers consider it the hardest to compose. It's worthy of your best effort. That opening prose should succinctly state the singular key message that needs to be communicated to your audiences. The lead can be one or two sentences or, if necessary, even one or two paragraphs. It summarizes the most important details of your article: who, what, where, when, why, how and so what. Not all of those are necessarily crucial for the brief lead, of course. Don't make it crowded with superfluous facts.

Sandell University

PO Box 1915
www.sandell.edu
Sandell, IN 47100
800-SANDELL

April 8, 2014
Contact: Jim Sunthimer
For Immediate Release
jims@sandell.edu
812-555-1111 cell

Sandell U Sponsors High School Workshop

SANDELL, Ind.—High school media students and their advisers can pick up skills and interview celebrities at Sandell University's Media Workshop this June.

Highlights of the week will be a news conference with quarterback Andrew Luck of the Indianapolis Colts and a free concert by country music singer Kenny Chesney.

Running June 16 to 20, the all-day sessions will provide training in writing, editing, online production, advertising, web design and photography.

"This is the tenth year Sandell University has offered this workshop for regional high school students," said Dr. Gail Roso, associate professor of new media and workshop director. "We had more than 200 students here last year from six states, as well as 28 advisers."

Students will produce an online magazine as part of their assignments, live in air-conditioned dormitories, dine on campus, and use Sandell's recreational facilities during the week.

Instructors for the workshops will be Sandell University faculty, regional journalists and award-winning high school publication advisers. Yearbook and newspaper advisers can attend seminars and help their staffs plan for next year's editions. College or continuing education credit is available for public school teachers.

Other guests include Sen. Yuko Utetsu, Sandell University President Chase McDowell and book publishing giant Preston Scott, a 1982 Sandell graduate.

"We're already enthused about the week," Roso said. "Having Andrew and Kenny will add to the excitement and create actual media experiences for the students."

Applications are available online at mediaworkshops@sandell.edu, or by mail to the Media Workshop, Sandell University, PO Box 1915, Sandell IN 47100.

Sandell University is a Christian liberal arts school located on 160 acres in southern Indiana, about one hour south of Indianapolis. It was founded in 1915 by Gustav Sandell, a Swedish minister who immigrated to the U.S. in 1910.

#

FIGURE 2-2

Those crucial details selected for the opening should be sufficient to encourage readers to finish the rest of the story. The same facts also need to tease media gatekeepers—editors, station managers and bloggers—that the release is newsworthy for their own audiences. That's one of the reasons successful PR writers almost always try to emphasize a local angle.

Residents in Tampa have little interest in a news release about Pittsburgh unless they migrated south from that region. To hook the interest of a Pittsburgh editor, a corporate communicator will emphasize the product, company or individual with western Pennsylvania roots in the opening of the story. Bury that local angle and the editor may not get that far down the page before the delete key or recycle bin gets another visitor. Lack of localization, therefore, remains as one of those key reasons why news releases are rejected.

A direct lead tells readers immediately what the story is all about.

A Sandell University media professor has won the grand prize and $10,000 in a national short story competition.

Although a summary-style, direct lead is used in a majority of news releases, PR writers have other options if the article warrants it. A delayed lead gives readers a hint about the story, but the main point is delivered in later copy. Feature stories (as described later in this book) often may be better suited to start with a quirky quotation or question. Here's just one example:

"You better be ready! You're starting Saturday," yelled the head coach to the 19-year-old redshirt freshman.

Another aspect of the lead that's crucial is including attribution for any opinion or statement needing it. Otherwise, it appears that the newspaper itself would be endorsing the subjective statements in the news release. Consider the necessity for attribution in the opening sentence's claim below:

The newly designed Prius x model will deliver an industry-leading 75 miles per gallon combined when unveiled next summer, Toyota officials said Tuesday.

After the lead is written, the supporting cast for those opening facts is brought into play. More details flesh out the summary lead, in descending order of importance. News releases written with the proper lead can logically unfold as the objective facts fall into place. But they need to follow typical journalism style. Only include newsworthy information. Use a variety of paragraph starts, not a boring "The . . ." for each opening word. When using direct quotations, try to start the paragraph with a full-sentence quote rather than burying it within the paragraph. Use attribution after the first sentence of a multi-sentence quote (as found in the Sandell release).

And don't forget to think multimedia. Most PR professionals have done that already for their online media rooms. They will increase their success rate when they decide to add photos, graphics and other visuals to their releases and blog posts. Study after study has confirmed that if PR practitioners can think visually when preparing their releases, chances of the story running and being read increase dramatically. This is nothing new. Journalists know to use visuals, of course.

They found out that photos, tables and infographics enhance comprehension. While websites have picked up that theme effectively with videos, slideshows and audio, a majority of news releases are text only.

Finally, at the end of most news releases is a short paragraph describing the organization or company sending the release (not the PR firm writing it). Called a **boilerplate,** the two or three sentences remain the same for every submission. It may not be inserted on local stories, of course, where readers already know about the nearby establishment. A typical one you just saw for a fictitious college might be the following:

Sandell University is a Christian liberal arts school located on 160 acres in southern Indiana, about one hour south of Indianapolis. It was founded in 1915 by Gustav Sandell, a Swedish minister who immigrated to the U.S. in 1910.

Pretend You're a Journalist

PR practitioners (or students) after reading this book will be skilled in concise writing, grammar rules, Associated Press maxims and public relations techniques. Another advantage to possess as they produce their organization's external documents is to think and write as if they were journalists. They already know what a newsperson considers to be the major writing principles for news. So they must adapt that writing style for all their outbound efforts.

Media professionals want news that is timely. Print, broadcast and online journalists all operate within the confines of deadlines. A successful PR practitioner understands that world and does everything possible to get information to the journalist early. Web editions keep writers on their toes constantly. Updates are mandatory, so PR pros cannot wait until the next print deadline to get information to the medium. They also need to provide timely details constantly.

With space at a premium in publications and computer screens, brevity is a virtue. PR writers should not embellish their creations with extraneous details, flowery expressions or long-winded quotations. Two pages of double-spaced text should be the *maximum* length for almost every release. Terse not only refers to the length of the release, but for the length of the sentences and words as well. This text will remind readers often that the average *ideal* sentence length is 17 words. Writers remembering that adage will create sentences that are easy to comprehend.

Yet another way to mimic journalists is to create copy that's truly newsworthy. Failing to do that creates a major reason why releases are rejected, and disdain for the public relations profession among many news media veterans. Not all corporate communicators can be blamed for the drivel delivered to newsrooms around the country. Most of those releases don't originate with legitimate public relations professionals. (Many stem from untrained writers over in marketing departments.) Nevertheless, such impostors create a negative image for authentic PR practitioners. Their writing is skewed and sloppy, avoiding any resemblance to that produced by journalists or truly professional PR pros.

Rather than providing solid news, many of these pretenders produce schmaltzy exclamations about how a great new product or service will solve all of humanity's ills. Instant puffery flags for journalists are long-winded quotes subjectively telling the bored audience all these marvelous features. Truly newsworthy stories will deliver objective information quickly, following specific style and format guidelines, avoiding first-person references, and limiting superlatives to one or two succinct direct quotes.

Another trait to mimic quality journalists is accuracy. Company writers need to habitually double check facts, figures, dates, phone numbers, addresses and websites to ensure their accuracy. If they're not comfortable with statistics-laden copy, they should run it by an appropriate individual with such skills. However, if stats dominate their story, all the percentages could turn off the lay reader who needs news nuggets, not numbing numbers.

Relying on a computer's spellchecker may be helpful, but it's never enough to count on it alone. Too many erroneous words slip by and correct words are frequently flagged for no rational reason. Many words have several spelling options.

TOOLBOX TIP

Watch for Mispellings

You would think professional PR practitioners wouldn't struggle with such minor issues as spelling. Tell that to the major league Washington Nationals' baseball fans. For one game during the 2009 season, some players on the team wore uniforms with the name "Natinals" across the front. Then, for its bobblehead promotion, it distributed souvenir items of former President "Teddy Rossevelt." In 2012, Minnesota's Jeff Manship's jersey had his name as "Mansihp." Yes, it is *misspellings* if you missed the purposeful mistake in the headline above.

A spell Czech can dew a grate job most of the thyme. Butt eye can knot rely on it four all my miss steaks, oar I May bee inn big trouble.

A public relations person with a less-than-PR-savvy employer should pretend to be a journalist writing about her own company. Of course, that doesn't mean she has to write such a balanced story that it involves getting damaging statements from her competitors. But it does mean she will avoid overloading the story with hyperbole, sickeningly syrupy quotations by a CEO, and legal but nevertheless obnoxious puffery about company products or services.

If her boss dreadfully insists on including such waste in narratives, she could try a split-run experiment. She can write one the old way and write one the journalism way about an event and send them to various media. Find out the success rate for each. Then she can contact journalists to whom her experiment was sent—but not while they are on their deadlines—to obtain their comments about the reasons for running or rejecting the submission.

Perils of Proofreading

Every public relations practitioner has at least one horror story of an important document that was printed with a typographical or grammatical error. Those of us who have suffered the embarrassment of an extra word, a forgotten letter, a misspelled name or some erroneous comma have learned the hard way the importance of meticulously proofreading everything you write.

As an instructor—both of college students and adult learners—I see the results of a lack of proofreading all the time. Students submit papers that barely see spellcheck, let alone a critical reading eye to ensure that the words on the page are correct. I understand that in most cases time is of the essence, but can you really afford not to put your best effort forth and your best work on display for your clients and the public? As a practitioner, I cringe at the times I see careless errors on everything from direct mail pieces to billboards to chalkboards and wonder just what people were thinking when they decided, without looking, that their finished work was just "good enough."

Consider this. According to reading expert William DuBay in Working with Plain Language, "Bad writing accounts for 40 percent of the cost of managing business transactions." How is that possible, you ask? Think about the amount of clarification needed because of misunderstood language, the cost of reprinting documents that are incorrect, the number of internal memos and letters that fail to motivate or instruct employees and the news releases that never get published in any media outlets. Whatever the root cause—bad writing or bad proofing—companies are spending a small fortune trying to communicate correctly and effectively.

So how can you become a better proofreader? First and foremost, start doing it. Too many people assume that they have proofed their work as they type it into the computer. Nothing could be further from the truth. It's imperative that you briefly set your work aside to give your brain a rest from the information and then come back with a critical eye to review it. Then, *really* review it. Don't just scan it—read each word, each sentence and each paragraph. Are words spelled correctly? Is your punctuation correct? If you have anything that you aren't sure of, consult an AP Stylebook for clarification. You'll be glad you did.

If the document is crucial, have a colleague read through it as well. So many times errors can be missed because you've written and read the words so many times. A new pair of eyes can find even the most common of mistakes.

Another good proofreading trick is to read the document backward. Yes, you read that right, backward. Start from the very last word and read backward right to the first word of the document. Why? Your brain is reading something new, and although the words are the same, the difference in the order forces your gray matter to notice misspellings and grammar issues it didn't catch the first time.

And, of course, use your software's spelling and grammar check, but don't put all your trust and confidence in it picking up every nuance of your writing and every possible error. A discerning eye and a few extra minutes will make all the difference in the final work you submit for class or for your profession.

Isn't your credibility and reputation worth at least that much?

By Linda Burkley, APR, former Central PA PRSA Chapter president,
Principal, Ardis Communication Strategy & Training
www.ardiscommunications.net

Using the AP Stylebook

Public relations writers need to adapt their external writing to the style used by journalists, namely the Associated Press. That doesn't mean that internal publications follow no formula, causing chaos for such writing.

To provide company communicators with a grasp of specific citations, a business or organization may wish to produce its own handbook of recommended style. All staff writers and freelancers who contribute to websites and various publications, therefore, can use the internal style manual to produce copy with similar spellings, abbreviations, titles, etc. And interns or new hires won't drive their supervisors crazy by constantly asking sundry style questions. Most university PR offices, as just one example, develop style policies to guide their own writers and any others who may write articles for internal audiences. (See such an example in the appendix at the back of the book.)

Almost all daily newspapers (and many nondailies) in North America today adhere to *The Associated Press Stylebook.* Therefore, it's imperative for public relations and business writers to be familiar with (if not master) contents of the latest annual version. A handy "What's New" page near the front clues readers in on updates and new entries for that edition. Helpful sections in the back discuss social media, food guidelines, punctuation, media law, business guidelines, sports guidelines and photo captions. A broadcast chapter was first added to the stylebook in 2012. Using correct style will build exceptional credibility with the media gatekeepers who decide the fate of any organization's external public relations writing efforts.

That new dictionary on the bookshelf or in the computer may be a nice tool, but whenever it differs from AP, corporate communicators will want to follow the latter. For example, what a computer spellchecker might approve (such as the word *advisor*) is considered a ghastly error by AP.

A busy news editor or producer won't take the time—even if it were available—to correct style errors scattered throughout a news release if a PR practitioner decides to ignore established journalism writing basics. Careless disregard of such standards may not be the most common reason for dumping 90 percent of media releases into the office recycling bin, but it undoubtedly ranks as another among the top three.

The annual AP stylebook (rightly called "the journalist's bible") has evolved over the decades from the 60-page stapled first edition in 1953 to the 400+ pages currently being produced.

Tom Curley, AP president and CEO, wrote in the foreword of the latest printing:

"Today, the 21st century Associated Press has become the essential global news network. And the AP Stylebook has become the essential tool for anyone who cares about good writing."

One problem style area, among many, is when some writers wrongly choose to adopt the commonly known postal abbreviations for state names instead of those advocated by AP. And don't forget those eight states never abbreviated by AP, even with a city.

Even seasoned public relations practitioners—along with print journalists—still have to sneak a peek at their AP books, especially with yearly changes and new additions. But by having flipped through it so often, they are familiar with its contents and don't waste too much precious time trying to find the proper page for their style question.

Let's say a public relations college intern is writing an advance news release about a speaker, from whom he has received her self-produced biography. She lists her degrees as a B.A. and an M.S. Is that proper style? Where does he look in his stylebook?

- ▶ Education? Nothing there.
- ▶ Initials B.A.? Nothing.
- ▶ M.S.? Not there, but there's something about the courtesy title Ms. if that's ever an issue.
- ▶ Degrees? No, but there's a suggestion to look up academic degrees.
- ▶ Abbreviations? No, but please notice the suggestion again to see academic degrees.
- ▶ Academic degrees? Well, why not? Bingo. Here he will find the correct usage rules detailing if, how, where and when he should write about such academic achievements.

However, now comes the difficult part. Will the intern remember to check out academic degrees the next time that issue surfaces (in two months or so) if he didn't recall the style statute in the first place? Good PR writers don't need to memorize all these stipulations about style, as long as they possess sufficient hunting instincts when they need their stylebooks. Much of that will come with additional experience. Probably the most frequent style investigations are for assistance concerning numbers, addresses, abbreviations and punctuation.

As for numbers, AP's general decrees want numerals spelled out as words if they are nine or below. Typical exceptions to try to recall are that Arabic numerals are always used for ages (4-year-old twins), money (5 cents) and addresses (6 Main St.).

Speaking of addresses, AP rules call for abbreviating Ave., Blvd. and St., but only when used with an actual address number (77 Sunset Blvd.). All other such words (Circle, Drive, Road, etc.) are never abbreviated, with or without address numbers.

AP warns writers not to use too many abbreviations or acronyms that would confuse readers. That admonition applies even more so to broadcast copy (as noted in your electronic media writing chapter). Titles before names are usually abbreviated, but AP suggests writers check its pages for courtesy titles, legislative titles, military titles and religious titles. Most months (all but March through July) are abbreviated, **but only** with a date: Dec. 11, 2016.

The best advice is to consider style manuals allies for conscientious writers rather than enemies in producing quality copy. The consistency in following the rules will make their prose easier to read, hear, comprehend and even write.

Flaunt Your (AP) Style

The best tip for budding public relations practitioners you will ever hear is: Learn to write—and think—like a journalist. Reporters complain more about PR people than anyone else. Their biggest complaints are PR people don't know what a good story is, don't recognize a nonstory/event that shouldn't be pitched to media and don't know Associated Press style.

Are journalists just that grumpy? Yes and no.

All of these deficits add up to extra time for the journalist, and editors and reporters don't have much time to spare. Deadlines, you know.

So, here are suggestions to keep most members of the media happy (if possible).

1. Know your AP style and use it in your releases and emails to media. Keep an AP Stylebook beside your computer anytime you are writing and editing—and use it.

2. Keep emails of releases and pitches to media short and to the point. Look at the first sentence of your email message as a story lead that must get their attention. The subject line should be like a headline to draw the journalist in. Boring will not get it. Then attach your release and photos.

3. Be sure you write like a journalist. Use inverted pyramid style, have a compelling lead (preferably not simply who, what, when, where) and get the basic information in the first couple paragraphs (and maybe **bold** it). Even with visual media nowadays, they want more story, so the days of shortening a release for TV are over. They want the info but want the 5W's and why it's important to visual media in the first few sentences. No flowery, opinionated phrases. Those are the trademark of the kind of PR people journalists either hate or make fun of or both. Keep it unbiased and concise. Even feature stories should not be padded or wordy.

4. You **must** have a strong hook for the story to even get a nibble from media. Journalists are getting harder and harder to entice. The release must be about something new, different, happening soon, groundbreaking or changing. If it's not, don't bother the media with it. You'll lose your credibility with media members if you send even a few stories that have no strong hook.

5. Each journalist looks for something just a tad different, so be sure to establish a rapport with editors, reporters and bloggers in your clients' locales or markets. Call them when you have good stories to pitch or send. Chat with them when you see them in public, about things other than business sometimes, too. Send them well-written stories that they don't have to edit to pieces with good strong story hooks they can use. And feed them whenever possible.

6. Yes, feed them. All other ploys generally are looked at as "schmoozing" or even ethically questionable, but a tray of mini-hot hoagies from a new sandwich shop or a couple boxes of fresh doughnuts can make lifelong—albeit still a tad suspicious—friends of many poor and eternally ravenous broadcasters, reporters and editors. They may not show it, but they will appreciate the thoughtfulness and happy tummies.

7. If it's at all possible, include photos. Take them yourself or get them from your client. A photo or two (or several) at least doubles your chances of getting the story in print and Web editions. Use head shots only when you have nothing else. Get action photos of people doing what the story is about, rather than just a machine or an empty room.

8. If you have B-roll video for TV media, send it! Just make sure it's in the format that the TV production folks can use. That means you will have to call or email to ask.

9. Do not badger members of the media. If they don't respond to your call or email pitch or releases, check with them one more time, then let it be. If they like it, you will hear from them. If you do not, they might use it or they might not. But they will start avoiding you if you call or email too much or often. Remember: Their time is extremely limited and valuable to them. Use it wisely.

10. Finally, get some experience in the media if you possibly can, even as a freelancer. Get some clips for your portfolio **and** learn how reporters and editors **think,** how they decide which story to cover, which stories get the best play.

If you can write and think like a member of the media, journalists may be leery of you initially. But once they see you know what you're doing (and how **they** do it), they will come to respect you, not mind your calls and emails, and use your ideas and pieces more often.

Successfully working with journalists and getting your client in the media not only pleases the customer—and keeps you employed—but it also lays a positive foundation for the times when the news is not as good. Next time you get rebuffed by media, try counting to 10 (above) and think like a journalist.

By Lise Cutshaw, Media and Marketing Coordinator,
School of the Arts, East Tennessee State University

Media Kits

Unlike the old paper-laden media kits from the 20th century, today's online newsroom contains a wealth of details that can be downloaded instantly. Poorly produced kits, in any format, can still alienate reporters if they don't provide what the writers need. Some media kits are still printed, of course, and their need to provide background information is still valid for certain occasions, such as grand openings or legitimate news conferences.

Whether printed or virtual, their content can be somewhat similar in either format. News releases, a CEO biography, a fact sheet and a backgrounder are typical inserts. A photograph or two slips easily into folders, while the online kit provides many more options in all areas, not just visual or audio.

Numerous advantages exist for companies that have adapted new technology for their requisite media kits. Having 24/7 instant access to limitless content is a major plus. TV station managers, for example, can choose video they desire, something missing from the traditional kits.

Updates and corrections can be quickly made with a few clicks of the keyboard. Saving landfills from outdated printed kits is one more benefit.

Costs are vastly reduced, of course, when an organization doesn't have to pay for printing, paper, photography, folders, visuals, production and postage charges. That's especially important for a nonprofit organization that's often asking the public for donations. Since regular postal delivery can be slow, some companies would use more expensive overnight delivery services to guarantee kits reached their intended audience before a particular date.

A few PR practitioners would annoy newsroom personnel by having their print media kit delivery messengers hand over a package that exploded with confetti when opened. Online options avoid those frivolous costs and that type of infamous office chaos.

Traditional journalists as well as bloggers, social media participants and consumers now directly retrieve news via apps. The public has voted with its viewing habits to get more of its daily news through Web-based media.

Eric Schwartzman, a designer of online media centers, wonders why so many companies still aim them strictly at journalists. In the June 2009 *Public Relations Tactics*, he advised PR communicators on the topic.

> *The Web enables organizations to talk directly with the public. So why design an online newsroom specifically for journalists, when you can design it for all of your key publics instead? . . . So why focus your online newsroom primarily on accommodating the press, when you can engage your most vocal, outspoken proponents and build a word-of-mouth army instead?*

PRactical TIP

Media Kit Contents

Traditional media kits had useful information that also needs to be available in online newsrooms. A few astute public relations practitioners would create special individualized kits for various media outlets (radio, print, television), but most were generic to be used by anyone for any occasion. Online items can include:

- ▶ News releases—these should be in dated order, with an archived PDF version list available online for journalists needing prior details. Sharp PR pros may produce both print and broadcast versions of their releases.
- ▶ Backgrounder—this lengthy report provides an historical perspective about a company or event. It's great fodder for a writer needing additional objective details on an upcoming story. Often up to four pages long with tables and subheads, the backgrounder can also be used by staff writers for internal publications. It needs to be objective.

▶ Position paper—this extended editorial provides the official company stance on an issue. It's a persuasive piece, so use good ammunition to draw conclusions for the reader.

▶ Fact sheets—these one-page documents simply list items of interest about an event, product or service. Often bulleted for easy access, the helpful fact sheet provides reporters with related details easily inserted into their articles.

▶ Biography—this can be written as an in-depth personality profile or a shorter one-page sketch of a chief executive officer. If needed, several bios could be prepared about other key leaders of an organization. They should be updated annually or after any major achievement by the individual.

▶ Social media links—journalists will want to know where to find RSS feeds, company blogs, Facebook/Twitter accounts or YouTube videos.

▶ Audio/visual links—these are necessary to fill the specific requirements of various media. In print folders, PR practitioners typically were limited to one or two photos. They might create an audio segment for a radio station in town or video files for a TV station. Now, of course, seekers can download whatever they need from your online newsroom—streaming video, podcasts, logos, PowerPoints, links and CEO blogs.

▶ Key contacts—it's vital for the media to contact a company representative to clarify a point or to obtain an answer to a question. Make sure your contact information is easy to find on your site. Reporters are often on your site because a deadline is quickly approaching.

▶ Q-and-A section—it's helpful to formulate common questions with simple and complete answers.

▶ Search box—this will provide journalists with the feeling a staff member is available to assist in their research tasks.

▶ Comment section—your interactive newsroom needs to collect comments. Seek ways to improve this two-way communication tool.

One of the most common creations after the news release for a PR pro is the fact sheet. As the name suggests, these are one-page items full of facts. They're the media kit's equivalent of Cliff's Notes. Almost always one-page long, a fact sheet will list tidbits of information on a company, an event or a product that can prove useful to a journalist. Organized often in single-space outline or bullet form, the fact sheet may tell about the chronological history of an event, list participants or give details about the host site. Sometimes a question-and-answer or the 5W format is used. Online newsrooms often contain several fact sheets.

The popularity of fact sheets may be that they are so practical for bloggers and reporters working on their stories, both now and in the future. PR writers issue them for nonprofits, government agencies and corporations, among others. Various particulars are used to fill out the prose, which give readers the impression that the writer worked hard to "dig out" all such details. Anytime you can make a reporter look good, you have done your job and won points with that journalist.

Multiple fact sheets are needed for major events, such as the 2014 Winter Olympics in Sochi, Russia. Examples would be for translation services, cultural activities, venues, transportation options and individual events. Here's just one about a venue site cluster among many possible fact sheet options.

Sochi, Russia
2014 Olympic Games
Fact Sheet
Coastal Cluster

Eleven athletic venues were built for the Sochi 2014 Olympic Games, divided into two clusters: mountain and coastal. Each cluster has an Olympic Village. A new railway transports passengers between the two venues in less than 30 minutes.

The central focus of the Coastal Cluster is the Olympic Park. It connects to all competition event venues, the parking zone and the infrastructure elements. For the first time in modern Olympic history, all ice arenas are within easy walking distance of one another. Sochi 2014 is also the most compact Winter Games ever. Seating capacity of Olympic Park is 75,000.

Jean-Claude Killy, chairman of the IOC Coordination Commission for Sochi 2014, had praise for Russia's efforts. "The results are quite impressive at all points. This is related to construction, planning, accommodation, transport and logistics. We have visited a lot of venues, and I am very impressed by what has been achieved."

The various recently constructed Coastal Cluster Olympic sites in Sochi are:

- **Fisht**—Olympic Stadium with a unique translucent roof is site of opening, closing, medal ceremonies; capacity is 40,000
- **Bolshoy**—Ice Dome is venue for ice hockey with seating for 12,000
- **Shayba**—Arena for ice hockey, seating for 7,000; the word means puck
- **Ice Cube**—Curling is held here, simplistic in its design, seats 3,000
- **Iceberg**—Figure skating and short track speed skating takes place in this 12,000 seat arena
- **Adler Arena**—site for speed skating, capacity is 8,000

Source: www.sochi2014.com/en/objects/sea/

Summary

Writing for the media remains a crucial skill for any public relations job seeker. Learning to write news releases for a variety of media enhances your chances for employment and advancement. That process involves imitating the style of quality professional journalists

Chapter 3

Business Writing:
How to Write Letters, Email and Reports

"The difference between the right word and the almost right word is the difference between lightning and the lightning bug."

Mark Twain

A Web page designed for college students tried to arouse a sense of activism in the students; unfortunately, the Web page referred to famous activists like Ralph Nader, someone the students didn't recognize.

An American T-shirt maker in Miami printed shirts for the Spanish market promoting a visit from the Pope. Instead of "I saw the Pope" (el Papa), the shirts read, "I saw the potato" (la papa).

The dean of a college sent email to the chair*men* of the five departments. Three of the five were women.

The national success with the "Got Milk?" campaign prompted it to expand to Mexico. Unfortunately, the ad writers used the following translation, "Are you lactating?"

These real-life examples exemplify what happens when you don't know to whom you are writing.

Know Your Audience

The first tip to effective writing is to know your audience. The more you know, the more you can tailor or customize your message for an individual or group.

First, think of the person or persons you write to most frequently. Visualize your supervisor or your key customer as you write. Try to obtain information such as age, education level, income and gender.

If you can uncover interests, opinions and values, you can persuade your readers more effectively. You need to know the reader's knowledge of your topic—is she an expert or does he know nothing about it?

In the earlier example about T-shirts, if the writer knew the language of the reader, he could have avoided using the wrong translation. The Web page for college students to arouse activism ignored an important demographic, age. The students were too young to remember or care about Ralph Nader. The email should have considered gender and referred to the chairs as chairpersons. The American Dairy Council failed to address the Spanish market by not even translating the slogan correctly. You can see that if the writers of these pieces knew their audiences, they could have avoided serious blunders.

What if You Don't Know Your Audience?

You have 15 minutes to write an email and you don't know much about the manager you will address. Here are some quick tips.

In most cases you can spend a few minutes determining which of the following categories most closely fits your reader (your supervisor or key client). Then you can easily adjust your writing.

Experts vs. Bottom Liners. It's helpful to evaluate whether your reader is a *layperson, expert, executive, user* or *complex* audience type. Here's a list of "Do's and Don'ts" once you categorize your reader.

Audience Types
   ► Layperson—no motivation to read
   ► Expert—interested in process and detail
   ► Executive—wants to know the bottom line
   ► User—wants to know how to use information
   ► Complex—combination of above-listed types
   ► Mixed—all types such as readers of a company newsletter

A **layperson** has little expertise in a subject matter. Therefore, laypeople usually have no particular motivation to read your letter. So, as an effective writer you must motivate or attract your reader. Starting with a benefit helps. A layperson is not versed in the topic; therefore, you must adjust your tone, style and vocabulary.

Do:	Find a way to attract attention.
Don't:	Bore your reader with detail.
Example:	A person who enjoys watching gymnastics, but has never participated in gymnastics.

An **expert** cares about process and detail. A chemist would want to know how to reproduce your results by knowing all the procedures you followed. A programmer would want you to go into particulars about how you develop a program and its ability to interface with other programs. Give experts the specifics. The same details would scare or bore the layperson.

Do:	Focus on procedure or process.
Don't:	Only give bottom-line data.
Example:	An IT person who writes software programs and wants to know how you designed a particular program.

An **executive** audience wants bottom-line information. Detailed descriptions that work for experts would not work with this audience. Use straightforward language and tone. Give a benefit and the needed information first.

Do:	Get to the point.
Don't:	Explain in detail.
Example:	The manager in charge of selling InDesign publishing software, who doesn't care how it works, but how she will sell it.

The **users** must carry out your instructions. For example, users of a software package must read your documentation to do their job. These people don't care how you wrote the software package, or about the process; they want to know how to make it work.

Writers make a common mistake with user audiences—thinking that the reader knows exactly what the writer knows. You may be familiar with zero-based budgeting in which you start from zero and build a completely new budget without taking previous numbers into account. Similarly, zero-based writing assumes a reader with a zero base of knowledge.

Do:	Realize this person might not know as much as you do.
Don't:	Be too brief.
Example:	The person who must use the grammar and style-checking feature of a word processing program.

Depending on your audience, you must adapt your writing. Unfortunately, one person might be a **complex** audience or a combination of styles.

An example would be a **layperson/executive,** a manager with no particular expertise in your field. Although this person serves as your supervisor, you must motivate him to read your work. Use benefits to catch his attention and a bottom-line style to keep his interest.

You might report to an **expert/executive,** an engineer who has worked her way up in the company to become CEO. An executive summary followed by a detailed explanation will work for this CEO.

An **expert/user** needs to know how the process works and how she can implement it. A communication manager who still writes and edits e-newsletters is an expert/user.

A **layperson/user** (an employee using the Internet) needs motivation and information. With no particular expertise or information, this person may have difficulty accessing certain websites.

Sometimes you may write for a **mixed** audience, meaning your readers comprise several audience types. When writing a company e-newsletter you must address laypeople, experts, executives, users and complex audience types. Once you've established for whom you're writing, remember to provide benefits if they read your memo, email, etc.

"You" vs. "Me" Attitude

Feature the "you attitude" and benefits to your audience. Many audiences are hostile or neutral at best. *Readers want to know what's in it for them.* Why should they read your email, letter or report? How will your document benefit them?

Many writers feature the "me" attitude. I have included some sentences from cover letters with this attitude. It's hard to persuade an audience. Featuring the "me" attitude may condemn your masterpiece to the trashcan.

Examples of excerpts from actual cover letters of writers/editors applying for a job:

Poor Choice
Although I would seem to be enormously overqualified for your position, I invite you to consider using my services. (insulting to reader)

Better Choice
My years of experience in the data processing arena could benefit your company. (benefit to reader)

Poor Choice
I read your ad for communications writer and said to myself, "This job is perfect for me." (benefit to writer)

Better Choice
I'm responding to your advertisement for a communications writer. I would like to put my writing expertise to work for your company. (benefit to reader)

Poor Choice
I'm writing to request that you do not hire me as a part-time writer. Instead, use me as a consultant. (insulting to reader)

Better Choice
I would like you to consider hiring me as a part-time writer. My consulting experience will benefit your company in the following ways. (benefit to reader)

Whether it's a letter, report or email, if it's worth writing, it's worth writing well. Don't set out to "dash off" something. Consider these guidelines from *Communication Briefings.*

Start with a purpose. What is your message?

Organize. Establish your ideas before writing. An outline can help you do this. Be brief and to the point, but also be complete. You owe your reader all necessary information.

Make a mental picture of your reader. If you don't know the reader, try to imagine what she or he is like. Try to see your writing through your reader's eyes.

Write to communicate and to get the desired reaction or response. Do not write to impress.

Have a conversation with your reader. Write in a way that comes naturally. Use words that come easily to mind. This approach helps your writing come to life and conveys warmth. Don't worry about style. Style will emerge the more you write this way.

Use simple, plain English. Write with nouns and strong verbs. Use short words. Lincoln used words of five letters or fewer for 70 percent of his Gettysburg Address. Keep your sentences to an average length of 17 words. Longer sentences discourage many readers. Make paragraphs no more than six lines long. Tight writing invites the reader to continue.

Use specific words. Avoid vague words that can be misunderstood. Don't say "office equipment" if you mean a personal computer.

Be careful with names, dates and numbers. Check everything. Don't expect someone else to pick out your mistakes.

Readability

Whether it's a memo, report or email, readability counts. Readers must be able to understand your message before they can act on it. Try the following hints for making your writing readable.

Feature Clarity, Economy and Straightforwardness

Readability includes many facets, but most important are clarity, economy and straightforwardness. *Clarity* is the opposite of ambiguity. If your writing is unclear, the reader can't be sure what you mean. In business or professional writing, you must ensure that the reader at least understands you. *Economy,* or using no more words than necessary, is one of the distinguishing marks of clear and forceful writing. Write tightly. And *straightforwardness* refers to the order in which you write, placing the subject close to the verb for easy understanding.

Clarity

If your message has more than one meaning, it's not clear. Don't use long words where short ones will do; it makes your writing dense and difficult to understand. Words ending in -ize, -ational, -ality, -ization and so on make sentences more complex than necessary. Use precision to make your writing clear. Make sure words you choose have exactly the right (and only **one**) meaning. Use specific words. Don't say "organization" if you mean "the American Red Cross."

1. My educational background basically centers around a B.A. in business administration as an economics major.
2. I spent two quarters studying the stock market and three quarters of finance which will allow me to handle your financial accounts.

The first sentence confuses the reader. Do you or don't you hold a degree? Don't use the term "centers around" as a center is a point. In the second example, what do the quarters mean? Five weeks? Ten weeks? If the information you offer is negative or not positive, omit it. Why say you've only studied the stock market for 20 weeks? Why not rephrase the unclear sentences like this:

1. I hold a B.A. in business administration with an economics emphasis.
2. I have finance experience as well as stock market expertise that will benefit your firm.

Economy

Quality business writers use a 17-word rule average when writing sentences. You want to vary the length of your sentences; however, when you use too many words, you may lose the reader. Sometimes you get to the end of a lengthy sentence and can't remember how it started. Elementary schools used to select primers about Dick and Jane and their dog, Spot. Not only were these sentences clear, but also economical, e.g., See Dick run. See Jane run. See Dick and Jane run after Spot. Not exciting, but effective!

If your message is delivered in long, arduous prose, no one may read it. Economy refers to the number of words in a sentence and the lack of redundant phrases or words. Active writing or verb writing reduces the number of words you use.

Straightforwardness

Straightforwardness refers to order and how close the subject is to the verb. Use S-V-O or subject-verb-object order with strong action verbs. If you write clearly, economically and in a straightforward manner, your audience will rate you high on readability.

Put your words in just the right order and use the right grammatical construction to make your point. For example, "We'll **only** write three major contracts this year," suggests the company won't do anything else but write these contracts. "We'll write **only** three major contracts this year," makes the meaning clearer. Also, try to keep your subject near the verb. Look at these next sentences to see what happens when you don't.

1. In response to your job opening notice concerning the public relations practitioner advertised in the October 12 issue of *The Washington Post,* I am submitting my job application letter.

2. In response to the letter you wrote to Dr. Busler, I am applying for the position of advertising assistant described in the aforementioned letter.

Not only do these sentences have an awkward order, but also they are unclear. Let's consider the following revisions. The subject "job opening notice" is nowhere near the verb "submitting," making this sentence confusing. The following revision seems more straightforward:

1. I am submitting this application in response to your advertisement in *The Washington Post* for a public relations practitioner.

   In the second example, *who* wrote the aforementioned letter is unclear. Try the following revision instead:

2. I am applying for the advertising assistant described in your letter to Dr. Busler.

Avoid the use of redundancy in your writing to ensure greater readability. When you use redundant phrases, you increase the sentence length and violate the 17-word rule. Research shows that if sentences contain up to eight words, they have a "very easy readability" rating, reaching 90 percent of the audience.

Toolbox Tips

According to The Communication Workshop in Port Washington, N.Y., and the *Secretary's Letter,* PR pros should avoid phrases and clichés like:

► To be perfectly honest
► Needless to say
► Enclosed herewith, please find
► If you should have any further questions, please do not hesitate to call
► For your perusal, review and consideration
► We deem it advisable; It has come to my attention
► The undersigned
► Pursuant to your request
► Transparent to the user
► Under separate cover

Consider the Following Readability Tips

► Use clarity—one meaning.
► Use economy—17-word average sentence length.
► Practice straightforwardness (proper order).
► Avoid clichés and jargon.
► Avoid negative writing.

▶ Avoid passive voice.
▶ Avoid noun and adjective stacks.
▶ Avoid italics and all caps.
▶ Avoid the "me" attitude.

Avoid Clichés and Jargon

If you use clichés and jargon, you'll likely bore or confuse your readers. Most people skip over dreary clichés, tired metaphors and overused expressions. In *The Careful Writer,* Theodore Bernstein offers good advice: Don't banish all clichés; use them with discrimination, not as substitutes for precise thinking.

When you use terms common within a particular field, but not necessarily understood by those outside the field, you risk negative reactions. If the audience misunderstands you, you've lost it. If readers feel you don't care enough to connect with them, you've lost again. If you need to use a term your readers may not understand, define the term or provide an equivalent.

Avoid Negative Writing

The quickest way to turn off a reader is to use negative words. Research shows that it takes the mind longer to understand a negative statement than the same idea expressed in a positive way. Many times writers give unnecessary negative information like in this cover letter. "ICI Americas is eliminating much of its corporate staff, including me." Why not get the interview first before you deliver all the bad news? A cover letter is a persuasive document and the purpose is to persuade the reader to review the attached resume.

So instead of providing unnecessary negative information, omit it. When you must provide necessary negative information, do so in a positive way. Sometimes giving a reason for the negative information softens the message.

Avoid Passive Voice

William Zinsser in *On Writing Well* says the difference between the active and passive voice is like life and death for a writer. In the active voice, the subject performs the action. "The president signed the proposal," versus "The proposal was signed by the president." To avoid the passive voice, don't use the verb "to be" or "to have." When you start a sentence with "there is" or "there are," you will most likely write in the passive voice.

Avoid Noun and Adjective Stacks

Whenever you see two or three adjectives in front of a noun or several nouns in a row, you'll confuse the reader and use unnecessary words. Why say the very pretty lady when you could say "beautiful" or "stunning"? Why say the very unattractive dog when you could use "ugly"?

In this case, don't worry about withholding information from the reader. Readers don't need to know the machinery was rugged, militarized and field accessible. They only need to know that the machinery works in combat.

Avoid *Italic* and ALL CAPS

Research shows the use of both italic type and all capital letters makes it 20 percent harder for the reader to understand. Use italic type for titles of literature, foreign words (*cul de sac*) or emphasis. Don't use it to "look pretty." You'll slow the reader down. Follow AP rules and avoid italic for news releases.

All caps have another problem. WHEN YOU WRITE IN ALL CAPS, IT'S LIKE SHOUTING AT THE READER AND HE DOESN'T LIKE IT! When you use acronyms and all caps, it can be quite confusing.

A memo from personnel read: BRING YOUR EARS DOWN TO HUMAN RESOURCES TO CORRECT THESE PROBLEMS. EARS was an acronym for Employee Action Requests; however, in a memo of all capital letters, we can't distinguish the meaning.

Avoid the "Me" Attitude

Avoiding the "me" attitude means taking the reader's perspective by focusing on the benefits for him or her. Why should that person read your email, letter, report or newsletter? You have to motivate readers to read your words. If you hit them with an immediate benefit, you're more likely to connect with them and to successfully answer that age-old question, "What's in it for me?"

Structure Your Writing to Reach your Reader

When constructing emails, letters and reports, newsletters and intranet entries, make sure you ask for what you need and explain why you need it. Many experts suggest ways to format internal and external communication. The following simple formats will help you write requests, informative letters, persuasive documents and good news/bad news emails. In most cases, using these principles will serve you well and provide structure for your reader.

Try Subject Lines and Postscripts

Use subject lines and postscripts as additional inducements for the reader. A carefully crafted subject line reveals the topic of the email, report, memo or letter and can motivate the recipient to skim the first paragraph. Similarly, most people read the postscript first. A P.S. can be a helpful device, especially for persuasive documents. Use it to list your most important point.

Traditional Letter Form

Let's start with the basic letter format. Since most managers today use their own computers, many also format their own correspondence. Let's use the following example in **Figure 3-1**.

Use a *heading*, including your phone number, even if you're writing from home so the reader can easily identify you or reach you, if necessary. Always use a *date* to identify the specific letter. The *inside address* fulfills two purposes: first, you can use the person's title, which most people like to see; and second, it routes the letter to the appropriate individual, even if someone else opens the mail.

The *subject line* clues the reader as to what you might cover in this letter. The *salutation* is also important. Always try to get a name. No one likes unsolicited letters or email. If you absolutely cannot find a name, use Dear Student, Dear Customer, Dear Homeowner or something that identifies the type of person you're writing to. Only use Dear Sir/Madam or To Whom It May Concern as a last resort. Never use Gentlemen unless you know no woman may read the letter. After the salutation, use a colon (Dear Dean Jordan:).

Remember to use a short first paragraph to intrigue the reader and to indent each paragraph for reading ease. Use one of the many good *closings* to end your letter: Cordially, Sincerely, Sincerely yours, Regards, Respectfully submitted, etc.

The *supplement line* usually benefits you, the writer, by indicating who formatted the final letter or where you can find this letter electronically. If you plan to enclose a check or another document, indicate how many attachments you included (Attachments 2). The reader can then look for the enclosed items.

Also, consider using a *postscript* to catch the reader's attention. If possible, put your main point in the postscript for emphasis.

Email Format

Most managers use emails for internal issues and letters for external communication. Sometimes the formality of the content suggests the use of a letter. Letters tend to be more formal while emails have a sense of informality.

In most organizations, email has taken the place of memos because of its speed and ease of use. However, many employees misuse email by sending private messages and by forgetting that others may judge their writing by viewing their sloppy email messages.

TOOLBOX TIP

When to Copy Someone

Copy a person's boss, particularly if your memo cites the person's achievements or accomplishments. When employees receive that kind of recognition, they tend to work harder. Also, many times managers copy employees on an FYI or For Your Information basis.

Heading

Judy Lord
699 Knox Road
Ardmore, PA 19077
(610) 259-1241

January 23, 2014   Date

Mr. James Penrod   Inside address
Vice President, Sales
ABC Computing
394 Vesper Road
Knoxville, TN 37966

Subject: QuarkXPress   Subject line

Dear Mr. Penrod: Salutation

I would like to order the most current edition of QuarkXPress. Would you please send me any appropriate documentation as well? I work at home as a consultant and prepare brochures and e-newsletters for clients.

Body

As I need your product immediately, please send it quickly, perhaps by overnight mail. I have always used your software products and appreciate your service mentality. Thank you for handling this request quickly.

Sincerely yours,   Closing and signature

Judy Lord
ALD/jl.245   Supplement line
Attachments (2)   Attachments

P.S.   I enjoyed your recent e-newsletter!   Postscript

FIGURE 3-1

Let's review the basic email format.

TO: All Employees
FROM: Human Resources
DATE: March 5, 2014
SUBJECT: Holiday policy

Because our employee committee suggested a more flexible holiday policy, we have adopted several options. You may now choose either Columbus Day or President's Day as a paid holiday.

Previously, you had nine paid holidays. You now have an additional "flexible" day. If you have questions about the policy changes, call Johanna at 4265.

c: Board of Directors
P.S.   Enjoy your extra holiday!!

Use a standard email format with the following headings: TO, FROM, DATE and RE or SUBJECT. Keep in mind the etiquette tips for checking grammar, spelling and content before you hit send.

Prior to the demise of the "carbon copy," the term "cc" was used at the end of a memo to indicate those who would receive carbon copies. Since the "carbon" copy is extinct, most writers now use "c" meaning copy. Consider using a postscript in your email or memo. It catches readers' attention, causing them to look at the subject line. Thus, you can lure the reader into your email in several ways.

Now that we've reviewed the basic letter and email format, let's look at five possible letter/email structures.

Direct Request Letter or Email

When writing a direct request, the most important piece of information you should include is why you need the requested item or service and *how* you will use it. Your reader will usually welcome the direct request. The reader's attitude is *positive;* he wants to hear from you. Try this format:

Paragraph One	Request for information or services.
Paragraph Two	**Show why you need the information and how you will use it.**
Paragraph Three	State the specific action for the reader to take.
Paragraph Four	List reader benefits and use a good will ending.

Direct Request Letter

If you write to a university asking about a master's program, the most important information you can give the university is why you need the information and how you'll use it.

Dear Grove City Admissions:

I'm writing concerning your master's program in Education, specifically for Special Ed. I'd like to enroll as a full-time student in Fall 2014.

As a full-time student, I'd like to complete the degree in one calendar year and to start teaching by September 2015 in a special ed environment.

Please send me brochures/collateral materials about the program as well as an application package. If you would prefer that I apply online, please let me know.

I've met some of the graduates of your program and they are well respected. Thanks for expediting this process for me.

Sincerely yours,

Lauralee Ebersol

Informative Letter/Email

Now, let's look at an informative letter.

Many times we write to provide information about upcoming meetings, policies or projects. Usually readers hold a *neutral* attitude toward informative letters, so the most important aspect of this letter is to capture their attention.

Paragraph One	**Capture the attention of your audience.**
Paragraph Two	Provide the necessary information.
Paragraph Three	Present any negative factors; show reasons for these factors.
Paragraph Four	List reader benefits.
Paragraph Five	Provide a good will ending.

Capture your reader's attention and then give the required information. If negative factors exist, embed them between other more positive paragraphs. For example, if an employer designates a room as a smoking lounge, a negative factor could be limited times when smokers could use the room. Never start or end with negatives! Always try to list benefits to the reader and use a good will ending.

Informative Email

> To: Employees of Parkdale School
> From: Lois Littlejohn, Facilities Manager
> Subject: Company Parking Lot
>
> I'd like to announce that the school board has approved plans to resurface the school parking lot. It will give us extra spaces to make parking easier.
>
> We'll begin work on August 12. We expect the project to take one week. Even with a delay, we'll finish before the school year starts.
>
> During the project, no one can use the parking lot. Let's put up with a minor inconvenience so that we'll have more room with clearly marked spaces.
>
> Hope you share my enthusiasm about this improvement of our facilities.

Persuasive Letter/Email

Sometimes we must not only inform, but also persuade our audience. Try the following format to persuade a resistant reader.

(Reader may *initially disagree* with request)

Paragraph One	Catch the reader's interest. Establish mutual goals or common ground.
Paragraph Two	Define the problem that will be solved if the request is approved.
Paragraph Three	Explain the solution. Show how any negatives are outweighed by advantages of the solution.
Paragraph Four	List all reader benefits.
Paragraph Five	**State the specific action you want the reader to take.**

Even if the reader disagrees with you, try to establish mutual goals, agree on some point or establish common ground. Since adult learners like to solve problems, give your readers a problem with multiple solutions. Most readers like choices; the multiple solutions allow readers the opportunity to select the option they prefer.

If you must list any negative information, make sure the advantages of the solution outweigh these negative factors. List any benefits that accrue to the reader as a result of her solution to the problem. And most important, state the specific action you want the reader to take. Many times readers feel persuaded by the message, but don't know what to do next.

Persuasive Letter

Dear Student,

I'm writing in hopes that you will consider registering as an organ donor. Registering as an organ donor means agreeing to donate organs to someone in need. According to the Cleveland Clinic, a nonprofit academic medical center, 110,000 people currently need an organ donation. Eighteen people die per day waiting for an organ donor. Organs and tissues from one nonliving person can benefit more than 50 people.

Organ donation is a personal choice and plays a huge role in the life of others. Christopher Sommer, a 16-year-old sophomore at Delaware Valley High School, recently surprised his classmates. He made an appearance on stage after the faculty gathered the student body in the auditorium for an assembly. He had received a heart transplant. His heart had failed, and he lived for several months because of a machine pumping his heart. Three months later, he received a heart transplant. His classmates followed his illness and recovery on Facebook.

Many like Christopher receive organ transplants because students like you made the important decision to register online or at your local motor vehicle agency. Others die waiting for a transplant.

Make a difference. Call the Gift of Life Donor Program at 1-800-4DONORS or visit organdonor.gov.

Sincerely,

Nicole Hodgson
Rowan University student

Good News Letter/Email

And now for an easy-to-write letter—the good news format that a reader happily receives.
(Reader's attitude is *positive*)

Paragraph One	**Deliver the good news.**
Paragraph Two	Provide any details.
Paragraph Three	Discuss any negative elements.
Paragraph Four	List the reader benefits and close with a good will ending.

Enjoy the opportunity to applaud a colleague or an employee by sending many good news memos. Research shows that employees perform better when they feel appreciated and recognized. In this memo, present the good news and any details of that news. Couch negative elements in-between the good news and benefits. List reader benefits to reinforce the good news and close with a good will ending.

Good News Email

To: Isabel Battaglia
From: Carol Pupis
Subject: Award

The photograph you submitted of the Bozorth Building has been chosen as the first-place winner in our annual photo competition. We will publish it in the next edition of the *Epson Magazine.* You have also won a cash prize of $1,000.

Will you be able to come to headquarters to receive your winnings in person? If that won't work for you, we'll issue it by mail.

Congratulations on your impressive photograph!

Negative Message Letter/Memo

Perhaps the most difficult letter to write, the negative-news letter, is one the reader doesn't wish to receive.
(Reader's attitude is *unfavorable*)

Paragraph One	Establish good will.
Paragraph Two	Present the negative message. **Present reasons for the message.**
Paragraph Three	Explain positive aspects and re-establish good will.

This letter or email most likely will inspire dread for you and your reader. Establish common ground or good will initially. Then give the negative message with the reasons, if possible. To close, explain any positive aspects and re-establish the good will of your reader.

Although no one desires to receive negative news, research shows that we prefer to know the reasons behind the bad news. And while most of us have received rejection letters, we feel less devastated when employers list the reasons for the rejection. Sometimes employers don't send letters at all or they send the "rejection form letter," which creates a poor relationship with the reader. As a writer, put yourself in the reader's place and you will write in an empathetic manner.

Negative-News Letter

Herring Interiors
296 Girard Avenue
Aurora, Ohio 44202

July 1, 2012

David Dinning
Decors by David
7 Oakmont Place
Media, PA 19063

Dear Mr. Dinning:

Thank you for your recent shipment of the furniture we ordered. We've enjoyed dealing with your company in the past.

However, as I mentioned to you on the telephone, we're disappointed by the condition of the six white mushroom chairs in this shipment. I've enclosed photographs of the chairs that show how the paint is flaking off in many areas. It appears that the paint was applied over a finish and is not adhering properly.

Please send replacements for these chairs as soon as possible. If you cannot guarantee the white finish, I will accept the natural finish as a substitute.

I know how much you care about customer concerns, and I look forward to a resolution of this problem.

Sincerely,

Nadia DegliEsposti
President, Herring Interiors

So, to design easy formats to guide your reader, consider using the aforementioned structures. Remember that having a purpose and identifying your audience won't work without an appropriate structure.

PRactical TIP

Writing Annual Reports

The annual report ranks at the top of the corporate communication pyramid. Surveys rank it as the single most important document. Company annual reports afford professional communicators with perhaps their greatest challenge. On one level they contain information required by the Securities and Exchange Commission (SEC) for reporting financial information for publicly traded companies. At another level they serve as a valuable marketing tool for organizations to attract potential stock investors. They typically are provided to members of the media to help them do a thorough job of covering businesses and nonprofit organizations.

While all reports contain information the SEC requires, most annual reports also contain optional features. Mandatory elements include:

▶ Auditors' report. Summary of the findings of an independent firm of certified public accountants to show whether the financial statements are complete, reasonable and prepared consistent with generally accepted accounting principles (GAAP) at a set time.

▶ Management discussion. A series of short, detailed reports that analyze the company's performance.

▶ Financial statements and notes. Provide raw numbers pertaining to the company's financial performance and recent financial history. The SEC requires three statements: statement of earnings, statement of financial position and statement of cash flow.

▶ Selected financial data. Summarizes the company's financial condition and performance over five years or longer.

In addition to these mandatory elements, an annual report may contain a host of optional items. Possible entries include financial highlights, letter to stockholders, management report, names and titles of key personnel and product information.

The bulk of an annual report's financial information takes the form of tables and charts. However, the optional information that appears in most annual reports prepared for major corporations includes lavishly designed information printed on glossy paper stock. Most annual reports over the past 10 years have become more reader-friendly, looking more like magazine spreads with color photos, generous white space and stunning graphics. They are the most expensive documents regularly created by public relations writers.

Fortune 500 companies typically use their own staffs to coordinate the colossal effort with outside consultants. Some PR firms specialize in annual report writing and production.

Well-designed and well-written annual reports should stand alone as respectable, hard-working publications. Their primary purpose is to recruit stockholders. However, they also present an interesting picture of the company, painting broad strokes about the culture and serving as a valuable image-building tool. Many organizations that are not required to file annual reports, such as nonprofits, still produce them for all the public relations benefits they create.

Writing Reports

Another common writing project for the public relations practitioner is reports. They range from simple, one-page articles about products or policies to lengthy, investigative documents with tables and charts. Many of the latter concern finances, feasibility or progress of a project, often issued monthly or quarterly.

Report writing is a treasured skill. Employees with solid experience in report writing are valuable staff members who are typically recognized and rewarded for their expertise. What we have covered previously in this text about quality writing applies as well to producing reports. Even if writing for a specialized audience, be careful of using too much jargon. Use enough specialized language so that your credibility is established with the readers, but simple English should be your goal.

The report's format itself is the major difference from many other writing examples. Organizational structure for the lengthy reports is fairly common, although not all documents use all the following elements. Their sole purpose is to ensure the report is well organized for ease of use.

Letter of Transmittal—Often clipped onto the entire packet, this letter or memo of transmittal (depending on the formality of the report) essentially says "here it is." It states that the report (requested by such a person or office) is now prepared to provide answers to the situation. The letter gives your report credibility by telling recipients why it is being sent to them. It usually includes a phrase from the authors about contacting them for additional information.

Cover Page—Heavy card stock is typically used, sometimes protected by a clear vinyl or plastic cover. The cover page simply presents (in a large font) the title of the report, often an explanatory subtitle, the parties for whom it's intended, the date and the authors.

Title Page—This is identical to the cover page, only it's produced on regular paper. The title page is part of the actual report, but it has no page number. Officially, it's considered page i.

Table of Contents—As the name implies, the contents page lists the various elements of the lengthy report and the page number where they begin. Do not list the title page.

Table of Charts and Graphs—Although often called other terms, this page likewise gives the page numbers for the various tables and illustrations used within the report. Some suggest that this insertion isn't necessary for documents with only two or three figures.

Executive Summary—We hate to tell you this, but for many reports this is the only page that is read by the busy CEO. Therefore, you need to produce a one-page document as if the rest of the report didn't even exist. It has to summarize the content and persuade convincingly. A compelling synopsis may encourage additional reading of your report by the organization's leadership.

Abstract—This is an even briefer, concise statement about the report's contents. Ranging from a mere paragraph to one page, the abstract does not attempt to summarize any findings. It merely provides a short description concerning the report's contents.

Report—The report itself consists of three main parts: introduction, body and conclusion. A brief introduction should state clearly what is the purpose of the report. Repetition of who or what department authorized the document is often found here as well. It might also flesh out the table of contents so readers will better understand the document's organization. The lengthy body of the report delivers details that have been researched. Internal headlines and subheads will help readers follow the logic and sequence of the written project. The conclusion repeats key summary points and often suggests future action.

List of Works Cited—Publication details about sources used in the report can be listed here. Often used only for long, formal reports, the list should have complete publication details (including publisher and date) for those who want to consult such resources.

Appendix—This final section might include questionnaires, graphics, maps, or charts and tables that may have been too awkward to include in the body of the report. Items in the optional appendix are individually labeled Appendix A, Appendix B, etc.

Writing a Technical Report

Every real story you read has some sort of logic and point to it. Technical reports are no different. Most technical writers look at a technical report as a laundry list of information—something that the reader must labor through. However, writers should view technical reports more from a story-telling perspective and add some warmth and personality to the project. After all, real live people read technical documents and these documents relate to real live people and events.

Business professionals, like many casual readers, have limited attention spans. They want to get to the conclusion quickly. They generally concentrate their attention to the beginning and end of technical reports. And, they find facts and figures compelling. They also like subheads for easy reading. Before writing the technical report consider the following:

- ▶ Technical reports written by someone with a reputation for careful work have greater credibility.
- ▶ Technical professionals respond favorably to well-organized documents.
- ▶ Warm, conversational tone adds to the persuasive intent of a technical report.
- ▶ Referencing authorities adds to the credibility and acceptance of technical reports.
- ▶ Technical writers must focus on the needs of the intended audience.
- ▶ Readers tend to resist information presented in a "pushy" tone and tend to reject arguments one-by-one.

Finally, don't assume that because you wrote the document and understand the technical nature of the information that the intended audience fully understands the information and jargon. A well-written technical report begins with a clear outline that first considers the desired outcome. It then weighs all the possible reactions that the receiver will have toward the message. Simply, it anticipates objections. It then writes with an eye toward clarity, conciseness and consistency.

Summary

Structure your writing to reach your reader. Try the aforementioned formats when writing letters or emails. Remember to indent your paragraphs, make your opening paragraphs short and use subject lines and postscripts. Mind your manner when using email. Treat them as carefully as you treat letters. Establish common grounds or state benefits to gain the attention of your readers.

Check your style, grammar, spelling and punctuation, no matter what type of report you write. Any report will be more effective if you focus on the specific subject, appeal to the reader's interests, address the reader's needs, provide the essential information and make it easy for the reader to use that information.

Chapter 4

Business Writing: How to Write Newsletters, E-Newsletters and Intranet Entries

"You can have brilliant ideas, but if you can't get them across, your ideas won't get you anywhere."

Lee Iacocca

Newsletters cater to both internal and external audiences. In fact, their varied uses enable writers to tailor creative, informative messages to selected audiences. Modeled after newspapers and news magazines, newsletters and e-newsletters provide information to a variety of readers through an inexpensive, yet powerful, medium.

The appropriate design and content of a newsletter depends on the audience targeted and the tone and style of the information needing to be communicated. Publications generally have two primary purposes:

1. They help present special information to selected audiences.
2. They reinforce organizational attitudes and opinions.

Newsletters contribute to an organization's overall communication program. In fact, their specialized use contributes to the overall organizational effectiveness and establishes another credible source for dissemination of relevant information.

Simply knowing how to use software doesn't necessarily qualify you to design and produce effective publications. Technology is merely a tool that relies on sound understanding of graphic layout and design coupled with clear and precise writing.

A basic, yet overlooked, element of a first-rate newsletter is to know what constitutes a newsletter. To qualify for newsletter status, a publication must first meet the criteria of serialization.

Serialization involves the regular production and distribution of a publication, whether hard copy or online. Organizations catalog newsletters by printing volume and issue numbers on each issue. This enables readers to keep track of the publication and gives a sense of permanence to the publication. Such durability adds credibility to the messages communicated and the communication vehicle as a whole.

PR practitioners use various formats to produce effective newsletters. Of course, before deciding on a format, communicators must first carefully analyze the audience and then select the design that best complements the planned messages.

Some design types to consider include:

Newspapers. Usually produced in four-column or five-column newsprint, newspaper design provides an inexpensive way to communicate hard news items.

Magazines. This style emphasizes more of a creative feel for your publication and generally capitalizes on the use of color photography and high-quality, coated paper stock. The style also works best with feature story copy.

Minimags. This half-size magazine style format (5½″ by 8½″) is generally used more like a brochure or for promotional purposes. Its simple design invites readers to sample the publication.

Maganews and **Magapapers.** These hybrid formats are unique for their generous use of white space and emphasis on graphic design. They provide a unique forum for conveying company information through a creative vehicle.

Key Design Issues

Proper production of newsletters begins with a thorough understanding of four basic elements of composition:

1. Body type (text). Use serif fonts like Times New Roman or Cambria.
2. Headline type (headlines, titles, kickers, hanging indents, etc.). Use sans serif type like Helvetica, Arial or Calibri for headlines.
3. Art (photos, drawings, graphic elements).
4. White space. Air or space gives a publication a sense of freedom.

Newsletter editors must also pay attention to:

Nameplate. The name of a publication. The front-page nameplate may also include a logo along with the volume and issue number of the publication.

Masthead. Block of text identifying the publication, including staff, address, website, copyright information and so on. Generally found on the second page of the publication.

Publications such as *Communication Briefings,* an award-winning monthly newsletter, stress a style known as modular design. Essentially, modular design combines a variety of geometric shapes to produce a publication that's easy to read and invites readers to spend time with the publication.

Despite a desire to produce super creative publications using a variety of graphic elements, an editor must remember these sound layout and design practices:

Emphasize white space. Publications that are too heavy in copy and graphics have a gray look that diminishes reader appeal.

Avoid butting heads. Publication designers must not place headlines directly next to each other in the publication. This causes confusion on the reader's part and can result in decreased readership.

Vary shapes. Consider the design of a publication like a mix of geometric shapes. Each different shape complements one another, yet maintains its own unique quality.

Focus on writing. Even the most creative and unique design can't make up for a poorly written newsletter. The design of the publication must work in combination with clean, crisp and concise writing. This provides an effective communication vehicle.

How to Write Newsletter/E-newsletter Copy

Although images and layout count, the written content is the major factor in whether your newsletter succeeds. Writing copy for a newsletter involves more than a grasp of English grammar. You need to write interesting, relevant and formatted copy to attract readers (see **Figure 4-1**).

According to wikiHow, you should first **consider your audience.** Gather both demographic and psychographic information about them. An audience of middle-aged women probably won't want detailed information about your product. But if you relate your product to how it will help them feel better, they might read on.

Content matters. If you include a variety of topics and sections, you'll appeal to a wider group of readers. Try using sections like newspapers do: opinion, letters to the editor, features, etc. Break up the layout with customer tips or reviews.

Ask questions. Use the "five W" questions to establish a news tone for your newsletter.

Research your information. Back up your articles with research. Without it, you risk including incorrect information and offending your readers. Use expert opinion and statistics and attribute them to your sources.

Make it readable. Use short, concise, clear language to improve the newsletter's readability. Use a style guide for consistency. Avoid jargon and slang: aim for the comprehensive level of a 12-year-old.

Use interesting headlines. Use action verbs to evoke curiosity. Otherwise, readers will skim your articles and never read them. Use subheadings to break up the text.

Proofread. You should read not only for typos but also for consistency of tone and voice. Don't leave proofreading to your spelling and grammar check tools.

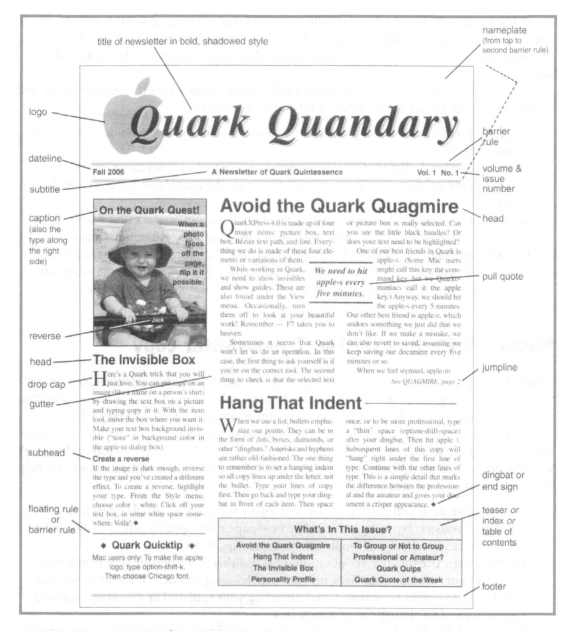

FIGURE 4-1 Anatomy of a Newsletter, page 1.

From *Communicating with QuarkXPress* by Claudia Cuddy. Copyright © 2012. Reprinted by permission of Word Nerd Publishing.

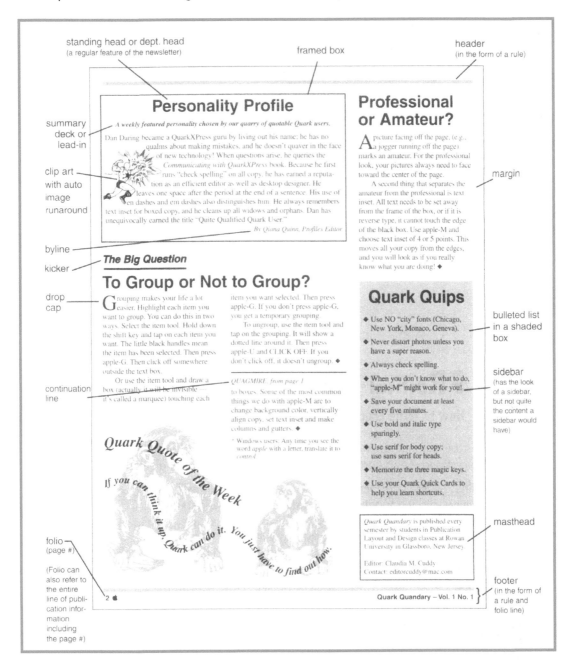

FIGURE 4-1   Anatomy of a Newsletter, page 2.
From *Communicating with QuarkXPress* by Claudia Cuddy. Copyright © 2012. Reprinted by permission of Word Nerd Publishing.

According to ProCopyTips (http://www.procopytips.com), corporate newsletters are an important tool to communicate with employees, clients, prospects or suppliers. Write regular, engaging, proactive newsletters/e-newsletters to maintain customer or employee engagement.

Writing Specifically for E-Newsletters

An e-newsletter is an HTML email that allows organizations to submit correspondence to their employees or clients on a continued basis using an email or e-newsletter system. For e-newsletters, an exciting subject line will arouse reader interest and encourage continued reading. Keep in mind that your readers will ask themselves the question, "What's in it for me?" Think about the benefits you offer or the results of using your services. Appeal to the emotions—anger, curiosity, greed, ego, vanity, hope, fear or insecurity.

Including testimonials establishes credibility with your readers. Remember that reading large chunks of copy is intimidating. Confronted with a page of solid text, many readers will close

PRactical TIP

How to Write Engaging Newsletter Articles in Seven Easy Steps

1. Know your audiences. What are their problems, motives and interests?
2. Have a strong, newsworthy angle. Try one of the following elements:

   Timeliness—did it happen recently?
   Proximity—did it happen close by to you or your readers?
   Prominence—was someone important involved?
   Consequence—did it have a major impact?
   Human interest—was it about someone who your audience cares about?
   Novelty—was it out of the ordinary?
   Progress—did it have to do with innovation?

3. Write a killer headline.
4. Follow it with a powerful lead.
5. Build your angle with a quote.
6. Use an image to create interest.
7. Finish your article with a call to action. Think along the lines of downloading the latest policy from the intranet, registering for training, requesting a product brochure, completing the satisfaction survey, etc.

your email. Instead, break up the text into bite-size paragraphs and use subheadings and bullet points liberally. E-newsletters often feature embedded links that lead the reader to websites where they can learn more about a certain topic or event.

For example, John Hopkins issues a monthly e-newsletter providing health information and insight from its experts. Each issue features information on common health topics and interests, health tips, patient stories and updates in medical research. (See http://www.hopkins medicine.org/news/e-newsletters)

Ezinearticles recommends that to keep readership high, you should have three main articles per e-newsletter. Include additional sidebar blurbs and links to information on your website and other interesting sites.

Figure 4-2 shows two pages of an e-newsletter written to graduate students and alumni of the graduate public relations program at Rowan University.

Writing for the Web—Externally and Internally

Our high-tech, high-speed business world demands to-the-point writing that gets its message across with no wasted words. According to Jack Gillespie, editor of *Communication Briefings,* even when sending email or writing intranet entries, we still need good writing techniques like these:

▶ simple sentences
▶ short sentences (17 words)
▶ "you" attitude toward readers
▶ active verbs
▶ avoiding verbs that masquerade as nouns like consideration (consider) or description (describe)
▶ clarity
▶ short paragraphs with subheads to help your readers

And, according to the *Online Journalism Review,* when writing for the Web, the shorter the better. Readers like writers who don't waste their time. You should use active voice so you don't bore readers with uninteresting prose. Use strong verbs that demonstrate action. And always attribute sources so readers don't think you've made it up!

TOOLBOX TIP

Online writers can communicate with their readers in many more forms than the traditional news article. Blogs, wikis and discussion boards dissolve the barrier between writer and reader, creating a more informal and interactive writing environment.

Blogging. Speak with informed, personal authority while engaging readers in a productive conversation. Write about what you know—your passion, which is well researched and reported.

Wiki. The ultimate exercise in writing by committee; presents facts and acknowledges controversies in clear, neutral language.

Discussion boards. Don't ask yes or no questions. Seek personal anecdotes to keep the momentum going.

TOUCH OF CLASS

News about the Rowan University Graduate Public Relations Program

VOLUME 19, ISSUE 4   SUMMER 2012

INSIDE THIS ISSUE:

Class Explores   1
Emerging
Career Trends

Experts Address   1
PR Support for
Foundations

Crawford,   4
Girone Earn
Graduate
Medallions

Graeff Named   4
NJSPRA
Scholarship
Winner

Class Explores Emerging Career Trends

By Cate Girone

Economic shifts, corporate reorganizations and technological shifts all contribute to big shifts in public relations career landscape.

To help students better understand and cope with these changes Rowan University's M.A.in P.R. Program hosted a Master Class this semester titled "Emerging Public Relations Career Trends."

Professor Edward Moore began the panel by sharing some interesting statistics about the future of PR careers. PR consistently lands a spot on the Bureau of Labor "hot jobs"

list, and appears again in 2012. The Bureau of Labor anticipates growth in the number of PR positions and in PR salaries. Moore then introduced the panel of experts, including PR veterans John Moscatelli, Raymond Daiutolo and David Burgin.

Moscatelli, a public relations counselor, PRSA Fellow, and president of his own consulting firm, currently teaches at Rowan. He spent 20 years on active duty as an Air Force public affairs officer before serving in top positions at various PR agencies, including Chief Operating Officer at Anne Klein Communications. Daiutolo, the corporate

communications officer for USPS and career USPS employee, provides internal and external communication support for the company's South Jersey, Delaware and central Pennsylvania regions. His extensive PR expertise spans issues from crisis communication to legislative affairs to employee communication.

Burgin, PSEG Nuclear LLC's corporate functional area manager for emergency preparedness, has more than 25 years of experience in the emergency preparedness and

Continued on page 2

Experts Address PR Support for Foundations

By Melissa Novak

Using public relations strategies to support education foundations was the topic of a second M.A. in P.R. Master Class this semester.

The event featured a panel of talented public relations and foundation executives, all with extensive experience in running and supporting educational foundations: Kathleen J. Corbalis, from Atlantic Cape Community College; Rich Bagin, from the New Jersey School Public Relations Association; and Tarence Smith,

from the Glassboro Education Foundation.

The session explored how education foundations benefit their communities. First, it is important to identify the need for a foundation. Second, a foundation must have "champions" or key people to act as initiators to raise awareness and attract interest. Third, a foundation needs fundraising and "friend-raising," as Bagin calls it, to grow and gain support.

Bagin pointed out public relation's huge contribution to creating an effective foundation campaign.

"Even when you try to raise money for a good cause, such as supplementing a school budget to provide additional school or community resources, someone will still be unhappy and want to use the foundation for other reasons. It's important to gain trust, support, and make the goals of the foundation known."

Continued on page 3

FIGURE 4-2 E-Newsletter, page 1

PR Career Trends—continued

public affairs sectors. He oversees the company's Salem and Hope Creek Nuclear Generating Stations, and has served on over 25 advisory boards for professionals in the nuclear energy field.

After the introductions, Moore and the students engaged the professionals in a lively conversation about what employers now look for in new hires and how to stand out during the application process.

One student asked about the classic job-search catch-22: new graduates want to get jobs to gain experience, but all job positions seem to require candidates that already have work experience. The panelists pointed out that Rowan graduate students have more experience than they think. Rowan students complete a series of PR plans, often for real companies or non-profit organizations, that they can discuss in interviews to show their strategic thinking and planning skills as well as what they learned from the experience.

The panelists then tackled some common resume conundrums, such as employers' desires for applicants to be "entrepreneurial" "team players." With HR departments screening resumes for these "buzz-words," Burgin suggests scanning the company website for words they prefer and using them in a resume.

All three panelists agreed that references still count but often are not as vital as they once were in the hiring process. Virtually every reference letter says something positive about the job candidate, but the letters' credibility is questionable. They admitted to relying on "unofficial" sources—such as respected peers in the public relations community—for a credible, third-party evaluation of a potential new hire. The panelists advised students to join and actively participate in professional societies to gain a positive reputation in the field. Knowing a member of the company is also valuable.

One student asked what to do when confronted with salary questions. The panelists advised researching to determine an appropriate range, and suggested that applicants note that their salary range is negotiable.

Overall, the panelists recommended developing a broad range of public relations skills with a focus on writing. As Moscatelli said, "Don't be trapped by technology. No matter the medium, strong, clear writing will get your points to your audiences effectively." ■

Touch of Class Staff—

Writer and Editor:
Cate Girone
   Graduate Program Assistant

Contributors:
Dr. Suzanne FitzGerald
         sparks@rowan.edu
Professor Edward H. Moore
         mooree@rowan.edu

Questions?
E-mail Cate at
   girone68@students.rowan.edu

Moscatelli, Burgin and Diautolo responding to student questions about job hunting.

FIGURE 4-2   E-Newsletter, page 2.

Minding Your Electronic Manners

According to Barbara Pachter, a communications trainer, sloppy Web writing illustrates bad business manners. She suggests that you use short paragraphs, limit each message to one subject or purpose and proofread your work.

Susan Perloff, writer for the *Philadelphia Business Journal,* agrees with Pachter that you can make your documents more readable (and mannerly) on the Web by:

1. writing short, declarative sentences (in other words, be concise)
2. writing in the second person (you)
3. using the active voice
4. using the imperative (command) mood to suggest what the reader should do
5. including a bullet list of choices
6. conceptualizing the hyperlinks as you write

Writing Intranet Copy

When writing for print vs. the Web, it's linear vs. **nonlinear,** author-driven vs. **reader-driven,** storytelling vs. **pursuit of actionable content,** anecdotal examples vs. **comprehensive data** and sentences vs. **fragments.** Remember the Web is an active medium where users become engaged and want to go places and get things done.

Jakob Nielsen in his Alertbox post (June 9, 2008) discusses an article in *The New York Times* titled "Coping with the Tall Traveler's Curse." That headline in print is enticing and might draw readers in. Because the article featured a photo of a tall guy crunched in a taxi, the content was clear to anyone reading the article.

Using that same headline online would fail because you must start with words like "tall traveler" because users scan down the left part of a list of items (**nonlinear**). They wouldn't see the last words in a link unless they're attracted by the first few words. The headline lacks keywords such as *airline seat* or *hotel bed* that work for search engine optimization. No one will search the word *curse* when trying to find hotel chains with extra-long beds. Even the words *tall traveler's curse* are not specific enough to tell users what the story concerns. Online, the headline alone must provide enough information to let users predict what they'll get if they follow the link.

The Web rewards **comprehensive coverage (data)** that's more specific than print content. On the Web, content for tall travelers should feature ratings of airline seats and hotel beds for major airlines and hotel chains. The content is searchable (**reader-driven**) and users can sort and personalize it.

Print publications contain linear content. In print, you can use anecdotes and examples that support a storytelling approach. On the Web, such content feels like filler. In print, discussing tall-friendly rooms in Las Vegas seems interesting. Online, if a user seeks tall-friendly rooms in Chicago only, the content won't work. Web content must be brief and get to the point quickly. Web users want **actionable content**—they're most likely on a mission. Websites must support the user's personal story by condensing vast information into something that meets the user's immediate needs. Thus, Web content becomes a user-driven narrative.

Print calls for complete sentences, while online content can make use of **fragments.** Finally, intranet users cherry-pick information and concentrate narrowly on what they want. To reach selfish readers, make your content actionable and focused on user needs.

In another Alertbox post (April 17, 2006), Nielsen refers to an F-shaped pattern for reading Web content: two horizontal stripes followed by a vertical stripe. In his eye-tracking study, he recorded how 232 users looked at thousands of Web pages. He found that reading behavior was fairly consistent across many different sites and tasks. This dominant reading pattern looks like an F and has the following three components:

1. Users read in a horizontal movement across the upper part of the content area. This forms the F's top bar.
2. Users move down the page and then read across in a second horizontal movement that covers a shorter area than the previous movement. This element forms the F's lower bar.
3. Last, users scan the content's left side in a vertical movement. This element forms the F's stem.

TOOLBOX TIP

According to http://www.therunninglibrarian. co.uk, these tips will help intranet managers succeed:

▶ Know your organization, especially its culture. How is the intranet used by employees?

▶ Know your users. What do they use regularly and what do they like/dislike on the intranet?

▶ Consult-consult-consult. Speak to users regularly about what you're developing on the intranet and how it will impact their work.

▶ Plan carefully. Use planning and project management skills to develop functionality on the intranet.

So if you design your intranet or Web content to attract readers, what must you then do to write well on the intranet?

A corporate intranet is fundamental for internal communication, collaborative work and sharing successes. According to http://betterwritinginbusiness.com, employees absorb an intranet's messages and tone, profoundly impacting their engagement and perception of the company's stability. When the writing is riddled with mistakes, employees may believe the company doesn't care about details. Your employees and colleagues deserve a well-organized and high-quality intranet. Work hard to create an intuitive intranet that includes engaging and insightful writing.

Summary

Newsletters cater to both internal and external audiences. Newsletters and e-newsletters provide information to a variety of business readers through an inexpensive yet powerful medium. PR writers use various formats to produce effective newsletters. Make sure you take body type, headline type, art and white space into consideration.

And for intranet entries, know your organization and its users and work to create an engaging and user-driven medium.

Social Media Writing

"Our head of social media is the customer."

McDonald's

Barriers to global communication certainly shrink as the world becomes increasingly connected. Public relations writers can now address audiences across continents with the same speed and simplicity as they once communicated with audiences down the block. The driving force in this, of course, is the Internet and the growing number of social media tools available on it.

Rather than relying on traditional media to hopefully get messages to intended targeted publics, you can now connect directly with consumers via social media. With an emphasis on two-way communication, these sites can create vibrant conversations between people and organizations. Huge increases in marketing budgets for social media have occurred every year this decade.

More than 1 million posts are available daily on the Web. More than 100 million Americans go online in a typical day. Two of every three online U.S. adults use social media. A large majority of journalists use Twitter or other social media devices. Yet no one has yet perfected the science of social media, a tool constantly in flux.

Nevertheless, all public relations writers need to embrace social media with the understanding that it will continue to evolve, expand and energize the communication process among

Guest author of this chapter is Stephanie Hines (B.A. and M.A.), who specializes in social media and development for Expectations Women's Center in Lewisburg, Pa. She has prior social media experience with Girls on the Run and the Autism Society.

target markets and the business community. These tools concern relationships and two-way communication, phrases often used in the definition of public relations. Properly used, they create conversations with consumers. Perhaps practitioners should take the chapter's opening quotation from McDonald's more seriously and apply the message globally.

References about social media are now the norm within print and broadcast outlet stories and advertisements. In fact, recent surveys found that about half of journalists use blogs to find story ideas. A contraction of *Web* and *logs,* blogs are free online journals on topics ranging from serious to silly. Bloggers, originally disdained by many as gossip mongers, have changed their perception to become legitimate writers and contributors to events (from sports, to fashion, to entertainment). Most professional bloggers have been recognized and given media credentials for covering events (White House, professional sports, news conferences, etc.).

But that wasn't always the case for blogosphere participants. Blogger Jeremy Porter, in response to a 2010 survey in which slightly more than half the bloggers considered themselves journalists, said: "Even if half of bloggers think they are journalists, that doesn't make it so. If I think I'm particularly good looking, it doesn't make it so." Critics of social media are increasing their attacks on its cure-all mentality. Recent book ventures include *Unfriend Yourself: Three Days to Detox, Discern and Decide About Social Media* by Kyle Tennant and *Social Media Is B.S.* by B.J. Mendelson. Others are quoting statistics that social media have not translated to corporations' bottom lines.

Operated by Brandware PR with headquarters in Atlanta, *Drillbits: The Brandware Blog* posted this interesting piece about the ubiquitous pink ribbon movement supporting breast cancer research (see **Figure 5-1**).

Most Popular Social Media

Social media exist everywhere and the ability for a user to consume them is easily a fingertip click away. As of publish date, the top five social media outlets (in order) are—Facebook, Twitter, LinkedIn, Pinterest and Google+. What does this mean for the public relations world? Simply, these sites get used for more than just social networking.

Today's social media invite curious viewers. Often, members of these diverse audiences are highly creative and analytical. They tend to reject traditional media with such great passion that they underscore famed communication scholar Marshall McLuhan's thesis that the medium is the message.

When writing for social media platforms, you need to remember more than the proper Associated Press style. Courtney Ramirez offers these hints in an article titled, "3 Cardinal Sins of Social Media Writing."

1. **Over sharing or selling.** While sales is a key goal, there needs to be an equilibrium between the sharing and selling. Ideas to share include other source materials and

THE **BRANDWARE** BLOG

Visit "Drill Bits" at http://brandwarepr.com/drillbits/

To Buy Pink or Not to Buy Pink, That is the Question

By Lindley Presley   **October 2012**

I support breast cancer awareness—not just in October, but year-round. I wear pink in honor of people I know who are currently fighting breast cancer and in memory of those who have lost their battle to the disease. I give money to breast cancer research organizations and have walked in a few charitable events for the cause. I have even purchased pink merchandise to support the cause, or so I thought. . . .

© Rihardzz, 2013. Used under license from Shutterstock, Inc.

I recently heard an unsettling news report that caused me to question all marketing around the pink ribbon campaign.

First used by the Susan G. Komen Foundation in 1991, the pink ribbon is now an internationally recognized symbol for breast cancer awareness. Many consumers are under the impression that sales of any product bearing the ribbon support the cause. Yet, in most places, the wildly popular pink ribbon is considered public domain, meaning that any company can use it on their product without actually giving money to breast cancer research.

As a previously uninformed consumer, I was disheartened by the news. Increasing breast cancer awareness and raising funds to research the disease are two reasons people purchase limited edition pink items each October. To think some companies take advantage of this enthusiasm and mislead consumers into purchasing their product under the guise that they are supporting organizations working towards a cure for breast cancer is despicable.

Now that my rant is over, here are three takeaways for responsible pink ribbon use and informed pink ribbon purchasing:

▶ **Companies Using the Pink Ribbon:** Don't abuse the power! If it's your first time dabbling in cause-related marketing, follow these steps for using the pink ribbon on merchandise. They include choosing an organization to support, clearly communicating what you pledge to donate and keeping track of your sales.

▶ **PR Professionals with Clients Using the Pink Ribbon:** Keep your clients honest. It's important that they're transparent about which organization(s) they plan to give to, how much they plan to give and that they actually follow through with the donation. Hold them accountable so they don't lose consumers' trust.

▶ **Consumers Considering Pink Purchases:** Do your homework. Don't be tricked into buying pink from just any company. Ask yourself these questions so you can be confident in your purchase decisions and trust that your money is actually supporting a charitable organization.

As someone who got her start in PR and marketing for a nonprofit organization that raises money for cancer research, I know that every dollar *can* make a difference. However, if consumers are making purchases simply because a portion of the proceeds is going to a cause, they'd be better off making a direct donation to the organization of their choice. Of course, if the goal is solely to raise awareness (rather than fundraise), then it can't hurt to have people everywhere—from your average Joe to your favorite pro athlete— sporting pink!

Drillbits—The Brandware Blog, Post by Lindley Presley, Source: www.brandwarepr.com.

FIGURE 5-1

content on your blog. Writers need to strive for sales but community building is important, too. Don't stuff the Twitter account with calls to action for a purchase all the time. Build value for the followers and get them involved in the conversation.

2. **Too boring.** Social media is a platform where viewers expect entertainment along with information. When they are seeking details, don't lecture them. Remember this dialogue is a conversation, not an advanced class on your business methodology. Think about the tone in the writing. Does it flow with what the business is trying to convey? Make sure there's that balance between the information and entertainment. Is there one staff member especially creative? This is a place for that person to shine. By having boring blog posts, lackluster updates and untargeted share, you'll be wasting valuable resources, budget and time.

3. **Lack of planning.** Just as a plan is crucial to the center of any marketing campaign, so is a plan for your social media writing approach. If not done properly, the entire plan can come apart. Having a plan will set the tone, give the right balance between sharing and selling and clearly set the objectives. Plans usually work best when done one month at a time, divided into eight to 12 posts.

"Forgetting to balance, being boring, and flying by the seat of your pants without a plan are three surefire ways to fail at social media writing," Ramirez concludes. Therefore, having social media writers aiming at the proper end results can produce the success companies strive for.

The often-repeated six Cs offer additional helpful tips for both traditional and social media writing:

1. Be Clear. Use simple words and straightforward sentences with active verbs. Try to keep paragraphs short—in general, six lines or fewer—and to use topic sentences to help readers follow your points.

2. Be Concise. Use the words you need to make your point, but no more. Don't give readers information they don't need.

3. Be Courteous. You catch more flies with honey than with vinegar. Write in a friendly, conversational tone. Imagine how you would respond if you were the reader.

4. Be Correct. Use a spell checker, and then proofread carefully.

5. Be Consistent. If you refer to someone as Susan in one sentence, don't switch to Sue in the next. If you use kilograms in one part of a letter don't switch to pounds in another.

6. Be Complete. Be sure to include all the information readers need. You don't want them to have to call or email you for important, but missing, details.

PRactical TIP

Three PR Rules to Follow on the Web

When it comes to the Web, PR writing has to walk a fine line between being too pushy and too passive. With so many different outlets to showcase your clients' messages—Facebook, Twitter, Instagram, Google +, not to mention the countless websites within any given industry—you must avoid overwhelming the marketplace while still allowing your information to be readily found. The Web continues to evolve, but some guidelines exist—for both etiquette and strategy—that will hold true, even when Web 12.0 comes around. Consultant Jenna Rose Robbins offers these tips.

1. **Don't Dawdle.** No matter what the next Web trend, be sure to stake your claim early to ensure that someone else doesn't pose as you or your client. For example, Twitter allows users to claim their name as part of a URL, but if someone else gets www.twitter.com/amazingbrand before you do, there's not much you can do about it short of taking them to court (and even then, you may not have a case). Even if you never plan on using a new site, claim your brand name before someone else does—just in case. And if you think an unflattering issue may reach the masses, act early to make sure your response to the matter is at the top of search terms. For example, lawsuits against companies are often written up on Wikipedia before the company's PR gets to them, at which point it's often hard to put an unbiased spin on the matter. Being first to acknowledge the issue—rather than pretending the issue doesn't exist—allows you to maintain more control as well as provide a level of corporate transparency that is becoming increasingly necessary in the success of today's businesses.

2. **Understand Netiquette.** Don't write in all caps (that's screaming). Don't send large files via email. Alert users when your link points to a PDF rather than a Web page. These are long-standing etiquette rules that, if broken, can mark you as unprofessional, antiquated, or, even worse, downright rude. And with each new platform comes new etiquette, so be sure to stay current on the rules. When in doubt, follow other leaders in your field for clues on how to behave—or just ask: There are plenty of online sources for best practices. Consider joining an online group in your field (e.g., LinkedIn has PR groups for most any industry), where your peers can act as an endless source of information at any given moment. For example, a travel PR firm recently began sending out a newsletter—as a 4MB PDF attachment rather than putting the copy in the body of the email. The firm's lack of understanding as to how e-newsletters work, the extra steps the user must go through, and the burden such a large file puts on a mobile user make the company look out of touch, particularly compared to savvy competitors.

3. **Patrol, Patrol, Patrol.** With monitoring tools such as Google Alerts and others, there's no reason you can't stay on top of what the Web is saying about your brand. If someone posts negative criticism, respond—promptly and courteously. If yours is an oft-attacked product, be prepared with responses to the most common criticisms so that your attacker, as well as those who read his diatribes, can become better educated. Go a step further and make certain these issues are always readily searchable, such as on your blog or as pages on your website, so users can find them and your proponents can point naysayers in the right direction.

By Jenna Rose Robbins
Founder of Siteseeing Media & Consulting
www.siteseeingmedia.com

Facebook

According to Ed Keller and Brad Fay, co-authors of *The Face-to-Face Book: Why Real Relationships Rule in a Digital Marketplace,* "Social media has helped us rediscover the power of 'social.'" The authors, specifically, believe people use Facebook to reconnect with friends from high school or college. However, they note users fail to engage in quality social networking time. Face-to-face dialogue offers more positive, meaningful conversations compared to exchanges via social media, despite its size.

"We are the largest community of engaged users anywhere in the world," said Facebook COO Sheryl Sandberg, in an October 2012 interview on CNBC. "Every day on Facebook, we have five Super Bowls, which means you can reach that many people." The social network passed the 1 billion mark in active members just before that interview.

For a business, using Facebook is akin to branding. When setting up a page for the company, the first rule is to not limit the number of fans. For a personal page, people max out at 5,000. When the "likes" begin to spread, the business won't have to respond to a request for a friend. Facebook automatically sets up for a person to get the updates by hitting "like." In late 2009, *The Facebook PR Handbook* reported that a mere 0.047 percent of pages have more than 1 million fans (297 in total).

Using the Facebook page for a company is more about the brand than it is about a specific campaign. Christi Day McNeill offers these tips for the branding of the page:

1. Specifically target users based on their profile information.
2. Use the status updates for your brand page.
3. Talk like a normal person.

It's important to continually update the status. Discuss news that you create. For example, post pictures and talk about social events during holidays when employees may be decorating the office or planning a party. What may seem like a simple event *is* something occurring. Use it.

Additional tips for writing a Facebook post from McNeill are:

1. Keep it short.
2. Avoid complicated wall posts.
3. Consider your audience.
4. Ask questions.
5. Use an eye-catching image.
6. Add links.
7. Keep variety in your posts.
8. Choose the right time.
9. Tell fans what to do.
10. Respond.

Next, consider the role of Facebook when pitching a story to members of the media. Top journalists weigh in on the Do's and Don'ts of Facebook PR. Steve Hall, Adrants editor, advises a DO: learn as much about the journalists as possible. Learn who they are, not just what they write. Follow and subscribe to everything they publish; even friend them on Facebook. Once a relationship is established, pitching a story from a virtual friend who understands the content the journalist is interested in will make the likelihood of receiving a positive response more likely.

Next, DON'T simply assume you can pitch via Facebook, warns Rachel Sklar of the Huffington Post. Once you've established a relationship, find out if the person would mind being pitched on Facebook. But Sklar strongly cautions against ever trying to chat with the people.

Learning about the journalists' other interests is a DO. Mark Frauenfelder, editor-in-chief of *Make: Technology on Your Time and BoingBoing* blog founder, and Garth Chouteau, head of internal PR at PopCap, struck up a friendship. Both share an interest in comic books and illustrators. This common interest keeps an email dialogue between friends during nonbusiness related topics.

Two varying perspectives on the Facebook pitch come from Patrick Gavin, associate editorial page editor, *Washington Examiner*—his is a DON'T—and David Kiley, senior business correspondent, *BusinessWeek*—a DO. Gavin advises against abandoning the email pitch. He states that in terms of PR, the email pitch remains king. Gavin doesn't want to check many different accounts to get information. People know his email. However, Kiley differs, finding the Facebook pitch acceptable as long as it's kept to a quick two sentences: "I have this cool thing about such-and-such and thought it might be a good fit. Do you want to know more?" Since some journalists are fine with the Facebook pitch and others aren't, Kiley recommends keeping a little book with names and preferred method of contact. Many seasoned PR practitioners, of course, have followed this practice for years.

More mistakes to avoid for aspiring PR writers include:

1. Profile Faux Pas: Pay careful attention to the privacy settings used for friends and be discreet when categorizing them.
2. Posting Faux Pas: Be careful when discussing religion and politics. One wayside comment could lead to arguments or disaster for the company. When posting under the company name, there's no need to update every five minutes or constantly market yourself and your work.
3. Photo Faux Pas: There's no need to ever have a compromising picture of you at a business party or another party. Just untag it. For that matter, change the privacy settings to avoid such a matter (see number one).
4. Social Faux Pas: Every day a new trend is coming out, different games to play, fields to build. Don't get sucked into using these and DON'T constantly send out requests to join in your quest.
5. Private Message Faux Pas: Take care whenever you are using the private message feature. One mistake here includes spamming friends with messages about work. Also when replying to a message in the email feature, be sure it's just to the sender unless you intend to send the message as a reply all.
6. Facebook "Event Invites" Faux Pas: When using this feature, really think about who is being invited. The business located in New York City, is having a cocktail hour this Friday and you're sending out a message invite to the entire "like" list, including those located in Hawaii? When it comes to relevant information, these people are more likely to ignore it. Also, don't communicate only through the invites. This is one of the fastest ways to get unfriended.

By learning to address the mistakes it made, Facebook has learned from its past issues to keep PR relatively disaster free.

Facebook and Twitter are also "friends," having done the whole "like" thing together. In other words, there's an app created to sync a Twitter account to the Facebook account. This is helpful for updating a 140-character message on Twitter and letting anyone read it on Facebook who may not be on Twitter.

Twitter

This social media platform began as a hack on top of AOL Instant Messenger by Jack Dorsey so he could view the status updates on his pager. The company began in 2006 as a mix between the IM and text message services. After some collaboration with Evan Williams and Biz Stone, Twitter was formed.
The first major growth spurt occurred during the SXSW festival in 2007. Live tweets were broadcast on plasma screens. At this time, Twitter saw approximately 400,000 tweets per fiscal quarter. Now it has about 230 million tweets per day. In 2012, the most popular topic was the Japanese Anime "Castle in the Sky," receiving 25,088 tweets per second. Today Twitter has half a billion users, posting 340 million tweets per day. They are younger overall than the typical Facebook user. The U.S. has the most registered accounts at 110 million, followed by Brazil with 33 million and Japan at 30 million.

Twitaholic.com lists the top Twitterholics, based on followers. As might be expected, celebrities always dominate the list.

When starting a Twitter account for a business, filling in the 160-character bio is an important first step. A well-crafted bio will make the difference between followers who ignore you and ones who click on every link you post. Potential followers want to know about you or the business you represent. However, people follow others on Twitter because they want to learn something new. Or share interests with you, and vice versa.

As the owner of the account, you want to target a specific audience that will share your content, learn something new from you and share it with their followers. And get re-tweeted. These followers are your diehard fans; they have the potential to become brand ambassadors on Twitter. This is why it is so important to have a well-constructed bio.

Think about why you are on Twitter. Is it to express your interests? Be the brand's voice? In the confines of 160-characters, answer for the audience why you're here, and stick to it. Don't constantly post pictures of Aunt May's doll collection. People will quickly un-follow. Key words are important and can be used as Twitter is a search tool. Think of what you represent, use these words, and the profile will appear in searches based on the keywords.

Some common mishaps in creating a bio include:

1. Quotes or song lyrics. Even if it has a strong personal meaning to you, it likely has nothing to do with the business. People want to know about you, not how Taylor Swift wishes she could go "Back to December."

2. Bio from another page. If you have a biography written on Facebook, LinkedIn or published in an article, chances are it's more than the 160-character allotment. Be sure to edit down imported information. Nothing looks sloppier than text being cut off. This is a careless mistake to avoid.

3. Empty space. The bio space is there for a reason. Use it. Does the company have a motto? Or what about linking the website? No matter what, don't leave it empty; it shows lack of caring.

Now that you know how to set up and attract followers, how are you going to keep them? By writing the perfect tweet, every time, bloggers and brands alike are ready to use this ultimate platform for sharing and exchanging link content. Shea Bennett offers these tips. Two big things to keep in mind when generating the perfect tweet:

1. Maximum readability
2. Maximum retweetability

One does not favor the other; both need to be used every time. It's easy, however, to make costly mistakes, leaving your content and tweet ignored like a badly produced, typo-laden community service flyer at the local market. As a self-promoter, you don't want to be known as a used car salesman. It's fine to link your own content, but by trying to over-sell it you'll find out quickly that you're either being overlooked, or worse, labeled as a spammer.

Seven additional tips to gain followers without annoying them are:

1. Think like your readers. You are trying to engage the largest amount of followers, not yourself; appeal to them. The exceptions to this rule are celebrities and brands with millions of followers. People will not always know what you mean. You know what they say about assuming? It usually will backfire. Take the time to be creative, accurate and pleasing to the majority.

2. Use consistent excellence to stand out from the crowd. When looking through the list of followers, some will stand out for the constant comments. Others for the avatar (picture) they select to represent themselves. Once you know the people who follow you, you'll learn to trust their judgment in the content and links they post. Sometimes we'll become robots just looking over this information, not always clicking on it. Then, someone will post something that just stands out. Maybe they're new or just someone you've not paid attention to before. But this message is excellent. Now you're more attuned to their posts because it is more relevant. You'll follow the links. However, if the quality of tweets and updates dips the opposite direction you'll ignore people. In extreme cases it will lead to being tuned-out and un-followed. Therefore, being occasionally excellent is good, being consistently excellent is best.

3. Sell the headline. But remember, you're not a sleazy used car salesman. Updates are always happening. Depending on how a person is viewing Twitter, a few words of a headline is all the attention you may get. Make it count. And, when the page is refreshed, you don't want the person to lose your tweet. You want it to stand out in myriad of other tweets. After it has captured the attention, the job is not done. You still need to have them click on it.

This is the difference between selling the link and selling the content. You need to gain the trust of the reader. Don't ever lie or promise something you can't deliver. While adhering to the "honesty is the best policy" statement is true, this doesn't mean you shouldn't use your rhetoric by giving it a new twist and maybe a little reverse psychology.

A great headline will often generate retweets immediately, even if the original reader didn't actually read the content. This is a pat on the back for you. You've gained the trust of the party and they believe in what you send out. This is the absolute loyalty you want.

When linking content from another site or tweet, don't be afraid to rewrite the headline and make it your own. Usually these were originated for a single purpose or platform that may not apply to you. And then, of course, there are times where they will just stink and are in need of a good revamp. People aren't going to object to you rewriting their headlines, especially if it means you're sending traffic their way.

4. Use correct and acceptable punctuation. You are the brand ambassador in the media world. It will reflect poorly on you and the brand or client if you have missing or incorrect punctuation, especially as a writer. This may be the readers' first impression of the company. You don't want them to think less of it based on your mistakes. Use periods and commas. Put apostrophes in the right place. Use quotation marks and parentheses. Be careful with the use of an exclamation point. Read the tweet out loud before sending it. Does it make sense? Did you pause in the correct spots?

5. Accept nothing less than flawless grammar and perfect spelling. Spellcheck is your best friend. If you don't have an autocorrect keyboard, type your message into a document before sending it. But even with autocorrect, make sure it's correcting to the right word. (Bad spellers of the world untie!) Use this as a quick checklist for each tweet:
   a. Always start with a capital letter. These are sentences you're writing.
   b. Use a capital letter at the beginning of each new sentence. Only one space is needed after the period.
   c. Learn the difference between your and you're, its and it's, and there, their and they're.
   d. An all caps message LOOKS LIKE YOU'RE SHOUTING!
   e. Avoid the speak-to-text option at all costs. The message is a maximum of 140 characters. These messages always come across like somebody who bungee jumped drunk.

While you want celebrities to follow you and you will follow them, don't use them for guidance. We all know rules don't apply to them (see Lindsay Lohan's jail stint).

6. Observe the magic retweet number. This is the total characters your tweet can be. Yes, 140 will fit in the space; however, to ensure maximum retweetability, some blank space at the end is needed. Many consider the ideal number to be 120 characters. This gives space for your copy and link and 20 characters for a retweet.

Believe it or not, this tweet is written to exactly 103 characters, showing how much space you have.

This rule will have to be bent from time to time. If you have an important message and it doesn't fit, take the space you need. If you never leave room for the retweet or any additional comments, your original amazing thought could be shortened to the dreaded txt spk. Everyone now will think that's how you originally wrote it and your reputation goes down the drain.

7. Shorten all links with bit.ly. These are the types of links that have the easiest retweetability. They take up few characters. Most links produced are already shortened with this URL as it was once Twitter's first choice and still super-convenient.

While these tips may seem a bit daunting for a 140-character message, by taking time to perfect the profile and message, you'll be able to drive sales and traffic for your brand. It's worth the hard work and extra effort. Soon it will become second nature.

A sample tweet under 100 characters, with a link to practical information for PR pros, follows:

4 ways to get maximum exposure for your press releases via@bianchipr #PR http://bit.ly/PTsO6R ^bss

The first time using Twitter, the coding will look like a foreign language. Be patient; eventually you'll learn the jargon and what each piece means. For instance:

The @APStylebook offers helpful #APtips. Send a DM with additional questions. Visit bit.ly/14CdnW for more information.

The @ sign calls out usernames for all to see in both parties' Twitter feed. When a username is preceded by the @ sign, it becomes a link to a Twitter profile. The # tag allows for the keyword to be searched. DM stands for direct message. These can only be sent once a party is following another. Both parties do not have to follow each other. The website was shortened with the bit.ly start. One last tip about the @ sign. If you begin a tweet with it, this is not calling out a person or company. It is sending the message directly to them. It will show up in your feed for being sent, but not for all to read. Know the difference.

@APStylebook, thanks for the helpful #APtips.

After understanding how to decode, you'll be on your way to writing the perfect tweet. To prove how popular Twitter is, consider this random fact. About 10.5 million tweets were sent during the 90 minutes of the first presidential debate back in the fall of 2012, making it the most tweeted event in political history at that time.

Google+

Having millions of users, Google is a popular platform and social media networking site. It has fewer users than Facebook, making it more attractive to many users who wish to avoid getting lost in the Web. Yet, it still baffles people on just how to use it, let alone how to write for it. This is a site that if you choose to use, you must spend time learning its quirks so you can garner its advantages. A big perk of using Google+ is that it comes with the vast array of Google media.

Mark Traphagen offers tips on the first five things to do with your business page.

1. Optimize your page for Search Engine Optimization. Since Google+ is part of the Google powerhouse, take advantage of the internal search site. Make sure the page is verified. There can be multiple pages with the same name, but you want to be the "official" one for your brand. Plus, verified pages get priority in searches.

   Here you are also creating a biography for your brand. Carefully create a subtitle, no more than 10 words, yet be as descriptive as possible. With the creation of the bio, be natural with the language. This is the main area to bring people from the SEO by using keywords, but use them sparingly. Don't just throw them in to attract visitors. It's always good to link other social media profiles (Twitter, Facebook, etc.). Also, have a list of recommended links.

2. Upgrade your page's visual appeal. Everyone knows the first impression counts the most and when a visual one is all you're able to give, make yours worth circling (the term for "following"). On the top of the profile area is where you can put eye-catching photos. This is known as the scrapbook area.

Photo courtesy of Stephanie Hines

3. Fill your post stream with quality content. As soon as you begin your page, you need to start posting even without followers. As soon as visitors wander to your page, they need something to read and your posting stream is the real first impression-maker. Seeing the blanket statement that your brand hasn't shared any posts yet, doesn't really inspire a call to action to circle the page.

   Google+ has its own set of formatting options. It doesn't give you an editing text bar. However, you can do a certain amount by keeping these in mind:

   ▶ To bold text, *put asterisks around it*.
   ▶ To italicize, put _underscores around it_.
   ▶ For strikeout, -use dashes around the text-.

   By using these simple tips, your post creations will appear more like blog posts. Likewise, use photos every time you make a post and video when you can. Google+ has won the loyalty from many top photographers for the way it allows photography to display. Plus, it's proven that a visual effect will more likely draw the attention to an article.

4. Begin to attract followers. You've done the basics of getting the page set up, but with any social media platform, this isn't *Field of Dreams*—"if you build it they will come." As mentioned before, link your page on other social media pages. Promote a Google+ badge on your website. Have others in the organization link their personal profiles on Google+ to the brand page. As always—be careful not to spam!

5. Engage. Once you've started the page, establish priorities of posting and engagement. This platform is one you almost can't post on too much. It's made for posting and is eager for content; just be sure it's value-added content. Follow back those who circle you. People get a notification when someone follows their page. For a brand's page, it shows followers there is a human aspect to the branding page. This is a great reinforcement for the person. Share content you find relevant from others and put these individuals in a special circle if you find you're using them as a constant source of information. This is great for cultivating relationships with them.

The circle feature on the main page is great to use as your online book of contacts. For each medium, create a circle. Here you can assign a name and even a picture. For the PR professional, Google+ can be relevant by having a large network of circles. The larger your network, the more likely your content is to appear in a Google search.

LinkedIn

LinkedIn, a professional networking site, has about 140 million users in 20 countries. A majority of those are beyond the United States. It's used for connections between current and potential colleagues. LinkedIn can also serve as a powerful tool in showcasing your writing abilities. As a public relations practitioner, your profile here should be written in Associated Press style, especially your objectives and status updates.

If you're just getting started with LinkedIn, Rebecca Odell offers this advice for the PR newbie:

1. DO: Share a personal message when asking to connect with someone (especially if you don't know the contact). Whether you've worked together for years, recently met, or this person would be a good contact to have, it's always important to write a reason why you should be connected. The generic message created by LinkedIn will not cut it.
2. DON'T: Cut straight to the chase. When you're getting ready to graduate, it's a given you're looking for a job. However, if this is all you try to use the connection for you're going to burn the bridge quickly. Remember PR can stand for Personal Relationships. By taking the time to build the relationship and seeking out advice, the rest will fall into place.
3. DO: Fill out your entire profile. Many recruiters do more than half their sourcing through LinkedIn. By filling out your title, industry and a short concise summary with keywords, you can use this to your advantage.
4. DON'T: Connect your Twitter and LinkedIn accounts. This is similar to giving someone access with your password. If they want to know what you're doing every waking moment, they'll subscribe to your Twitter feed. You don't want to turn off potential employers by constantly flooding their feeds with information that's irrelevant.
5. DO: Give yourself the option of sharing relevant tweets with your network. This can be done by adding the "#in" in your tweet. Any additional information can be found through a Twitter tutorial.

Pinterest

This visually oriented network started in early 2011. Within two years it drew close to 20 million unique visitors. Early on, most U.S. visitors were female. In the U.K., it was just the opposite. Businesses have jumped on board Pinterest, valued at close to $1 billion, to captivate audiences and potential customers. These include American Express, Coca-Cola, General Electric and Nordstrom.

Any journalist will tell you a graphic is preferred with a news release or pitch. A new trend in the social media world is the infographic. An infographic is a graphic visual representation of information, data or knowledge. Popularized by *USA Today*, these tables and charts are favored by information-seeking readers.

The image-bookmarking and social networking site, Pinterest thrives on businesses using the infographic for the creation on its pages. Public relations writers should simply let the infographic speak for itself.

However, it's not all about the graphics, even though this site is a virtual pin board. Blogger Lisa Pluth offers these tips on how words play an integral part in not only gaining followers, but getting repinned.

1. Use keywords—not only for categorizing the pins, but also in the comment section of a pin. By taking the time to fill out information about the pin, users are able to quickly find it based on the keyword or phrase.

2. Be funny—never underestimate the power of humor or laughter. In a graphic with words, retype the words in the comment box for searchability. Users enjoy the site because for five minutes they can easily get a good laugh and a breath of fresh air. Under your description box is a section for others to comment.

3. Offer A/B testing—has two different pins that link to the same origin. This is a great way to see what preference people have for pictures and wording.

4. Make comments—this spot is almost as important as the pin description. Here you can interact with others who have pinned your pin and made comments. This shows an interest in people, being social in a social network.

5. Be lengthy and complex—this is a mystery of Pinterest. Unlike other sites, a description here can be 500 words, not characters. Longer posts take up more screen space and this makes it more popular. When a viewer is glazing over many small photographic images and comes across a large story, she will pause to give it a second glance. This can lead to a "like" or even better a re-pin. Remember, however, that length does not mean wordiness.

Photo courtesy of Stephanie Hines

Even though the Pinterest site is based on pictures and graphics, words remain your friend. By using the correct terms and keywords, you'll be able to watch your pins take off.

Summary

No matter how hard you try, it's impossible to keep up with every new social medium. New ones come along and prior ones can become outdated, controversial or security concerns. The more you know about social media, the more valuable you will be for your client and its customers, goods and services. And you can communicate in a two-way conversation directly with the public by eliminating the media gatekeeper.

Chapter 6

Electronic Media Writing

> *"Storytelling reveals meaning without committing the error of defining it."*

Hannah Arendt

Professional communicators who view media equally and believe they can satisfy all their media relations needs with the print news release commit a fatal error that dramatically reduces their potential to reach target markets with persuasive and powerful information. Reaching key publics today requires adherence to narrowly tailored messages, a vast understanding of media channels and the ability to use video and audio in an informative and creative manner.

Failing to disseminate information in a style and manner that meets the needs of the electronic media often dooms messages, or results in them being off target when reported. Strategic planning requires communication professionals to produce information with a keen eye toward clarity and a willingness to construct messages in a variety of formats.

Today's communication experts must be schooled in writing for a variety of media outlets. Writing for the electronic media requires a firm understanding of how modern audiences process information. That being said, communicators must be well versed at writing for television and radio as well as online media. Television, with its unique blend of video and audio, must grab viewer attention and persuade and inform in a seamless message that combines strong visuals with powerful prose. Radio combines a delicate blend of the right level of language and an easy-to-remember format, interspersed with memorable phrases. Blogging and writing for the Internet combines the power of reporting with the ability to package news in a style widely accepted by today's sophisticated target markets.

Broadcast news has been a mainstay of society for almost a century. It has evolved from its early roots of radio to its younger cousin, television, to its newest family member, the Internet. While the technology has changed and the style altered somewhat, the fundamental principles remain the same. At the heart of all electronic communication remains the need for sound reporting, enhanced storytelling, critical thinking, ethical standards, and, of course, solid writing.

A video news release (VNR) is the television version of the print news release. VNRs translate printed words into moving images appropriate for broadcast on television. Generally distributed via satellite to television stations worldwide, the VNR includes completed video stories, broadcast roll (b-roll), and sound bites. VNR producers should be careful to exclude dissolves and fancy effects so that television outlets can edit stories. The bits and b-roll VNR afford television outlets the opportunity to tailor the story to their needs.

Television journalists, like their print counterparts, focus on newsworthy stories. While the process takes a different shape, the fundamental principles of newsworthiness, accuracy and truth remain the same.

Several years ago news went video. Consumers' active involvement in print, particularly newspapers, continued a downward spiral. The movement toward visual imageries in news exploded more with the growth of online news coverage. Simply, consumers prefer viewing an engaging video news release rather than reading long blocks of gray text.

Before launching into a deeper understanding of writing for electronic media, the authors must first emphasize that good writing is the foundation of all successful journalism. Successful professional communicators must learn to write, rewrite and write again before they can release a polished story. Professional communicators must rise to the challenge of engaging the attention of the audience and motivating the half-interested to become involved in the story. Writers must communicate the essence of stories in little time and with an eye toward accuracy, succinctness and perfect imagery. Of course, they must do this with an audience that most likely will give it only one chance to grab its attention and retain its content.

Spoken stories must be clear, concise and economical. Communicators engage audiences by stimulating the sense of hearing. The ear rejects the story that plods along and hurls fistfuls of facts and details at a passive audience. Print can be verbose. Broadcast must be succinct. Effective broadcast writing can capture a phrase of two or three words and make a memorable impression. While facts remain important, simplicity and clarity reign supreme.

VNRs engage the senses in a way that text-only releases cannot. While in theory the VNR offers the same information as the traditional news release, it adds a powerful dimension, visual images, which enhance the storytelling element of news stories. Research shows that consumers exposed to VNRs take further action on the persuasive intent of the message 50 percent more frequently compared to the same message sent in text only. Business recognizes the impact of VNRs so astute public relations professionals have become increasingly skilled at packaging their messages in electronic form.

Public relations counselor Peter Shankman, speaking at an Internet Marketing Conference, spoke about the rise of the sewing circles. Shankman stated that personal recommendations and word-of-mouth had been replaced by the PR and the press providing consumers with information. Now, Shankman believes, video and smart content marketing strategies have enabled public relations professionals the opportunity to appeal directly to consumers with video.

The widespread use of VNRs has transformed the way many industries gain media exposure. For example, the music industry has moved well beyond the need for record labels and promoters gaining an audience for new acts and has instead embraced a form of the VNR called an electronic press kit or EPK. The EPK generally contains prominent audio tracks of the artists' music, sound bites, artist-narrated biographies and music video clips or live performance coverage. A host of local, national and international businesses have recognized the success that the music industry has experienced with EPKs and shifted their media efforts toward producing VNRs and sending them to television stations, and sending the messages directly to consumers through the use of the Internet and sites like YouTube. In fact, companies such as Easton Pharmaceuticals and Toshiba have VNRs published on YouTube. A growing number of other companies have increased their marketing exposure and visibility by embracing the use of VNRs and online streaming of messages as an alternative to traditional print coverage.

Broadcast news writing generally takes one of two forms. News features, stories between three and seven minutes long, report past events. Communicators craft news feature storyboards that explain in detail how the audio and visuals present the researched background facts and information. Breaking news and daily announcements happen today or in the near future. The stories generally get read by a studio reporter from a teleprompter and run on average from 15 seconds to 1 minute in length. These timely stories contain little in the way of source credibility so writers need to carefully monitor the story after to clarify any discrepancies in the information. Writers should follow the general rule of thumb that for every 30 seconds of airtime, the writer can write about 65 words (roughly two words spoken per second).

Writers should adhere to the following rules in writing both news features and breaking news.

1. Write with a conversational tone. Writers need to inject enthusiasm into their stories by keeping a warm, conversational tone.
2. Write concisely. Write with an eye toward simple sentences. Avoid the tendency to write to impress rather than to express.
3. Simplify complicated ideas. Writers will likely get only one chance to reach an audience. By simplifying complicated ideas and making them understandable, writers can quickly get a reader's attention and make their point with bold, easy-to-understand facts.
4. Research and verify all information. Check all facts twice. And remember, remain objective. Stories often have two different points of view. News reporting is objective, not subjective.
5. Avoid newspaper construction in your writing. Professional communicators must be well versed at packaging information for different media. Therefore, they cannot merely take the print news release and turn it into a broadcast release. Carefully check the tone of the broadcast release and make it sound conversational.

6. Use strong verbs. As stated throughout this book, strong verbs energize writing. Get the maximum impact for the story by concentrating on strong, active voice verbs. Too many adjectives and adverbs bloat the story and rob it of its vigor.

7. Be objective. Let the reader decide whether a story is good, bad or shocking. Present the information, not the commentary.

8. Avoid participle phrases or dependent clauses. These may be fine for a print story, but they simply don't work for broadcast.

9. Nix the "There is" and "There are" phrases. Beginning a sentence with *there is* or *there are* immediately signals weak construction. Rewrite the sentence and use active voice.

10. Stay away from leading with an unknown person. When writers begin a story with an unknown name, they tend to lose the reader's interest from the beginning.

11. Talk *to* the audience, not *at* it. Don't make factual errors. Writers who lose credibility lose their audience. Audiences hate being lectured *at.* They prefer being spoken *to.*

Writing the Broadcast Lead

Perhaps the single most important part of the broadcast news story is the lead. The lead must catch the interest of the audience and hold it for the rest of the story. Simply, the lead captures the crucial spark necessary to grab attention.

Broadcast leads work best when containing 12 words or fewer. Print leads attempt to answer as many of the traditional 5 W's and the H (who, what, when, where, why and how). Broadcast leads often answer only one or two of the most important questions: generally, *what* and *where.*

Leads should be catchy. But writers should avoid flippant or insensitive language. Broadcast leads must also be clever and creative. They should also be conversational but written with an eye toward crisp and concise language. Clarity is king. Finally, broadcast leads must be current.

Some important characteristics of broadcast leads include the following.

1. Attribution. Broadcast puts attribution at the beginning of the sentences for better flow.
   (**Newspaper**) Revenue dipped this quarter largely because of unforeseen capital expenditures, reported company President David Morton.
   (**Broadcast**) Company President David Morton said that revenue dipped this quarter because of unforeseen capital expenditures.

2. Time element. Broadcast strives for immediacy. Try to avoid references to yesterday. Focus on what is happening now or today.

3. Use of quotes. Direct quotes in broadcast work very differently from direct quotes in print.
   (**Newspaper**) "I will work diligently to avoid a total collapse of the labor negotiations," the governor said.
   (**Broadcast**) The governor said . . . and these are his exact words . . . I will work diligently to avoid a total collapse of the labor negotiations. (Don't use quotation marks)

4. Middle initials. Broadcast is more informal and avoids middle initials unless part of a well-known person's name.
5. Use of names with titles or positions and age. Broadcast puts titles and ages before names for better flow.
   (**Newspaper**) Dr. Gerald Carter, 56, a Food and Drug Administration supervisor, said…
   (**Broadcast**) Fifty-six-year-old Food and Drug Administration supervisor Dr. Gerald Carter says . . .
6. Round off numbers. Broadcast rounds off big numbers for greater clarity.
   (**Newspaper**) Medford Township officials reported the tax revenue shortfall at $727,593.00.
   (**Broadcast**) Medford Township officials report the tax revenue shortfall at more than $700,000.
7. Use present tense verbs. Broadcast uses present tense to sound more timely.
8. Use active voice. Broadcast uses active voice for better flow and stronger copy.
9. Contractions. Broadcast uses more contractions because it sounds more conversational.
10. Abbreviations. Avoid abbreviations in broadcast copy.
    (**Newspaper**) 8811 Lincoln Blvd.
    (**Broadcast**) 8811 Lincoln Boulevard
11. Hyphens. Broadcast uses hyphens to separate initials.
    (**Newspaper**) EEOC Officials
    (**Broadcast**) E-E-O-C Officials
12. Symbols. Broadcast spells out symbols.
    (**Newspaper**) Revenue grew $75 million.
    (**Broadcast**) Revenue grew 75-million-dollars.

Leads Open Stories. They grab audiences' attention and try to hold them for the remainder of the story. With today's fragmented audiences, writers must clearly identify audience characteristics and write in a manner that will grab their attention. Writers therefore must have at their disposal the ability to craft different types of leads and use them according to their audience makeup, the purpose of the story and the manner in which the story gets disseminated.

Summary Leads. The summary lead focuses on one or two essential facts to grab audiences' attention and capture the essence of the story. Summary leads focus on why the audience should know about the story.

   Example: Apple Computers may be forced to recall its newest smart phone, officials of the Cupertino, California-based company say.

Hard News Leads. Hard news leads strike to the heart of the story. They present breaking news or update already established news stories.

   Example: More than two thousand ACME Company workers staged a strike yesterday over stalled contract negotiations.

Soft News Leads. Soft news leads are used most often for feature stories. They work best for human interest stories.

Example: Many residents of Minneapolis find the lure of small town living and the lure of wide-open spaces an antidote for the hustle-bustle of their daily commute to their urban jobs.

Suspended Interest Leads. These types of leads delay the conclusion of the story to the very end.

Example: A local inventor could never figure out why he kept losing things in his lab so he devised an elaborate plan to protect his things.

Story Organization

Broadcast news stories generally get organized using one of two basic structures. The newspaper structure incorporates use of the traditional inverted pyramid. The inverted pyramid style summarizes as many of the traditional 5 W's and the H as possible (who, what, when, where, why, and how) into the lead. The format places most important information first and gradually ascends to the least important information.

The conversational story structure uses a more traditional pyramid style. Here the story begins with a concise lead that includes only the most important aspects of the story, with emphasis on only one or two parts of the traditional 5 W's and the H. The story generally gets told in chronological or narrative form and may even begin an anecdotal lead, which begins the story with an eye-catching tale or anecdote rather than the most important information. Sometimes writers will also use a question-and-answer type format.

Good broadcast writing is both uncomplicated and highly demanding. Its straightforward, matter-of-fact style provides clarity and eliminates waste. However, since the story generally gets heard only once, it must be crisp and creative to break though the daily clutter of mounds of news stories. Five components must be present in all broadcast stories.

1. Conversational tone. Writing that has a breezy, warm tone helps writers avoid awkward, often stuffy prose. It achieves a rhythm and flow that mirrors a conversation rather than a report. Often we achieve this conversational tone by using contractions that shorten sentences. You'll grab readers' attention and engage their brains by simply making it sound like a conversation. However, you need to avoid the tendency to throw grammar out the window. The most brilliant ideas get lost with jumbled structure and poor grammatical focus.

2. Relate to the listener. In today's 24-hour news cycle, listeners must often labor through a deluge of information. Consequently, they become adept at dumping and mentally blocking stories. Broadcast writers must tie the story in with some relevant part of the audience member's world. Try to answer the all-important audience question, "What does this have to do with me?" early on to engage the listener.

3. Creative style. Vary the style and flow of broadcast stories. Broadcast writers rewrite and refine stories often before they capture the right tone and style. Great broadcast stories incorporate news and art to create a seamless flow of ideas.
4. Make sense. Conversational tone does not give license to rambling, long sentences and unruly structure. Conversational tone means connecting with readers without being sloppy and unclear.
5. Technical correctness. Broadcast writing requires properly constructed sentences with clauses that flow together. Remember that technical crews depend on clear, concise script commands to execute the various audio and video commands.

News Judgment

At the heart of the broadcast story rests the need for writers to have precise news judgment. News judgment encompasses the quality of thinking to determine the relative merits of one story or one idea over another. News judgment helps writers sort out where the story fits in relation to the audience needs. It shifts though the facts and determines whether to use a hard news approach or a soft news approach. Simply, we use news judgment to figure out what about the story makes it news.

News judgment puts into focus the vast amount of time and energy spent filling a limited news hole with a virtually unlimited amount of news. Writers must consider what ideas stay and what ideas go. Broadcast writers—even more so than print journalists—must cut stories or story elements that might be considered good somewhere else. The complexity of deciding what facts are placed in a prominent position also plays an important factor in the reporting process.

Sometimes a little bit of news judgment is all that stands between an insignificant announcement and a much better story. Carefully analyzing the merits of the story helps the writer structure the story. News judgment develops over time and considers the personal perspective of the audience and the relationship between the story and its context to the audience's daily life.

Feature Stories vs. Straight News Stories

Feature stories combine the hard news style of investigative journalism with the serious treatment of highly emotional, personal stories. Well-crafted features draw people into the story and make them care more about the facts than they would normally care about in a straight news story. While both straight news stories and feature stories have as their basis the traditional 5 W's and the H, feature stories place greater emphasis on the Why. Feature stories speak of the consequences of the story. They evoke human emotion and hold audience attention with emotion.

Features blend both art and craft with a combination of words and visuals. The strongest features generally contain these elements:

- ▶ a lead that tells up front the story focus
- ▶ a script light on details the audience already knows
- ▶ a blend of natural sounds that add realism to the story and enhance the storytelling element
- ▶ a point of view
- ▶ historical context of the story when needed to help set the stage for the story
- ▶ a flair for the unexpected
- ▶ short sound bites that enhance the storytelling
- ▶ a limited number of points—generally two or three—in the story to avoid confusion
- ▶ a strong close that presents the story in its entirety

Unlike the straight news story with its emphasis on the inverted pyramid style, the feature places greater emphasis on a dramatic close. The feature story should unfold into a memorable conclusion.

Video News Releases

With increasing regularity, news directors, especially those in the areas of science stories and health and medical news, accept VNRs. Often edited to usable news segments ranging from 30 seconds to 90 seconds, VNRs also provide additional footage or "b-roll," as well as some additional actualities. Writers must focus on real news and avoid the tendency to write commercials. VNRs must contain facts, sights and sounds relevant to broadcast news.

In addition to completed edited stories, writers can also provide fact sheets to reporters along with the appropriate b-roll. This offers reporters the opportunity to build the story at the studio. Typically these fact sheets contained bulleted lists of relevant information organized in an easy to read manner. The b-roll may also contain some staged event appropriate to enhance the visual appeal of the facts. Writers must also include the appropriate audio files.

Most broadcasters prefer to get VNRs by satellite. They also tend to shy away from talking head videos, preferring more action and movement. VNRs must appeal to both the eye and the ear. The words must be clear enough to be understandable the first time through.

Keep in mind this brief checklist for producing broadcast news.

- ▶ Keep it technically correct. Edit carefully for proper grammar, spelling and punctuation.
- ▶ Gear it to the appropriate target public. Even the best of stories targeted to the wrong target public result in nothing more than a failed communication.

▶ Be persuasive. Craft the story with effective content and an eye toward persuasive strategies.

▶ Determine the news peg. The news peg is the story element that makes the story timely or newsworthy now rather than two weeks from now. News pegs differ from a news hook in that the hook focuses on something or an event taking place that ties the news peg in with a local angle.

PRactical TIP

Sample Video News Release (VNR)

STARBURST CASINO HOTEL
Brighton Place and The Boardwalk
Atlantic City, NJ 08401. (800) 222-STAR
Contact: Victoria Marie Parker, Director of Public Relations

EDITED STORY + B-ROLL AND EXTRA BITES
TRACK 1 – VOICE OVER ONLY TRACK 2 – NATURAL SOUND ONLY**

Atlantic City Welcomes New Casino Hotel

(SUGGESTED INTRODUCTION)
Atlantic City New Jersey's gaming industry welcomed its newest gaming hall today with a gala reception on the city's famous Boardwalk.

(SCENE)
Ribbon cutting outside Starburst Casino Hotel
[Sound-on Starburst CEO Abner Greenbaum]
(10 Seconds)

(VOICE OVER)
"Today marks a new era in Atlantic City gaming and entertainment as we welcome the city's most opulent casino hotel."

(SCENE)
Aerial shot Starburst with graphic of Starburst features
(15 Seconds)

Continued

(VOICE OVER)
Atlantic City's largest gaming hall features:

▶ Two hundred thousand square feet of gaming space;
▶ Fifteen restaurants;
▶ Two-thousand five hundred rooms; and
▶ The largest indoor amusement park in the world.

(SCENE)
Tourists walking on Boardwalk
(10 Seconds)

(VOICE OVER)
Atlantic City legalized gaming in 1978. The industry has struggled the last decade because of increased competition—especially from Pennsylvania.

(SCENE)
Legislators on floor of New Jersey Senate in Trenton
(15 Seconds)

(VOICE OVER)
Officials hope Starburst energizes tourism and breathes life into a sluggish state economy. While Atlantic City's number of visitors grew at a anemic rate, its revenue has declined five years running.

(SCENE)
Bathers on Atlantic City's Beach
(10 Seconds)

(VOICE OVER)
Starburst's owners are confident the city's fortunes will turn and the city will regain its market share in regional tourism.

Writing for Radio

An audio news release, generally a 60-second packaged news story, includes a 15- to 20-second sound bite from a designated spokesperson. Writers pitch stories and feed them to interested stations and networks. Radio stations have skeleton staffs, so public relations writers need to use this medium frequently. To increase the chance of the story being aired, writers produce 30-second and 15-second versions to meet the needs of the broadcast outlet.

Just as with a VNR for a television station, writers should supply radio stations with a script to complement the audio. The script should be set in triple space to make it easy to read. Don't forget to leave time for music or sound effects in calculating your word count. The lead-in gets the reader ready for the story. The lead itself should be about 16 to 20 words for ease of reading. Finally, difficult-to-read words should be spelled out phonetically to help the station's news presenter.

Sometimes organizations distribute interviews to radio stations for publicity purposes. These interviews, distributed either by phone or by audiocassette, are called actualities or audio feeds. They provide a wealth of information and news programming for radio stations, particularly those in small markets. A cataloging number appears after the date of the release to help the organization keep track of the number of radio releases it sends each year. Following the last two digits of the calendar year include the sequential number for that release. For example, 13:3 would indicate that the particular radio release is the third release produced in 2013.

Public service announcements (PSAs) provide advertising time, free of charge, to organizations that wish to promote messages for the public interest. Prior to the deregulation of broadcasting, television stations and radio stations were required to provide a percentage of their time to nonprofit organizations to air public service announcements. Now, the Federal Communication Commission only requires that radio and television stations operate in the public interest. They no longer must devote a percentage of their broadcasting time to PSAs. This has led to dwindling opportunities overall, particularly on radio. However, well-written news items that connect with a station's local listening audience will still get airtime. Exciting, well-written and newsworthy PSAs break through the clutter, though, and get coverage.

Television PSAs range from low-cost, announcer-read scripts to high-quality productions created by international advertising agencies. Today, most radio PSAs offer only short, announcer-read spots. Radio PSAs often provide an opportunity for local nonprofit organizations to air their messages. The same writing techniques apply for PSAs. The focus remains on newsworthiness and clean, concise prose. Most radio PSAs run 10, 20, 30 or occasionally 60 seconds. Offering a variety of spot lengths can increase the chances of the PSA fitting seamlessly into a station's broadcast schedule. Television PSAs should be 10 and 30 seconds in length. Longer PSAs generally appear in overnight broadcasts when stations have difficulty selling advertising time to a smaller viewing audience (see **Figure 6-1**).

Radio Writing Guidelines

Brevity is essential when producing conversational copy for radio stations. With small news staffs, stations are dependent on news submissions. According to some studies, almost 90 percent of radio outlets will use releases, especially if they are localized for their listeners. Radio reaches a large audience daily, especially during morning and afternoon commute times. Broadcast outlets repeat news throughout the day, helping to cause word-of-mouth promotion.

A writer needs to tell the essential facts quickly in the lead. While print articles could easily reach a thousand words, most stories aired will be about 100 words long. The best way to

Habitat for Humanity
Union-Snyder County Chapter
Contact Randy Hines (rwh@habitat.org)

June 14, 2014
30-Second PSA
Run until June 27, 2014, at 6 p.m.

Want to <u>Own</u> your own <u>Home</u>?

The Snyder County Habitat for Humanity chapter is having an information meeting at 6 p.m. Wednesday, June 27, at Sharon Lutheran Church in Selinsgrove.

Habitat for Humanity provides housing for families who cannot obtain conventional financing. In turn, families invest <u>sweat equity</u> hours into construction housing projects, and repay a No-Interest Mortgage.

That meeting again is 6 p.m. Wednesday at Sharon Lutheran Church, downtown Selinsgrove. For information, please call 3-7-4-24-24.

# # #

FIGURE 6-1 Sample Radio PSA

gauge the time is for the writer to read it aloud in a slightly slower speaking pace. Common news releases average under 60 seconds (or 125 words), often with a sound bite from an organization's representative. Although word count may not seem crucial to the writer—only to the announcer—it's imperative for public relations practitioners to send appropriate-length news stories to radio outlets. Word totals are crucial, however, for public service announcements, discussed below.

To make radio listening easy, writers need to use simple words and short, simple sentences (subject plus verb plus object). It's nice if the announcer can finish a sentence in one breath. Audience members cannot go back and read a passage again if they aren't sure about a phrase. They can't even see any words on the screen, as TV viewers can. Of course, visual materials sent for a station's website or online newsroom can provide those extra details. But for broadcast copy, conversational language is always best for this medium, even when a variety of sentence structure is used. It's important to make things crystal clear for listeners. Many PR writers will capitalize key nouns for emphasis, ignoring AP print guidelines. Avoid clichés and jargon. Homophones, for instance *bear* and *bare,* should be avoided whenever possible.

Contractions are useful to create that informal listening atmosphere. However, to especially emphasize a news event, two words are stronger than the contraction: Mayor Mallory Pope said she *will not* run again for the office this fall. PR writers should be cautioned that a few contractions can be confusing to the radio audience. It may be best to avoid the following: there'll (there will), it'll (it will), they'll (they will), that'll (that will) and shouldn't/wouldn't (should not/would not).

Facts must be clearly stated. A PR writer for broadcast needs to remember that it is news, not commentary, being produced. Loaded words need to be avoided, just as they are in print. Active voice is almost always preferred over passive voice. The subject is doing the action rather than the action being done to the subject. Speaking of facts, it's wise for writers to verify information before it's dispatched to their local radio stations. They should verify details and provide objective information. PR practitioners should not put quality labels on their broadcast news releases. What is *good news* for one set of listeners (no increase in property taxes) may be *bad news* for others (closing one local elementary school because of funding problems).

Weak phrases to start sentences, for both print and broadcast, include "there is, there are, it is." Recasting the sentence will make it stronger and often shorter. The opening must hook the listeners so writers should avoid any wasted words. Likewise, it's best to avoid using the names of average citizens at the start of radio news releases. They do not attract the listening ears. Rather than writing "Maria Perkins won a national award . . . ," use "A 19-year-old Daytona Beach woman won a national award . . . ."

An appositive is a common grammatical tool, using a noun or noun phrase to rename an adjacent noun. "Sonya Wise, the incoming journalism instructor from Germany, will advise the school newspaper this year." Fine for common usage in print, those long, interrupting appositives should rarely be used for radio writing. A similar shunned device, a relative clause, can be created by simply inserting *who, where* or *which* in front of an appositive: "Sonya Wise, who is the incoming journalism instructor from Germany, will advise the school newspaper this year." Placement of appositives and relative clauses at the end of any sentence (except the opener) is not as confusing: "The school newspaper adviser this year will be Sonya Wise, who is the incoming journalism instructor from Germany." By the way, dropping *who is* from such constructions will shorten the sentence without losing any meaning (see **Figure 6-2**).

When possible, most radio newscasts prefer present tense rather than past tense. It gives the news more immediacy—one of radio's best assets—rather than sounding old. Radio likes to keep listeners up-to-date as much as possible. Even for something that's already occurred, it sounds fresher to say, "Rail service to Philadelphia from Harrisburg *is ending* today for a month-long bridge repair," rather than use *ended*.

Direct quotations are infrequently read on the radio. If a news source's words are uniquely stated, a sound bite can present the key quote for on-air usage. PR writers must remember that quotation marks in their news releases are not seen by the radio audience. So paraphrased material is inserted instead. Some stations like to keep attributions in the present tense, with *says* rather than *said*. It makes the news sound more current for their listeners. The morning newspaper indirectly quotes that the CEO *said*. The radio at the top of the hour indirectly quotes that the CEO *says*.

Metropolis State University

Communications Office
Oct. 17, 2014

Contact: Tim Duncan
tduncan@metro.edu
555-555-5555

Slug: Metropolis Professor Wins Award

A Metropolis professor has won the Grand Prize *and* Ten Thousand Dollars, in a national writing contest.

Joy Forry will receive the Southern Quill Award, in a special ceremony next week in Atlanta. Her humor book, called *The Bone Lick Beacon,* is an account of life in a fictional, small southern town, as told by the newspaper's editor.

The winning author has this to say about her honor: "I'm thrilled that my zany characters in *The Bone Lick Beacon* have been recognized with this prize. The book is fiction . . . but these characters are *real.*"

Forry, who teaches Journalism at Metropolis State University, will be available at M-S-U's Campus Bookstore to sign autographed copies of her new book, from 2 to 4 p.m. this Saturday.

# # #

FIGURE 6-2 Sample Radio News Release

As mentioned earlier, it's wise to consult the main outlets used for individual policies on this and other matters. Although *said* may seem repetitive, it's much safer than using words such as felt, hoped, thought. Such attribution words imply intimate knowledge of the speaker and should be avoided. The writer cannot determine how the speaker feels, only how she said she feels.

Summary

Writing for electronic media uses a different style from print releases. Keep in mind that radio copy is writing for the ears. Sound bites and actualities increase chances your release will be read on the air. Television, of course, needs visuals (color, movement and dialogue) for its audience.

Persuasive Writing

> *"If you wish to win a man over to your ideas,*
> *first make him your friend."*

Abraham Lincoln

News releases require public relations practitioners to write objectively, but in some instances practitioners need to provide persuasive messages for particular audiences. These convincing communications help an organization tell its side of the story, convince a targeted public to take action (vote) or alert the public about impending legislation. Practitioners often receive the task of getting audiences to change or modify their opinions or behavior—a daunting endeavor.

Historically, public relations counselors have acted as advocates for their organizations. Ivy Lee and Edward Bernays both displayed genius in influencing publics to adopt new beliefs and behaviors. More recently, the Public Relations Society of America Member Code of Ethics, in fact, lists advocacy first under its "Statement of Professional Values."

According to the code, practitioners serve the public interest by acting as responsible advocates for those they represent, and they provide a voice in the marketplace of ideas, facts and viewpoints to aid informed public debate.

Advocacy, in fact, has become so crucial to the public relations profession that the organization established its own Advocacy Advisory Board (See **Figure 7-1**).

FIGURE 7-1 PRSA dvocacy Advisory
Board Logo

Don't throw out all the rules about objective news release writing that you've learned so far, but use the same writing and research skills to produce plausible arguments on behalf of your client. You need to know an issue thoroughly to convincingly present your case and also to rebut the opposite side.

This chapter discusses those instances when PR professionals need to craft persuasive messages for pitch letters, position papers, letters to the editor, op-ed/guest editorials, brochures and direct response pieces.

Persuasion Theory

According to both the International Association of Business Communicators (IABC) and PRSA, a primary goal of PR professionals is to influence or persuade audiences. Knowing the theory behind persuasion can help you construct persuasive messages that resonate with your audience. Earl Newson's theory of persuasion rests on four principles: **Identification, Suggested Action, Familiarity and Trust** and **Clarity.**

Identification means that individuals/audiences will relate to an idea or opinion if they can see the connection with their own wants or hopes. Radical demonstrator Saul Alinsky says it well, "People only understand things in terms of their own experiences . . . If you try to get your ideas across to others without paying attention to what they have to say to you, you can forget about the whole thing."

Suggested Action means that people will adopt new concepts only if they align with a proposed action—the simpler the action, the better.

Familiarity and Trust means that people don't want to accept ideas from sources they do not trust. Thus, a goal of PR practitioners is to build and enhance the confidence that the public places in organizations or clients.

Clarity means that to persuade, the meaning of an idea in an event or message has to be clear. Journalists often complain about jargon and doublespeak that clouds clear communication. Many news releases (up to 90 percent) are discarded for this reason. Keep in mind these principles as you write persuasive products.

Persuasive Efforts Begin with Clear Audience Analysis

You should have a clear sense of what you're trying to accomplish to produce a persuasive effort. Addressing the attitudes of the audience and moving it to action are the most important goals of any persuasive communication.

Motivating your reader to take action offers the most difficult challenge for any scribe. Writers must overcome situational forces that cause readers to say one thing but do another. For example, the writer may influence the reader to adopt a particular political position. However, if the reader gets opposition from family or friends concerning that position, he or she may reject taking action for fear of scorn. Consequently, persuasive writing must anticipate objections or constraints and address them to solidify the message in the reader's mind.

Public opinion is the sum of individuals' opinions on a subject that affects them. Writers must determine how differing opinions affect individuals before crafting a message. In doing so, writers must distinguish between opinions and attitudes.

An opinion is a predisposition to think, speak or act in a given way about a specific subject. Attitudes are learned and some are deeply rooted. When tied into other attitudes, beliefs and values, they are most likely hard to change.

Consider the following four attitude types:

1. Active audience—already involved with the issue.
2. Latent audience—an existing audience that has yet to form an opinion.
3. Aware audience—an audience that knows about an emerging issue, but holds limited facts.
4. Passive audience—an indifferent audience that's also unaware.

After establishing the overarching persuasive goal, you must then decide on the type and direction of the changes. These four persuasive aims help define the nature of the overall persuasive goal.

▶ **Adoption.** You attempt to get the reader to adopt an idea or plan. Write the message clearly. If you want residents to approve a school bond referendum, use clean, crisp language like, "We urge every resident of Cumberland County to get out and vote YES next Tuesday to support two new schools in the district."

▶ **Continuance.** You want the audience to continue a behavior. Using the above example, "We need residents of Cumberland County to continue their support of our schools and vote YES next Tuesday to support school expansion."

▶ **Discontinuance.** The writer or you want the audience to stop doing something. Continuing the previous example, "Residents need to reverse the failed bond referenda and support a plan to infuse the district with much needed funds."

▶ **Deterrence.** You, as the writer, want to convince the audience *not* to do something. "Residents of Cumberland County have voted against the last two bond referenda to infuse needed funds into our school system. Next Tuesday, let's reverse that trend and vote YES for school expansion."

Pitch letters, position papers, op-ed pieces/guest editorials, brochures and direct response pieces provide an ideal platform to convey controlled messages to targeted publics. They might shape a client's future, determine how laws will affect its operation, and create favorable public opinion, especially following a crisis. Naturally, creating these documents and using them proactively is the optimal way of getting the most mileage from them.

Now that you know persuasion theory and how to analyze your audience, let's tackle an individual persuasive product: pitch letters.

Pitch Letters

PR writers use pitch letters or short persuasive documents to entice journalists to cover an event or interview a client. You should address a pitch letter to a particular media contact using a business letter format. Unlike a fact sheet or a media advisory that provides primarily information, the pitch letter should persuade. You spell out why it's crucial for the media outlet to provide information on this specific topic to its audiences. You politely convince the media gatekeepers that this is the "smart" thing to do as professionals.

For print, the letter goes to the beat reporter or editor who covers your organization. If you don't know who that individual is, get the name from the publication and spell it correctly. Nothing upsets a journalist more than receiving generic mail unless it's mail with the name spelled incorrectly. For most television stations, the key contact is the assignment editor, whose job entails directing camera crews to specific locations at specific times.

TOOLBOX TIP

Points to Ponder in a Pitch Letter

▶ Include enough facts to support the full story you intend to write.
▶ Provide an angle of interest to the readers of the specific publication you have chosen.
▶ Offer the editor the possibility of alternative angles.
▶ Indicate your willingness to supply or aid the editor in securing quotes, interviews with credible sources, important statistics, arrangements for photographs and illustrations.
▶ Explain your credibility or authority to deliver the article, and mention that you will call the editor for his/her decision.

(Fran Pelham, "The Triple Crown of Public Relations: Pitch Letter, News Release, Feature Article." *Public Relations Quarterly,* Spring 2000.)

Importantly, having a relationship with editors gives you a foot in the door for making your persuasive appeal. If you have a reputation for suggesting solid news coverage, your future pitch letters should get noticed when they arrive. Make sure you provide specific details about the coverage you desire as well as its significance to the medium providing news to its community.

The following is an example of a pitch letter.

Tula Karras, Senior Health Editor
Seventeen Magazine
1440 Broadway, 13th floor
New York, NY 10018

January 24, 2014

Dear Ms. Karras:

Plastic surgery used to be considered nose jobs or altering the shape of a pointy or too large nose. Today, it covers everything from liposuction and Botox injections to breast augmentation. According to *The Huffington Post,* more than 300,000 women and teens will have breast augmentation this year, excluding mastectomy patients.

At 17, Cassie Mendez made a deal with her parents. If she maintained her 3.75 GPA throughout her senior year, her graduation gift would be breast implant surgery. A well-rounded B cup, Cassie never felt confident wearing clothes and felt that a larger bust size would improve her self-image. While her friends spent their summer cruising around in new cars or on vacation, Cassie spent six weeks recovering from her surgery, unable to hug anyone, or sit up because of the intense pain. The following six months would be no pleasure cruise either, as Cassie dealt with dizziness, nausea, hair loss and infections inside and out of her left breast.

Little clinical testing has been conducted on the long-term safety and risks of saline breast implants in girls under the age of 18. The FDA has not yet approved saline breast implants for those under 18. Yet doctors perform the surgeries despite the number of risk factors.

Take a look into the trend of the "grad gift" for young girls like Cassie. Investigate the FDA's claim that breast implants put women's lives in danger. Consider the article idea "A Grades for C Cups." Let me know if you're interested and we'll get you the information.

Sincerely yours,

Janet Nieberle
Public Information Officer
Federal Drug Administration

Position Papers

Simply stated, position papers are persuasive documents written by a company's public relations team for a variety of audiences. They can be sent to the media, employees, legislators, investors, etc. Often called "white papers" in the corporate world, these are expanded editorials, often four pages long for PR purposes that provide the organization's policies and position on a current or future situation. Somewhat similar to the much more objective backgrounder, the position paper gives writers the opportunity to conduct research, present the facts and then take a stand on the best option or course of action, and why.

Industry may go overboard at times with white papers, setting up a scenario as to why its product or service is necessary for other companies' survival. Radian6 produced a white paper in 2012 after considerable debate ensued over the value of social media to an organization's bottom line. Titled "The ROI of Social Media: Myths, Truths and How to Measure," the free downloadable document provides success stories and measurement suggestions for social media.

Whatever the focus of your white paper, keep jargon and other technical language to a minimum. Avoid other "inside" language, such as acronyms. To win your argument, you need the readers to understand the situation as well as your credible solution. Talking over their heads will have the opposite effect. Their lack of understanding will be coupled with a sense of frustration. Chances are that your audience won't even read to the finish if you annoy it with jargon.

Position papers have sundry uses, which is why the public relations department has to be vigilant in seeking out possible topics on the horizon. These can be local, regional or even international in scope. The media will often need position papers from your organization because of a timely news occurrence. Getting your company's reaction and perspective on that issue is a legitimate news function. So the PR staff needs to prepare for media inquiries about such events when possible.

However, do not send your position papers in a mass email to all regional media outlets. Editors and publishers like exclusives on their editorial pages. That's why syndicated columnists, by contract, cannot appear in competing newspapers within the same market. So parcel out your executive's essays so one medium doesn't feel slighted.

A quick rewrite with a different lead will enable you to send the treatise on a hot topic to another publication if needed. Once a potential issue has been identified, the PR staff alerts management with a draft outlining the organization's ties to the subject and implications for the future. After several drafts, a final version is formed. Whether intended for internal or external audiences, most white papers take a similar approach. A brief introduction and historical overview broaches the matter. As in a backgrounder, the position paper brings the readers thoroughly up-to-date on the topic. After informing, however, the latter document begins to persuade its audience. An organization's official stance on an issue must be effectively supported with convincing, objective documentation. As in typical newspaper editorials, opposing something is best supported if one can propose a better alternative solution.

Rather than ignoring the other side of the argument, successful position paper writers will acknowledge the opposite point of view. Then, with good, solid specifics, rather than stacking the deck, they will refute such merits with better solutions. Be careful, however, about exaggerations or overstating the facts. You need credibility with your print and online readers if you want to persuade them. That involves research, so you need to be familiar with such techniques as Internet searches, clippings from publications, speeches, books and specialized sources. But be careful about overloading the document with too many statistics or numbing numbers. You may want to cite references, where interested readers can go for further information. Clear, logical arguments are most effective. Irrational and emotional pleas get less response, especially from the informed, educated audience that you're probably targeting.

Many white papers have a conclusive summary to appeal to busy readers who often turn to that, and nothing else, to form an opinion about the document's merit. This is especially vital if the paper gets lengthy, since some of them can reach 20 pages or more. Knowing that the length typically decreases readership and acceptance rates by the media, public relations staffs should strive for much shorter documents than technical writers from industry. One of the key things to keep in mind for brevity is to focus on only one main point in your position paper.

According to Anthony Fulginiti, professor emeritus at Rowan University, you can write an effective position paper by using four sections: Problem/Issue, Effect, Position and Benefits.

In the **Problem/Issue** section, you should clearly state the issue, problem or challenge that your organization faces. Include historical background, if relevant.

In the **Effect** section, list the effects of the issue on your organization. You may want to use a bulleted list. It's important to list the nature and extent of the influence on your organization while providing believable evidence for each effect.

In the **Position** section you should state the position of your organization in a clear bottom-line statement. Then, argue that position by citing detailed evidence.

Finally, in the last section of the position paper, **Benefits,** list the benefits your organization will enjoy if society takes your position. You can also use a bulleted list for these benefits. Make sure to include the public interest and socially responsible aspect of these benefits. The more you can show that others benefit from your position, the more persuasive it becomes.

The following fictional example shows the New Jersey Department of Transportation's position on elderly drivers.

Problem/Issue

The New Jersey Department of Transportation (NJDOT) strives to ensure the safety of all state drivers. Most individuals take the privilege of driving seriously and thus drive carefully and responsibly. However, as adults get older, the effects of the aging process can dramatically impair their driving capabilities.

Effect

The aging process that includes hearing loss, reduced vision and a decline in motor skills threatens not only the safety of these older adults, but also the safety of other drivers on the road. As a result, too many accidents occur daily in New Jersey. In addition, this accident rate helps to further increase the high cost of auto insurance for state residents.

Studies conducted by the National Research Board find that:

► A driver's chance of involvement in an accident dramatically increases with age.
► The accident rate for motorists over the age of 75 doubles that of the average driver.
► The accident rate for motorists over the age of 80 triples that of all other drivers on the road.
► New Jersey auto insurance rates remain among the highest in the nation.

Position

NJDOT believes that older adults create a driving hazard and therefore recommends that the State of New Jersey require all motorists over the age of 75 to take an in-car driver's exam at regular intervals to determine their current ability level.

Benefit

This policy implementation will benefit all New Jersey drivers by:

► Reducing the total number of accidents and injuries on the road, of drivers young and old
► Ensuring the safety of elderly adults and all other motorists
► Reducing the high costs of auto insurance
► Creating new employment opportunities for state residents as driving exam instructors

Letters to the Editor

Op-eds and letters to the editor are short articles in a newspaper's valuable editorial section. Letters typically run 250 words or fewer while op-eds are approximately 800 words. Newspapers vary on these word counts. *Op-ed* can stand for either *opposite the editorial page* or *opinion and editorial,* depending on whom you ask. Letters to the editor usually respond to a previous article in the paper.

Both letters to the editor and op-eds can prove useful tools to get your message out. In particular, letters to the editor can help you:

► have access to policymakers who track constituent issues
► use an inexpensive channel to influence public opinion
► explain a complex issue
► revive an old issue

To write a letter to the editor:

▶ Plan your message. Use just one.
▶ Choose your target. If you want to affect public opinion, look for a paper or magazine with a large circulation.
▶ Read the publication and check out the writing style used.
▶ Contact the publication to find out how it wants your letter submitted.
▶ When you write, keep it short.
▶ Use real life stories to engage readers.
▶ Bring up an opposing point of view and discredit it.

Letters to the editor in local and regional papers are read by local activists, government officials, legislators and community members. Your letter can support and expand on an issue already in the news, make a point that someone else omitted, or disagree with information from a news story, editorial or another letter. According to ReclaimDemocracy.org, you should respond directly to breaking news or commentary published in the previous two days or the previous week in case of a weekly paper. You should focus on one important point and use verified facts. If the publication publishes an online version, you should hyperlink the relevant websites or emails. Don't overstate your points and don't insult your opponents.

According to Grace Fleming, writing for About.com Guide, submit your letter by email if the publication allows it. If you respond to an article you've read, do it quickly before the topic becomes old news. Widely read publications receive hundreds of letters so you might want to start with a smaller publication. Since the publication will edit your submission, get to the point early. Don't bury your point in a lengthy argument. Don't appear overly emotional. Limit those exclamation points. Remember that short letters sound confident. Long, wordy letters give the impression that you're trying too hard.

Op-Ed Pieces/Guest Editorials

Op-ed contributions and guest editorials often stem from condensed white papers. In fact, those are fairly common methods to get more mileage and wider exposure from a well-drafted document. Op-eds and guest editorials are great opportunities to have an organization's viewpoint explained in great detail. And if you think about it, an op-ed piece is like a position paper in that it expresses the opinion or position of a person or organization. So if you've mastered the position paper, op-ed pieces should follow naturally.

Furthermore, this public relations tool is rarely subject to any editing by the media gatekeeper. The four-page position paper, however, is probably way too long for a newspaper or magazine opinion article. It's wise to always check with the medium's guidelines regarding submissions for both op-ed pieces and guest editorials so they can be boiled down to the proper length and submitted before its deadline. These articles appear in a prominent position in the publication and usually get high readership, especially among opinion leaders.

Research at *The New York Times* revealed that its editorial section is second only to the front page for readership. Studies elsewhere show that editorial sections are consumed more by older, higher-income and higher-educated citizens than the average reader. Daily newspapers often rely on guest submissions to help fill the section, especially in weekend and holiday editions. We're familiar with one Tennessee newspaper that devotes one-third of its op-ed page to a local community leader's column each day during the latter half of December.

The op-ed page took shape across North America when newspapers decided to make their publications more open to community voices. The traditional editorial page still pronounced the institutional positions on a variety of topics, from local zoning proposals to international conflicts. But another key page in that section opened up to other viewpoints to allow a community dialogue to take place. In this way, publishers were attempting to show that the power of the press did not belong to only those who owned printing facilities. Credit for instituting the first op-ed page goes to Harrison Salisbury of *The New York Times* on Sept. 26, 1970. Some insist that *The Washington Post,* after being informed that its New York competition was about to launch such a page, actually beat *The Times* by inaugurating its own op-ed page a few days earlier. Many newspapers in big and small cities soon copied the leaders and adopted similar versions, with expanded letters to the editor, syndicated columnists, guest editorials and op-ed contributions.

An article in *Political Communication* by Brown, Waltzer and Waltzer (2001) pointed out the value of this location:

> *"The op-ed page is a hospitable environment to disseminate an organized interest's message. The newspaper and the page lend their prestige, authority, and credibility to the organization's message. While the op-ed page may not offer the breadth or quantity of readership of some publications or the audience of television and radio, it does offer quality of readership."*

You as a public relations writer need to proactively seek out opportunities for the placement of both guest editorials and op-ed pieces as promotion tools for your client or company. Some regional print media may ask for submissions occasionally, but why wait for that rare occurrence? Be alert to current events or future trends that could be developed into op-ed pieces. For maximum impact, enlighten and sway your audience without crass commercialism from the bylined author's organization.

The following op-ed piece concerns an author's view of energy drinks.

Energy Drinks That Deplete, Not Energize

According to Sari Harrar in *The Philadelphia Inquirer* February 20, 2012, teens and young adults spend an estimated $2.3 billion annually on energy drinks laced with caffeine and herbal stimulants. These expensive products do more to deplete health than encourage it according to Oklahoma State University researchers.

According to University of Miami researchers in *Pediatrics,* more than 5,000 reported caffeine overdoses in recent years—(46 percent in kids age 18 and younger)—have been attributed to so-called energy drinks. Besides containing dangerous levels of caffeine the drinks often contain herbal stimulants like guarana and yerba mate. University of Miami researchers indicate liver damage, kidney failure, respiratory disorders, agitation, seizures, psychotic problems, muscle breakdown, off-rhythm heartbeats, high blood pressure, heart failure, heart attack and even death have been reported in energy drink users in Europe. Many of those European countries ban energy drink sales to kids.

Canada requires new warnings and stricter caffeine limits. But what about the U.S.? Should we worry about our kids?

▶ **Energy drinks marketed in the U.S. enjoy no FDA restrictions.** The level of caffeine is set for cola drinks only. Beware those drinks with herbs that increase the amount of caffeine in each drink.

▶ **Marketers go after the teen audience much like Joe Camel ads aim at a young audience.** Energy drinks use coupons, samples and celebrity testimonials to intrigue young buyers.

▶ **Energy drinks don't energize much like a sugar high.** Energy drinks with excessive caffeine causes a burst of stress hormones and a fast descent sometimes called a crash.

▶ **Watch out for multiple servings in one can.** Many energy drinks contain up to four servings per small and expensive can.

Entice your teens/preteens to enjoy water, lemonade, ice tea, or juice. While some contain sugar, most contain no energy-depleting caffeine.

PRactical TIP

Writing Op-Ed Pieces from National Conference of Editorial Writers

▶ Put your main point on top. You have no more than 10 seconds to hook a reader. One of the most common mistakes is using too much windup before throwing the pitch.

▶ Make a single point—well. You cannot expect to solve all the world's problems in 800 words or less. Be as specific as possible.

▶ Avoid jargon. Simple language does not mean simple thinking. It means you are being considerate of readers who lack your expertise and are sitting half-awake at the breakfast table.

▶ Use the active voice. Don't write, "It is believed . . ." or "It is shown by studies . . ." Write instead, "I believe . . ." or "Studies show . . ."

▶ Tell the readers why they should care. Ask yourself, "So what? Who cares?" Explain why readers should care. Appeal to their self-interest.

▶ Relax and have fun. Newspaper editors despair of weighty articles, called thumb suckers, and yearn for items filled with spirit, grace and humor. Readers seek to be entertained and learn something in the bargain.

▶ Avoid tedious rebuttals. In writing a response to an earlier piece that made your blood boil, mention the earlier piece and then argue your own case. A point-by-point rebuttal makes you look petty, and it's a safe bet many readers didn't see the first piece.

Brochures

Unlike newsletters, which are serial publications, brochures are generally published only once and distributed to special publics for a single purpose. University interns often get their introduction to publications through newsletters and brochures. Brochures differ from fliers and leaflets because they are more lavish in design and generally convey more detailed information.

Designers must begin by writing copy using active voice verbs and with an emphasis on short sentences and short paragraphs. Bulleted lists add clarity to a brochure and help communicate information quickly. The use of subheads also adds to the clarity and visual appeal of a brochure.

Carefully planned folds can add design creativity and functionality to a brochure. Special tear-off panels can be used for mail-in promotions or as coupons for consumer goods. They provide an attractive and cost-effective design element (see Figure 7-2).

6-panel standard folder horizontal, two parallel folds
Z-fold or concertina fold
6-panel standard folder vertical, two parallel folds

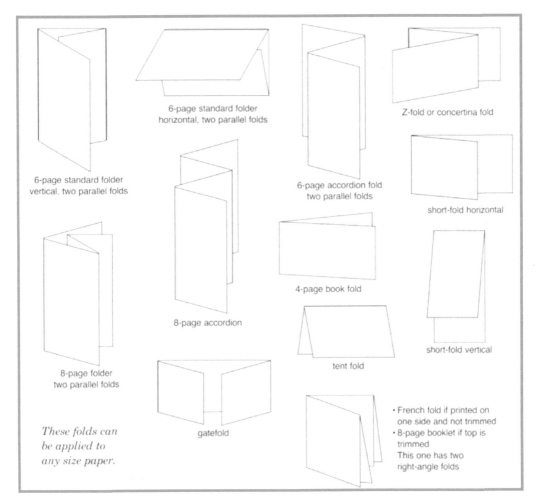

FIGURE 7-2 Options for Brochure Folding

From *Communicating with QuarkXPress* by Claudia Cuddy. Copyright © 2012. Reprinted by permission of Word Nerd Publishing.

These folds can be applied to any size paper.

French fold if printed on one side and not trimmed
8-panel booklet if top is trimmed, this one has two right-angle folds
6-panel accordion fold, two parallel folds
short-fold horizontal
4-panel book fold
8-panel accordion
short-fold vertical
tent fold
8-panel folder, two parallel folds
gatefold

Brochures can also include a mailing panel. Use of a mailing panel eliminates the need for sending the brochure in an envelope. The decision to design the brochure as a self-mailer or one that requires an envelope must be made after considering a number of factors such as budget for the project and the message tone the designer wishes to convey.

Finally, brochure designers must be bold enough to take chances with their design but also fundamentally skilled to follow the rules of good writing and the principles of effective design.

Writing Brochure Copy

When writing brochure copy, try listing the features of your products and services. Then list the benefits users will receive from these products and services. If you use an attention-getting headline and subheadings that support your headline, you'll make it easy for readers to scan. The back page of the brochure contains your contact information: include the many ways people can reach you.

According to eHow, before you write brochure copy you need to know how much space is reserved for copy. Next identify the key points that you need to cover. Decide what you want the brochure to accomplish (inform, sell, persuade). Choose cover copy first—focus on an idea important to the target audience. Establish credibility for your organization so that consumers will read your brochure. Outline what the business has to offer. Quote appropriate facts and statistics. Focus on why consumers should care about the service or information provided by the business. Challenge, entice readers into reading on. Get rid of obstacles—figure out the objections a reader may have and dispel them one by one. Deliver a call to action. Never make the customer guess what to do after reading the brochure.

TOOLBOX TIP

According to Jamie Turner, use these 14 words—the most powerful, effective words in marketing: *free, now, you, save, money, easy, guarantee, health, results, new, love, discovery, proven* and *safety*.

According to John Kuraoka, an advertising copywriter, the biggest mistake you can make in writing a brochure is to focus on informing rather than persuading your readers. Persuasive brochure copy starts on the cover by issuing an intriguing idea that positions an organization. Think about your readers or customers first, not your product or service. You want to make the readers feel that you understand their key problems. Each page of your brochure presents the reader with the opportunity to stop reading. That's why each spread should contain elements that attract and intrigue readers. Don't lose readers on technical points. Many brochures can overwhelm readers with jargon, diagrams or technical information. Your brochure is a key marketing piece and must take full advantage of the time with a potential customer. Customer testimonials help establish your credibility as experts. Finally, brochure copy should end by directing the customer's next step. Ask for the vote, the order or the behavior you want.

Direct Mail Letters

According to Richard S. Hodgson in his book *Direct Mail and Mail Order Handbook,* we've all received direct mail letters that we read. However, many end up in the recycling bin. How should your letter read? The following checklist suggests ways to make your direct mail piece stand out.

- ▶ Be friendly—write your letter/mail to convey warmth and personal regard for the prospect.
- ▶ Be clear—put yourself in the reader's position. Remember that he/she may not have any background knowledge of your problem.
- ▶ Be Anglo-Saxon—don't adopt a literary style for your letters that you don't use in conversation. Write at a 12-year-old level. Most newspapers in the U.S. are written for 6th–8th graders. Use words that express your meaning most clearly.
- ▶ Be concise—it doesn't have to be short to be concise. Tell the whole story and only that. Cover all the reasons why a prospect should do what you want her to do and answer all her objections.
- ▶ Sell benefits, not features. Uninterested audiences like to know what's in it for them. Promise the benefit in the headline or lead.
- ▶ If possible, offer something free.
- ▶ Back up your statements with proof and endorsements.
- ▶ Tell the reader what he might lose if he doesn't act.
- ▶ Rephrase your prominent benefits in your closing offer.
- ▶ Incite action now.

Each year approximately 80 billion pieces of direct mail go out from charitable organizations, government agencies and advertisers. The U.S. Postal Service receives revenues from direct mail marketing. Benefits of direct mail or direct marketing include individualized communication, measurable response, lead collection and customer feedback. Drawbacks are the high cost, customer avoidance and small reach.

B A G i N EDUCATION FOUNDATION INC.

900 Route 168, Suite B2 ■ Turnersville, NJ 08012
bagineducation@comcast.net ■ (856) 582-0943

January 8, 2013

Dear NAME:

The past year has been another busy one for the Bagin Foundation and its efforts to support Rowan University's MA in the PR program with enrichment opportunities and resources for students and faculty.

Along with sponsoring student field-research activities related to thesis work, the Foundation also helped the program sponsor its annual Mentor Night event, as well as two master-class workshops bringing recognized experts to campus to meet and work with the students.

Last year's master classes covered the topics of *PR Career Trends* and *Public Relations Issues for Education Foundations*. Both well-attended events were held in the historic Holly Bush Mansion.

Since its creation, the Foundation has supported events and activities important to enriching the educational experience of public relations students. Along with helping the faculty promote events to help students in their public relations education, the Foundation also accepts applications directly from students seeking assistance for their research and other work.

For example, along with funding previous master classes and other educational events, the Foundation has:

* Sponsored graduate students in developing theses research for those invited to present their work at professional conferences.

* Supported graduate assistants for the graduate PR program.

* Supplied funding for new reference books and other materials now available to students in the PR resource room.

Work is already under way to develop master classes and other special events for the coming year. And we expect to hear from this year's students to identify ways in which the Foundation might help them reach their goals.

Dr. Don Bagin's career was dedicated to building and improving the graduate communication programs at Rowan and supporting motivated students who needed special attention and resources to achieve their goals. Clearly, the work and vision of Don, a long-time professor and founder of the Public Relations program at Rowan University, continues through the efforts of the Foundation he founded and the ongoing interest and support of many people, like you, who helped Don in this important mission.

I invite you to visit us at www.bagin.org to keep up to date and, of course, to get in touch if you have any ideas or suggestions to share. Please continue to support the Foundation and keep Don's dreams alive and thriving for his students.

Gratefully,

The friends and family of Don Bagin

FIGURE 7-3

Writing a Direct Mail Letter

According to David Ogilvy, you can test everything direct mail writers do—from words to appeals to visuals or length. And, according to Bergh and Katz in *Advertising Principles,* the two most important things a direct mail writer must do are (1) get the reader to notice and open the piece, and (2) influence the reader to respond to the offer. The envelope, cover and headline will open up the direct mail piece while the interior copy will make or break the offer. A call to action must come at the end of the interior copy.

Wells, Burnett and Moriarty, in *Advertising Principles and Practices,* said the critical decision whether to read or toss is made on the basis of the outer envelope. To get the audience to open the envelope, some use a written offer on the outside. You can use an envelope that looks like it contains a check with no return address. Others use a peek-through envelope that announces an offer.

After recipients open the envelope, how do you get them to read on? Use a personal style that includes the target's name. The first paragraph should work like a headline to convince the reader to continue on. The body of the letter should provide support, explanation and details about your offer. You must write hard-sell copy. Because the postscript will draw readers' eyes first, use it as a teaser or a wrap up to your offer.

Often, a brochure may accompany the letter. The brochure should use graphics in the same way the letter uses words to convey your main point. *Remember:* When writing a direct mail letter or a brochure, you need to persuade readers, not just inform them. So it's good to review the principles and design of a persuasive letter (see Chapter 3). **Figure 7-3** provides an example of a direct mail letter written not only with a request for additional funding, but also touting the benefits of the Bagin Educational Foundation.

Summary

This chapter discusses many types of persuasive writing that PR pros must develop regularly. Whether it's a direct mail piece or a letter to the editor, you need to follow persuasion principles like Newson's Theory of Identification, Suggested Action, Familiarity and Trust, and Clarity. To craft a persuasive message, you'll need to know your audience, dispel its constraints and give it a reason to act.

Feature Writing

"Write a lead that invites an audience into the story."

MediaStudies.ca

For a relaxing change of pace for a writer, nothing beats getting a feature story assignment. Features use a variety of writing styles, quite unlike the typical straight news release. Not only enjoyable to organize and research, features are fun for almost every reader.

"Show them the forest; introduce them to a tree," says William Blundell to aspiring feature writers. Repeated readership surveys have told editors and publishers that storytelling or narrative journalism is the best way to reach and hang onto readers. Aware of this growing trend, the Associated Press started producing feature lead options along with its traditional news stories during 2012. Human interest angles still work. Readers recall what they feel. They're interested in how things work, how people think and what they do. The enjoyment of feature stories is universal, as studies from other countries have confirmed. Author Natalie Babbitt said, "Good stories are always a pleasure to read, and we like pleasure, regardless of our ages."

However, despite any rumors you may have heard, these features aren't necessarily easier to write than hard news stories. They take skill and dedication. It's not an exercise in writing at will on whatever is interesting with no concern for factual accuracy, research or background information.

Rather than simply delivering objective facts, a feature writer will tell a story with humor, color, drama or emotion. Elizabeth Sims provides tips in the March–April 2012 *Writer's Digest* on how to make readers laugh ("7 Simple Ways to Make a Good Story Great").

Note that wit is not exactly humor: We might laugh reading a scene where a vain person gets a pie in the face, but that's humor and takes no intelligence to perceive. Wit is more of a brain thing.

We laugh when we're given a perspective we'd never have dreamed of. We laugh when we can see absurdity that others can't. We laugh when we're surprised, and when we're caught off-guard by understatement.

On the other hand, straight news articles almost fall into place, in fact, as events unfold for a writer: *City Council Approves Downtown Zoning Request* or *Gividen Home Builders Recalls 100 Workers.* Feature facts don't automatically organize into a logical order as they do for straight news. The inverted pyramid is not considered part of the writing process.

"Writers usually say that they use the inverted pyramid because readers stop reading after the first paragraph," says veteran writing coach Ann Wylie. "Meanwhile, readers typically say that they stop reading after the first paragraph because writers use the inverted pyramid." It's not the way to attract an audience.

Scribes will hook the reader quickly with the enticing story's human interest introduction, and then provide details as necessary. A major reason to write a feature lead is that it will make the audience want to read more.

> Beyond being clear, concise and error-free, good writing "sings." It has a rhythm and a flow that helps propel the reader along, even if the subject matter is mundane or highly technical. This is probably the hardest aspect of writing to teach.
>
> Andrew Hindes, president, The In-House Writer

Readers today suffer from information overload more than any other time in history. A recent study, for example, found that online viewers see almost half a million words daily. Storytelling is one of the best methods to cut through all that clutter. Writers need to produce feature stories like a storyteller, not a collector of facts. The American Society of Newspaper Editors, in one survey, found that articles containing storytelling elements had higher readership and comprehension levels than inverted pyramid examples.

"Hispanic news outlets are more likely to use a feature article than a regular press release," said Jesus Hernandez Cuellar, editor-in-chief of Contacto PR News. Likewise, he said, features attract the attention of readers more than news releases.

According to an article in the summer 2012 Journalism and Mass Communications Quarterly, narrative-type stories produce more favorable reactions from readers and more compassion for subjects in the articles. Authors Mary Beth Oliver, James Price Dillard, Keunmin Bae and Daniel Tamul titled their article "The Effect of Narrative News Formats on Empathy for Stigmatized Groups."

Scholars and journalists have long noted that news stories do more than simply present information. Rather, the way that information is stressed or downplayed and the examples provided to illustrate issues play important roles in readers' understanding and retention of information, as well as the perceptions and beliefs that follow from exposure.

Many have probably heard the classic newsroom definition of news: Man bites dog. Roy Peter Clark of Florida's Poynter Institute has determined that a feature could be any one of the following examples:

▶ Several men bite several dogs.
▶ Several men bite the same dog.
▶ Why are men biting dogs?
▶ What makes dogs bite?
▶ Fred the letter carrier holds city record for being bitten by dogs. (Has never bitten back.)
▶ Diablo and Spike: Why owners give docile dogs vicious names.
▶ How to protect children from dangerous dogs.
▶ Martha the vet cares for good dogs bitten by bad dogs.
▶ Nature or nurture? What makes good dogs turn bad?
▶ Why we love vets and hate dogcatchers.
▶ How dogs help cancer patients.

Even though it's worth the effort to write human interest stories, public relations writers might be waiting a long time for feature assignments for traditional media outlets to be handed to them. That's why they need to always think of feature pieces they can come across to craft for their internal audiences and pitch to other media. PR writers have plenty of feature opportunities with their company or clients. There are founders, officers, board members, employees, retirees and volunteers, just along the people angle of feature options. Then there are the how-to articles, new product or service features and the application piece that addresses how a company solved a situation.

An informal feature story typically covers a topic not considered hard news. So the timing aspect is rather minor on many features, rarely written for an immediate deadline. In fact, features used to be called evergreens, always fresh, ready for dropping into a news hole when extra room was available. PR Newswire, which sends more than 2,500 feature stories a year, keeps them available in its archives for two years. Unlike yesterday's news release that's now history and deleted from a reporter's computer, a feature can be used whenever needed. That's enough incentive for some PR writers to create features ahead of time to use when things are too hectic to find material for the next e-newsletter, blog or Web content entry. A snappy headline and a strong lead paragraph can intrigue readers at first glance.

As mentioned above, one of the more frequent terms heard around newsrooms the past few years is storytelling. The American Press Institute conducts seminars for reporters on the trend, encouraging them to take a multimedia approach. It's a way to help readers see and understand a topic, not merely read about it. Feature writers should think of themselves as storytellers, not news reporters. They uncover and explain the offbeat, humorous and emotional events not appearing in traditional or social media. Their writing is informal and conversational, entertaining readers. Advertising guru David Ogilvy, when talking about another form of writing, summed it up well when he said, "Nobody ever sold anybody anything by boring them to death."

Annette Simmons provides PR feature writers with advice and encouragement in her book, *The Story Factor: Inspiration, Influence, and Persuasion Through Storytelling.*

> *People don't want more information. They are up to their eyeballs in information. They want faith—faith in you, your goals, your success, in the story you tell. It is faith that moves mountains, not facts. Facts do not give birth to faith. Faith needs a story to sustain it—a meaningful story that inspires belief in you and renews hope that your ideas, do indeed, offer what you promise. . . . Storytelling is the most valuable skill you can develop to help you influence others.*

Michael Hauge, author and Hollywood consultant, said storytelling elements can fit when enticing the media with various feature ideas. "The elements of great storytelling are universal," he said in *Bulldog Reporter's Daily 'Dog* (March 2, 2009). "They apply equally to PR pitches and good feature stories in the media as to Hollywood feature films. Any compelling story has character, desire and conflict—those are the three corners." Hauge advises feature writers to make sure their story has all three of those before sending it to media contacts.

Any feature story may use those three elements of character, desire and conflict by taking a different slant on a current news event or go behind the news. For example, instead of talking about the high-mileage hybrid motors produced in the local Honda assembly plant, a feature angle could look (with photos and video) at the 38-year-old brainchild (character) behind the improved robotic assembly line that speeds up production 25 percent (desire) without displacing workers (conflict). Or it could be even lighter than that. A feature could talk about the assembly line materials made from recycled plastic bags or the history of Honda's restored building—a former blimp manufacturing plant back in the 1960s.

Speaking of hybrids, another term you will hear is newsfeature. This is a feature story directly tied to a contemporary news event. Yet the treatment is not hard news. It will have emotions and a human interest touch, similar to a regular feature described in this chapter. Newsfeatures often appear a day or two after a headlined news story, when writers have more time to develop the interpretation and depth to the original piece. Popular newsfeatures every two years are the struggles and sacrifices of Olympic athletes.

You can base many features on current events or related news items. A feature that ties in with newspaper and magazine sections—such as health, travel, sports—is a great way to promote a client's product or services. This type of related feature article will build off the news, but perhaps in a lighthearted way. A jet crash with no injuries may create sidebar features about airport runway improvements, better seat design, fire-resistant cabin materials, flight attendant preparation or pilot skill. Of course, it will enhance chances of getting published or viewed if public relations staffers have media convergent material to share with the appropriate journalists and bloggers, such as photos and video.

Types of features are too numerous to list, since there is no definitive classification. However, a few common examples are personality profiles, interviews, background pieces, new products or services, research/survey results, newsfeatures, sidebars, and historical (including anniversaries).

Features still need to conform to quality writing standards and AP style, but they stray from most news release format basics. Rarely will a feature story follow the inverted pyramid style of writing. Many of the who, what, where, when, why and how developments can wait until the middle of the piece. The story doesn't unfold as it happens in a sense of most important to least. Rather, a feature lead may consist of a

TOOLBOX TIP

Brainstorms Create Ideas

Just contemplate all the numerous features a PR writer might develop about the 2016 Summer Olympics in Rio de Janeiro. Remember, a brainstorming session is not the time to evaluate the merits of every idea, only to get them listed on an overhead or easel. In fact, most quality ideas develop after several inferior ones get posted. Writers can use informal brainstorm sessions to think of releases they could write for clients providing travel, security, cameras, clothes, cell phones, credit cards, sunglasses, sports equipment, cultural sites, energy drinks and overnight lodging, just to name a few possibilities. Can you think of more?

quirky quotation, a puzzling predicament or a strange situation. A feature writer has great latitude in starting the story. Anecdotal leads are effective starters for entertaining feature articles. The final paragraph of a news release contains the least important aspect of the story, of course. For a feature, however, it may form the crucial punch line. In many cases, it ties in with the feature's opening.

Leads, of course, can range from one sentence to a few paragraphs. Summary leads rarely appear on features, but they may be inserted as nut graphs. A direct quotation could make a good feature lead. It quickly absorbs the reader into the action. It creates a personalized, conversational start to the story. Full-sentence direct quotes are effective ways to start any paragraph. A feature writer must remember not to use direct quote leads too frequently or to use mundane quotations anywhere, especially in the lead.

You should reserve question leads for features rather than news stories. The problem for readers is if the writer phrases the question lead so they have no concern for its answer. "Are you worried how long a hybrid car battery lasts?" For those who don't own or plan to soon buy such a vehicle, the reading experience could end with an emphatic "no" after reading that opener. So the wording of the question should avoid eliciting a negative or nonchalant response.

Again, unlike straight news, you might write a few feature leads in chronological order. Readers can get hooked at the beginning of a quality chronology lead, who then beg to know what happened next, and then next after that.

PRactical TIP

A Mat Release Is Not a Wrestling Hold

On-the-ball PR writers have obtained local coverage using mat (or matte) releases. These are feature stories, almost always teamed with a photograph or other visual element, about a company's products. Nonprofits can even use them to promote their services. Mat releases are produced by the PR staff in a ready-to-use format for small daily and weekly publications. If they are the proper column width, editors can drop them into the page as is with no or few changes.

These small papers with even smaller staffs seek local coverage. So your feature should use that same angle—local workers, local resources, and local distribution network—whenever possible. Of course, with a wider appeal, you can obtain broader coverage with regional newspapers. Perhaps a mat release with a photo of your company's new and improved batter's helmet for Little Leaguers could be used nationally if written from a safety angle, not a sales angle. If you want to concentrate on a wider scale, PR Newswire (among others) has a national mat release distribution system.

In any case, play down the marketing pitch. Make the features informative and practical. Always gear them for small-town media. Papers that then post mat releases on their Web editions could multiply your exposure with minimal expenditure. You can pin your hopes on mat releases if you have the right moves.

As mentioned above, colorful features don't have to tie in with current news developments. You can write them about any subject: people, pets, pests, plants, places, pain, passion, plans, prejudice and prayer. These topics touch audiences. Universal themes such as emotions are always perfect for feature treatment.

Even obituaries can lead to award-winning feature stories. Jim Sheeler, formerly with the now defunct *Rocky Mountain News,* won a Pulitzer Prize in feature writing for an extended obituary. Many of his finest examples are collected in his book, *Obit: Inspiring Stories of Ordinary People Who Led Extraordinary Lives.*

> *"When I began writing obituaries, my goal was to write about people whose names had never appeared in the newspaper, to find the stories that had never been told—and, just as important, the lessons they left behind. . . . For me, the answer is simple: these people teach me how to live."*

Rather than seeing his assignment as a terrible job, Sheeler interviewed people about the deceased to find their many positive traits. He noted that everyone deserves a good feature story, rather than simply a brief obituary notice. So he resolved to develop a feature every week about an individual who had never been in the newspaper until the death notice appeared. Sheeler proves that even features about death—and life—can have widespread appeal.

Here's the intriguing start for one of Sheeler's masterpiece leads from *Obit*. It's titled "Your Life Must Be So Dull."

> *Depending on his mood or the time of day, the crusty old man on the park bench might brush a hand through his enormous, filthy gray beard and tell passers-by about his life as a Benedictine monk. While keeping an eye on a shopping cart filled with his only possessions, the artist, scholar, and priest in the funky homemade clothes would sing in flawless Latin.*
>
> *He could quote obscure Russian novels and cite esoteric philosophy but could also describe the way a carburetor works or the intricacies of horse saddles through the centuries.*
>
> *Then Severin Foley would say something to ruin everything. He always did.*

Deborah Petersen, deputy features editor of the *San Jose Mercury News,* said localizing broad trends is a benefit for her readers in the Feb. 18, 2009, edition of Bulldog Reporter's Daily Dog. And if public relations writers can produce features for both print and online they will be noticed.

> *"We all want to hear if you have video or multimedia that can help a story be more interactive on our sites," Petersen said. "Think Web first, not print."*

She suggests public relations writers should focus on visuals in a narrative writing style when pitching the media.

Because most journalists like to put their own personal style on features, corporate communicators will find few opportunities to place them with traditional major media. National and state press competitions recognize excellence in feature writing, but only by journalists. Therefore, it's wise to recognize this reality and allow reporters to create these newspaper and online features for fun and profit.

So why devote a whole chapter to feature writing? A major reason is that reporters still need plenty of help researching, writing and, in many instances, thinking of feature ideas concerning any company or a PR firm's clients. Public relations writers should send regular beat reporters a personal pitch letter, describing a possible feature story proposal. If it's appealing enough, the journalist may be enticed to take on such an assignment. (It's always wise to make sure to take turns spreading those feature suggestions around, so one medium doesn't feel slighted.) Since the writers and their employers are now investing time and resources on that idea, it stands a better chance of getting printed, put online or aired. Being a skilled public relations practitioner, you'll also be expected to quench the journalist's own thirst for unusual slants and profiles. So the PR staff must encourage and supply such details. They can provide access to individuals and any relevant material unavailable on their online newsroom.

Another—more practical—reason to discuss feature writing is because PR practitioners will continue to conceive and create feature stories for their own organization's internal print and online publications (e-newsletters, magazines, quarterlies), its Web site, blogs and online newsroom. Their unique features can also be sent to understaffed, small-market television and radio stations in the region, all nondailies in the area, and those invaluable trade publications with their priceless editorial pages. Needless to say, there will always be abundant outlets for their written feature stories.

Be a Serious Reader

"All serious students of writing must also be serious readers. You can't expect to flourish in a field that you do not enjoy and also aren't very familiar with. Read everything you can get your hands on. Read books, magazines, newspapers, and online articles. Study what other writers are doing."

The Complete Idiot's Guide to Getting Published

Not a Dime a Dozen

One of the hardest aspects of feature writing for many is coming up with gems—brilliant ideas that become compelling reading. Actually, the task is not as complicated as it seems. Ideas are all around the workplace daily. Almost every organization creates services, ideas or products. What about its archived publications? Company and product anniversaries can make good feature ideas when they roll around. The company has employees, managers, and perhaps customers and volunteers. Writers could enlist the help of employees and others to suggest story ideas with a good shelf life. That's one of the best reasons to encourage two-way communications between management and the workforce. Maybe the PR staff can even find a few guest storytellers in the process.

A task taught early in communication classes is to be a keen observer. The maxim holds true for feature writers. Classified ads, personals and blogs can get them thinking. They should tune in to radio and TV talk shows. They can surf the Net as part of their cross-training duties. Veteran feature writers read bulletin boards and direct mail, talk to people, and listen to conversations at work (lobby, elevator, lunchroom, parking lot, etc.). Has the PR department conducted any polls recently? Survey results usually turn up good feature article ideas. PR staffs need to observe trends and how they might impact their own client or company.

Ideas don't have to be unique to be effective. What one company writes about in another state or country could easily and legally be "translated" into a local organization's features folder.

An astute PR pro can just add her own twist to the original idea. It's lawful as long as the words are changed, since ideas cannot be copyrighted. That's a great benefit for reading out-of-town publications. Scanning trade magazines or websites totally unrelated to her own organization can also give her material to adapt.

PRactical TIP

Top 10 Typical Sidebar Topics

Sidebars are developed in a variety of styles. There's no exact description or category, since many of them can blend into other types. Our top 10 listing includes what are typically the most common.

1. Localization—This might interpret new developments from Berlin or Washington, D.C., into local significance.
2. Resources—Your readers may want more information about a product or service. Provide appropriate social media sites, email addresses, phone numbers in the sidebar.
3. Lists—Even before David Letterman popularized his Top 10s, lists have been favorite reading material.
4. Background—Many readers want more details than one story can tell them. Provide those eager learners with a time line, history of an issue, or particulars about how a product or service developed.
5. Informative—Provide instructions on how to obtain flood insurance or make arrangements for a wedding.
6. Quiz—These short tests get high reader marks, whether serious or whimsical. Make sure to include an answer key.
7. Quotes—Usually you don't have adequate space to include enough good quotations in the main release. The sidebar can be the perfect place for their placement. Sometimes they are boxed in a Q-and-A format.
8. Personality—Rather than detract from the major article, the sidebar can include tons of biographical information about a certain individual.
9. Related Event—Give readers a look at what happened during a similar situation in the past: recession, flood, fire, earthquake.
10. Details—For readers who want to know every minute detail on an issue or product, you can satisfy them with sidebars without slowing down others.

Another great source of feature ideas is current events. Stories related to big news can easily take a feature slant. Busy journalists often don't have the time to conduct follow-up stories on original major news items. PR writers can also consider getting a local angle on a national trend.

Many of those fit into the sidebar category, smaller tidbits related to the major news story of the day. Readers have a fascination with sidebars, which are often boxed or have other typographical devices to set them apart from normal copy.

Because they're short, websites and print editors can usually find room for sidebars. PR scribes should follow the style of the ones they read in their targeted media, since they have passed the media gatekeeper's seal of approval. Typically they include practical information that will help the publication's readers. Often written in an informal and entertaining style, sidebars need to be referenced to the main article without repeating the same information. It seems only appropriate for this chapter to show readers a sidebar, since they're reading about them.

Quality ideas for feature stories may not be "a dime a dozen," but they are plentiful for the watchful PR practitioner. Whether long descriptive feature stories or the shorter versions that link to a major news item, feature ideas are found everywhere.

Overcoming Writer's Block

Public relations writers aren't immune from dull prose or the occasional writer's block, especially when they need to be creative for a good feature story. They stare at the blank screen but the words just won't flow. What can be done then (or earlier in the process) to overcome such obstacles to produce writing that sings with crispness and clarity? One or two of the following tips may prove effective when no words are forthcoming to fill that blank screen.

Relearn Creativity—Rather than insisting that they have no creativity, writers merely have to think as they did when younger. Children are naturally creative, until schooling, social pressure and adults rob them of that wonderful trait. So writers need to recover and reinforce such right-brain traits as intuitive, curiosity, independent, visual thinker, inventiveness and open to new ideas.

Vary Circumstances—Perhaps a change of scenery will help the creative juices flow. Rather than writing at the typical desk, they can take a tablet or laptop with them to the roof or a nearby park. Likewise, some scribes are able to produce creatively at a time other than 9 to 5. Many prolific writers arise at 4 to work on projects before starting the workday; others might set aside a 10 p.m. to 1 a.m. block of time solely for writing.

Read Regularly—A PR pro's daily reading habit should lead to a spark that says, "I could slant that type of story to my organization." Again, ideas **cannot** be copyrighted, only the expression of those ideas. Writers aren't cheating—just being creative—to ponder over an interesting story to see how they can find a new angle. They should rip out (and file) creative articles they find in newspapers, Sunday supplements, flight magazines, websites, blogs, etc. They can download other great examples they come across while surfing the Net.

Blank Screen Syndrome—Several techniques are available to meaningfully fill that blank computer screen. When working on a feature piece about mass transit and the writer hasn't ridden the bus or subway within the past month, he needs to get out of the office and hop on board. Some experts suggest writer's block victims retype the previous page of an ongoing writing project so they'll get into the creative flow of what they have been working on.

Try Free-Flow Writing—One technique often useful is to start writing as quickly as possible. The advice continues: Don't worry about spelling or punctuation issues or even a lead for now. The task is to just get those thoughts down on the screen. A rewrite and edit job can work on those issues later. Sometimes the physical act of clicking away on a keyboard will help the creativity to transform from the deep recesses of one's mind to the tips of one's fingers. Another thought is to pretend the written document is a letter being sent to a friend at work. Related to free-flow or free association writing is brainstorming, when writers merely list as many ideas or concepts as possible, without stopping to consider their individual merit.

Of course, writer's block doesn't just occur for those producing features. It's a universal problem for all writers contributing to a variety of media. Jerry Lanson, in his 2011 book, *Writing for Others: Telling Stories in an Age of Blogging,* suggests that writers should also consider a change of scenery to get the writing juices flowing. "The secret is to go where you can relax enough to solve writing problems, not merely worry about them. In our overcrowded, overscheduled lives, it is advice too few writers heed."

Naturally, writer's block will seem less of a problem if the PR practitioner's research activities have uncovered enough information and resources to help the writing process flow effortlessly.

Researching Features

Experienced reporters always gather much more information than they will need to write their stories. The same should hold true for PR writers of feature stories. It's wise to cover all the bases instead of getting sidetracked during the writing process to unearth some minor, time-consuming details they should have researched the first time. Writing is easier when the preparation gives them confidence they sufficiently know their material. And the story's credibility will determine its worth in readers' (and journalists') eyes. That's why a second opinion or corroboration is necessary. Relying solely on *Wikipedia,* not a valid resource, brands a writer as an amateur. For starters, a feature creator should interview all possible sources, just not put them all in the story. Too often, writers want to show off all their background research so they include extraneous details just to prove how industrious they were.

"In the end, only blood relatives of sources will read the story, and some of them will only say they have," says William E. Blundell in his classic *The Art and Craft of Feature Writing: Based on the Wall Street Journal Guide.* He adds:

A good writer is merciless in deciding who gets into his piece. Each person must have a story purpose or be excluded; scores of sources may have been interviewed, but that's the worst reason for putting them into the story. . . . As the number of characters diminishes, those remaining loom larger in the reader's mind. They become more than talking heads and begin to take on identities of their own. The storyteller wants this to happen and works to advance the process.

If the feature is indeed targeted toward a specific medium, part of a writer's research is to examine that publication thoroughly. She needs to go through a few recent issues. What are its audience characteristics? What slant do most newsfeatures take? How long is the typical feature? She will need this knowledge so her article resembles all the others an editor examines for the next issue. If it includes links in its feature pieces, for example, make sure she has appropriate ones for her feature. She'll probably want to obtain helpful links anyway for online uses.

A frequent practice for public relations writers is interviewing. It's useful for gathering information for news releases, backgrounders, position papers, biographies and features. Since many features are personality profiles about individuals at work, quality interviewing skills are essential when talking to one or more people for a story. PR writers must remember not to limit the list of feature subjects to the CEO or other executives. Many employees and volunteers have fascinating lives, interesting hobbies and feature-worthy interests.

It's imperative to conduct preliminary investigation before a scheduled interview. Ideal questions are informed questions. So the feature writer doesn't want to waste his own time and that of his source by asking mundane questions already ascertained with a little computer and archive searching. He should read what others have said about the individual with an open mind. It's wise to develop and write down a series of questions, but not be glued to asking them all if the interviewee opens up other opportunities for new or follow-up questioning. The writer needs to keep in mind that he is in control of the interview process. So he can't let his subject ramble endlessly. He will have to come back to those questions as needed.

Open-ended questions are always better than ones providing simple yes-or-no responses. A writer can't quote himself (or even his long-winded inquiries) in the interview account. It's necessary to get the various sources' actual words. Their comments create the story's content, not his own questions. As everyone can tell from reading other features, brief direct quotations make up quite a bit of the story. Those popular quotes humanize the selected subjects for readers, who enjoy getting in on the verbal action. They can "hear" the actual words of individuals. They make features and news stories more personal and more conversational.

You'll also notice that feature story quotations are mixed in with indirect quotes and other details. Writers shouldn't quote generic statements, but unusual expressions, strong emotions and subjective opinions. They need good quotes, concrete examples and colorful descriptions. Attribution is always needed for someone's words. Interviewers can't leave "naked quotes" in their feature. They must tie them to the specific person who said them in a variety of ways, such as:

▶ After the quoted material: "We pulled off the biggest event in years," she said.
▶ Before the quoted material: She said, "We pulled off the biggest event in years."
▶ After the first sentence of quoted material longer than one sentence: "We pulled off the biggest event in years," she said. "Ideally, we can do this again for the next conference."
▶ Identify a second speaker in a new paragraph *before* that individual's actual words appear:

> "We pulled off the biggest event in years," Michelle Earl said.
> However, Brett Carter countered, "The 2011 conference actually was much larger than this one."

▶ Please note that only one attribution is needed per paragraph, no matter how long it is. For consecutive paragraph quotes by the same speaker, attribution is needed only for the first use. Thereafter, you should not put closing quote marks at the end of a graph if quoted material follows. Quotation marks are always used to start all such paragraphs, but closing quotes are placed only after the last graph.

A feature writer must keep the jargon to an absolute minimum. When her source starts using too much technical lingo, she must lasso him back to reality. She can remind him she needs to explain this information to an untrained, general audience. Newspapers are still targeted to about a ninth grade reading level. Literacy levels in this country are declining, rather than increasing. If she doesn't understand terms the interviewee is throwing at her, chances are the online or reading public will draw a blank also. She can simply ask, "How would I best explain that phrase to our audience?"

TOOLBOX TIP

Imagery's Power

1. **Simile**—a comparison of dissimilar things using either like or as.
   Example: Good prayer is like a beautiful garden.
2. **Metaphor**—a comparison of dissimilar things without like or as.
   Example: Good prayer is a garden.
3. **Personification**—giving human qualities to an inanimate object.
   Example: The clover applauded our team's victory.
4. **Exaggeration**—overstating (hyperbole) for dramatic impact.
   Example: Our team moved mountains to win this championship.

If there's a brief silence in the interview during the response time, she should not get uptight. Perhaps the person is thinking how to phrase a statement or if it should even be shared. If she moves on too quickly, that gem could be lost from the storytelling experience.

As the interview process starts winding down, she should thank her sources for their time, even if they are not that friendly or cooperative. Unfortunately, she may have to check back with them for one other piece of information or to confirm a fact. And she always wants to leave on a good note in case that person becomes another interview subject again. If the interviewee asks to see the story before it's published, she can say that it's not company policy to do that. Except for the CEO, most people will accept such a response. Or she can get back later to the source with just the direct quotes or technical details to ascertain their accuracy, if she feels the need. This might be more likely if it's a complex or scientific feature piece.

A person quoted in a feature story is often asked by the media to respond to additional questions. This is a great opportunity for a public relations practitioner to extend the impact of that initial media event. Sharp quotations can thus become the springboard for an interview and more exposure for the client or organization.

Nut Graphs Set the Stage

Feature writers frequently start their stories with an anecdote or some similar device to rivet the attention of their readers. Rather than talking about a national trend, the first two paragraphs may personalize the plight of an unemployed father of four. Then the writer brings the overall topic into better focus with what is called a nut graph. The practice can appear in newsfeatures or even analytical news articles.

Often more than one paragraph long, the nut graph gives the story an overall sense of why it's important to keep reading. The anecdotal opening helps capture the readers' attention, even if the audience doesn't know where the article is going. The nut graph that follows serves as a bridge, explains the significance of the newsfeature, and helps set the stage for the rest of the story. It clues the often clueless but intrigued reader what the story is all about. Sometimes called a second lead, the nut graph should not be buried more than 100 words into the story. The one below follows 74 words of introductory text.

An example of a nut graph—in this case, two paragraphs because of length, which occurs frequently—appears in paragraphs three and four following two introductory anecdotal graphs. It summarizes and localizes the national topic for Podunk readers.

> *Yuko Kumata recalls her excitement when she arrived in the United States last fall for classes at Podunk State University. The 19-year-old registered for classes in her sociology major and eagerly started reading her books.*

> *Her anticipation of meeting new friends and getting to know more about American culture didn't happen, however. "I felt like a prisoner on campus," she said, which is why she and three of her friends returned to Japan after only one semester at the rural campus.*

> *More than 600,000 international students annually flock to American shores, with about 60 choosing to study at Podunk every August. But after recruitment, few efforts are made at schools to make these typically timid visitors feel at home.*

So PSU received a pilot grant to create a new position of International Student Director to help visiting students get involved in activities and go on field trips so they won't feel so isolated on campus.

This anecdotal opening creates an emotional storytelling setting and creates some anticipation of whether there could be a solution to this problem. Readers are wondering if this trend might continue when the news peg transition hits them in paragraphs three and four. The nut graphs above provide the reading audience, in a "nutshell," what the rest of the story is about. They will soon learn how this pilot grant is providing shuttle vans for regular trips to an area mall and recreational facilities, since international students don't have cars or drivers licenses (and mass transit doesn't exist). The newsfeature continues how the new director has involved host families in the somewhat rural community who will "adopt" one or two students to make sure they are included in holiday events and not left stranded on an empty campus.

A nut graph emphasizes understanding more than simple facts. It may often tease readers without giving away the ending. Some say it gives readers a reason to care about one's writing efforts. Its goal, of course, is to fascinate them into answering their own question: "Why should I read the rest of this story?"

Don't Quit Yet

A major advantage of features for the writer typically is the lack of an immediate deadline. Just because he has finished the story, he shouldn't send it off or post it online yet. If possible, he needs to set the work aside for 24 hours and come back with a fresh mind and an editor's perspective. His summary, unlike the news release lead, is the most important part of many features. (He should never include a boilerplate at the end of his feature story. If left in a feature, the boilerplate would interrupt the flow for readers.) The summary may be brief, but the conclusion contains the idea he wants to leave with the readers or viewers. Unlike the deadline-zaniness of a developing news release, time is on his side. He can rewrite that earlier draft if necessary. The biggest complaint from editors about features is overwriting. To avoid that problem, can he eliminate those extra words he didn't notice the first time through? Can he tighten one of his colorful descriptions? Make a point clearer?

If possible, he should have someone else read his work. He knows he typed "well" in that fourth paragraph. He has read it over three times, and spellcheck caught nothing wrong. However, a sharp colleague may find the word actually appears as "will" in the feature. Another set of eyes always seems to improve anyone's writing efforts.

Publication editors have been telling their staffs to think about photos, artwork and graphics for their news stories ever since 1982 when *USA Today* started revising American

© Bedrin, 2013. Used under license from Shutterstock, Inc.

reading habits. The same holds for feature writers. An eye-appealing package can contribute to the feature story's popularity with readers as well as those gate-keeping editors. But with media convergence, that feature could wind up as an on-air video report, a blog, an online package with extra photographs and charts, and still see some print visibility in traditional media and internal outlets. Public relations communicators must be planning visuals as they begin the feature writing process. A writer should take along a digital camera to those interviews and supply accurate captions. Even old photos can be used effectively in feature stories. Pictures and illustrations are especially important when you consider a society that has become accustomed to less text.

Effective visuals are one of the best methods to get page flippers to become page readers. Online content demands a multimedia approach with fewer words but more visuals. Web reading is up to 50 percent slower than regular print documents, so public relations practitioners should not overload the online audience with abundant text. Video and audio clips will enhance any feature story's placement success.

Pitching Tips

Before even considering providing a reporter or blogger with a feature idea, public relations scribes should put themselves in that journalist's place. A carefully crafted pitch won't even be in the playing field if it's targeting the wrong outlet. Would the journalist be interested in this topic for her particular publication, station or website? Will it be of genuine significance to that medium's audience? Would her editor or station manager think it's a wise use of corporate resources to pursue such a feature? Can this item be used across various platforms (with sounds and visuals)? Only after successfully answering such inquiries, can PR writers now attempt to deliver the pitch.

Gini Dietrich, CEO of Arment Dietrich, said research efforts to effectively pitch journalists pay off in her Ragan's PR Daily piece, "For the Love of God Stop Sending Terrible PR Pitches" (June 15, 2012).

She suggests getting to know bloggers and journalists. "If you build a relationship ... and you pitch them what you already know they write about, you will hit a homerun every time. It's not that hard."

Thanks to the Internet, Dietrich adds, that task is simplified. PR practitioners need simply to check out specific journalists to see what topics they cover. She recommends reading their blogs or online articles before sending a pitch.

One of the most convenient ways to time and aim the pitch is to check with a magazine's media kit and editorial calendar. Almost always available online, these two tools will help any PR writer to direct appropriate offerings to the proper audiences at the proper time. They also prevent pros from wasting everyone's time with meaningless feature pitches. Media kits, often incorrectly thought of strictly for advertising purposes, provide tons of valuable demographic and even psychographic data about a magazine and its readership.

Executive Travel, a six-months-per-year magazine from American Express, produces an editorial calendar that provides the cover story topic for future issues. Its annual technology issue is every November/December edition. Destinations featured in the 2013 issue included Mexico City, Miami, Orlando, San Diego and Toronto. With plenty of lead time, a savvy PR employee could have pitched features for clients in those locations or for those with new tech toys.

PRactical TIP

Pitching Practice

As in baseball, a good promotional pitch is fast, on target and irresistible to your audience. The catch is first to win over the client (editor, news director, etc.) for whom you're writing. If not, game over.

© Alex Staroseltsev, 2013. Used under license from Shutterstock, Inc.

Good Aim

Research is central to any effective pitch. You must be familiar with not only what you're promoting, but also your target audience and media outlet (print, broadcast, Web or other). Study your product or service and determine its attributes. Then think about a likely consumer and how they might benefit from those attributes. Distill that information to find the hook.

Next, consider appropriate media for your message. Audience demographics will help you narrow your search, but don't stop there. Absorb each medium from the user's perspective—pick up an issue, watch an episode, browse online. Familiarize yourself with the medium, and you'll better hone the message.

Signal the Pitch

Once you've identified the target audience and medium, introduce yourself to the contact person. You're selling yourself as much as your message, as a dependable contact is a most valuable long-term asset. Be sure your client has time to talk and *briefly* outline your product or service. Resist the urge to elaborate on every last bell and whistle.

Should they express interest, offer to send them detailed information by the means of their choice (mail, email, fax, mule train). Schedule a follow-up phone discussion or meeting at their convenience, and at all costs *keep that appointment.*

The Delivery

A professional pitch should be flawless, from perfect grammar and punctuation to the right letterhead and envelope. Reread your copy for any errors or disconnects and have a proofreader comb through it for extraneous adjectives or other redundancies. Pitch directly to your contact in a tone appropriate to their character and position. When in doubt, err on the side of formality.

The pitch itself should be no longer than a page, your narrative spare and direct. Lead with your most compelling hook. Entice, amuse, provoke—take a risk. Whatever you do, don't bore them with statistics or boast your knowledge of their company. Support all claims with sourced facts and figures.

Follow Through

End your pitch with a simple salutation or, better yet, a promise to follow up in person. Always be mindful of deadlines, and offer to help with planning details. Impress them from the first pitch, and you'll quickly develop a go-to network of relevant media.

By Dave Lauterborn, senior editor of Weider History Magazines
www.historynet.com

Speaking of timing, bloggers typically work on their own schedules, so PR writers should try to keep track of who works late and who works early. Online deadlines never end, unlike the nightly news or the morning newspaper cycle. By following the pitching preferences of bloggers public relations staffers will deliver more strikes than wild pitches.

A related thought is to pitch when news demands are higher than normal but staffing is low. Summer schedules are often filled with vacationing personnel. (August is the most frequent month Europeans take off from work for their *holiday*.) The last two weeks of December represent rather ideal times for public relations practitioners to make inroads. Not only are media outlets understaffed, but many corporations and organizations slow down for the holidays. Video releases and news releases are typically not coming in to media as frequently during this time. Some practitioners try to pitch on slow news days, such as weekends and around holidays. There might be fewer pitches headed to the media then, but there could be fewer journalists around to absorb them. That's why viewers often see the second- or third-string local TV broadcast crew on holiday weekends.

One of the obvious differences with broadcast stations is television's need for audiovisual materials. The pitch should let the journalist know what B-roll footage or recordings from an organization are available in those areas. TV obviously needs visual and audio material to put on the air. Primarily an at-home medium, it reaches 92 percent of the U.S. population daily.

Unfortunately, many PR pros overlook radio since it seems so common and "old school." But that omnipresence can be its strength. Much more mobile than TV, radio needs sound; live streaming is another option. According to the Radio Advertising Bureau, it still is a valid medium in this social media world. Radio every week reaches 93 percent of all Americans aged 12 and up. It's often used to drive listeners to websites. Radio too needs visuals to post on its own Web presence. Some material, in fact, goes straight to the online route without getting aired.

Radio is able to target specific consumers with its various formats, including Internet, cable and satellite programs. So it becomes much easier to reach almost any niche audience. And practitioners can't overlook the growing Spanish-language radio market. A timely pitch could see quick results (especially on a slow news day) since you'll find small staffs and lots of air time. Radio news is repeated throughout the day, often to captive commuters. But the targeted pitch must be kept short. Few stations will devote a large segment since radio time is measured in quarter hours. Except for lengthy talk radio programs, news shows themselves are typically five minutes long, including commercials. So a feature pitch could result in a 30-second plug. Fridays and holidays seem to be the best times to pitch radio, when the news cycle is often in hibernation mode. Late night and weekend staffs enjoy bite-sized feature pieces, often with natural sounds, to help entertain their listeners.

As mentioned earlier, online news cycles are ongoing. Interactive features are favorites for social media and should be mentioned in the pitch. Whether it's a reader quiz, a clickable graphic or an interactive map, it helps increase consumer interest.

Public relations counselors must be careful of getting a blogger upset. He will tell the world about promotion blunders. Rather than using the word *pitch,* some feel a better term is *conversation* with this growing phenomenon. A PR pro should consider simply passing appropriate tips along to social media creators. It helps build relationships that can pay dividends both ways over the years. Determining the pitch preferences of social media journalists is crucial as well. Some bloggers, for example, prefer to receive pitches via Twitter. And a blogger appreciates a courteous thank you note from a public relations writer after a pitch is picked up.

Dan Patterson, digital manager of ABC News, provided tips for pitching social media outlets in an April 23, 2009, *Bulldog Reporter's Daily 'Dog:*

> *"You can pitch me however you want. I don't care how you pitch me, but don't assume I know who you are. We all have busy lives, so you need to tell me why I should care. And do this as briefly and as quickly as possible."*

Regardless of when they send pitches, PR pros need to get to the meat of the story in their appeal to the reporter. Appetizers, salad and dessert can come later. This brevity rule holds true whether the pitch is verbal (such as a phone call or personal encounter) or if done in writing (such as a fax, tweet, email or regular mail). Journalists do get bombarded with pitches that are hundreds of words long, perhaps lengthier than the actual story would have been had they the patience and interest to follow through. It bears repeating that a succinct subject line that zeroes in on the topic is essential. So don't waste time with a lengthy introduction.

"Your goal is to pique their interest and compel them to click a link or make a call so that you have ample time to share more details," advises Ryan Zuk, APR, in the May 2012 *PRSA Tactics.*

Magazine editors relentlessly remind freelancers to save time and effort by first reading their publications before sending query letters about a proposed story. That's the top complaint repeated by editors in every annual issue of *The Writer's Market.* The same argument is as valid for PR practitioners trying to land their offerings with a wide media audience, whether print, online or electronic. They shouldn't send consumer-slanted article ideas to trade publications, for example. *Seventeen* is a beauty and fashion monthly targeted for 12- to 19-year-old females. Inappropriate pitches would include just about anything directed at males or grandparents.

Consider the impact a generic pitch would have versus an exclusive one that's personalized for a specific journalist:

> *I enjoyed your Editor's Page in the current issue of* Special Events Magazine, *Lisa. Those five crucial points you listed for your event planner readers are covered in a new e-book by Maura Olsewski.*

Such a concise initiative has immediately mentioned the journalist's name, title, publication, a specific issue, a specific department, specific aspects of an article, its readership and positive comments about its contents. Not by chance, the PR pitch also quickly mentions the practitioner's own initiative—a client's new book that ties in with the publication's targeted audience.

The worst problem about pitching, as hinted above, is the haphazard spamming of story suggestions to every media outlet known to lazy PR pros. Perhaps their illogical thinking is more is better. A lengthy Cision White Paper, "When in Doubt, Don't Send it Out: Quick Tips for Targeting the Media," warns PR writers about spamming pitches:

> *Still, some PR people are not aware of the damage this type of indiscriminate and impersonal communication causes to their industry, their organization or client, and their personal reputations. If you—a person tasked with helping journalists and influencers do their jobs better and faster—cannot quickly and clearly articulate why the story you are proposing is important to an outlet's specific audience,* don't make the call, don't send the email, and don't send the release.

Summary

Features are entertaining for readers, but not necessarily easier for writers to create. You create storytelling techniques to enlighten audiences on a variety of topics. Most PR writers scan for feature ideas about their clients they can pass along to media professionals who put their own handprint on the finished product. Internal publications and websites, however, make ideal outlets for your own feature creations.

Chapter 9

Advertising Copywriting

"I have always believed that writing advertisements is the second most profitable form of writing. The first, of course, is ransom notes..."

Philip Dusenberry

Public relations practitioners often choose between public relations and advertising. According to Public Communications/West, a marketing communications firm, no communication plan is complete until it embraces elements of both public relations and advertising.

Many people lack the knowledge of the difference between public relations and advertising. Public relations is usually thought of as unpaid and "earned" while advertising is "paid-for" publicity. Using public relations means giving up control of the MAC triad or the Message, Audience and Channel to garner third-party credibility from a media outlet. A major strength of advertising is that it allows you to **control** all three aspects of the MAC triad. But, because advertising is considered paid-for space or air, it lacks third-party **credibility,** public relations' major strength.

When asked, "What is the difference between public relations and advertising?" These experts said ...

"I view advertising as part of public relations—just one of the many tools those in public relations use to reach their audiences."

Jack Gillespie, editor, Communication Briefings

"Advertising is what you pay for, PR is what you pray for."

John Elsasser, Editor, PR Tactics

"Simply stated, advertising is space or time purchased with the message controlled by the advertiser. Public relations delivers messages through various techniques and the media control what the intended target audience actually hears and sees."

Rene Henry, Director, Office of Communications and Government Relations, EPA

Public Relations vs. Advertising

Public relations and advertising are closely related and good practitioners use techniques from both to produce comprehensive communication programs. Public relations and advertising differ in several important ways including: the level of control of the message, audience and channel; the credibility factor; and the way they use the media.

Control—When PR practitioners need to control the message, audience, channel or all three, they should choose advertising. If achieving credibility through a third-party endorsement (or implied endorsement) overshadows the need for control, they should use a public relations technique.

Credibility—The credibility of public relations generally outweighs that of advertising in that a third person recommends or conveys information for you rather than an identified sponsor providing the information. Public relations cannot control the way that gatekeepers use the information it provides, but it can develop media relationships that produce more accurate coverage.

Media Use—By paying for time or space, advertisers maintain control over their message, audience and channel while guaranteeing access to the media. Public relations practitioners, on the other hand, use media gatekeepers to carry their messages. Public relations writers must trust these gatekeepers (editors or producers who control the flow of information by deciding how much of a story, if any, they'll use) to maintain the intended meaning of a story.

As a practitioner, you should decide how to best deal with media gatekeepers. If you need control, such as in a crisis or when dealing with a controversial issue, use predominantly advertising. If third-party credibility is more important, use primarily public relations. Then, construct your campaign based on the most important factor.

Public Relations Advertising

When most people think of advertising, usually a brand commercial comes to mind. However, because PR pros often deal with issues like advocacy, image, persuasion and public information, they tend to use certain types of advertising more frequently. When public relations writers use paid-for media, the message is usually to feature an image, advocate a position, or evoke a behavior other than buying. The following section briefly discusses common types of public relations advertising.

Advocacy/issue—Advocacy advertising seeks to change public opinion concerning an issue or an organization. Sometimes referred to as issue advertising, it adopts a position on a particular issue or advocates a particular cause, rather than promoting the organization itself.

You can use advocacy advertising to: 1) counteract public hostility toward corporate activities, for example, you might write an advocacy ad featuring the benefits of a new nuclear energy facility or to allay the fears of its opponents; 2) communicate views on issues that affect an organization's business, for instance, you might use an advocacy ad to address the regional power shortages and your position on the reliability of your industry; 3) promote the organization's philosophy, for example, public relations practitioners for domestic violence shelters could use advocacy ads to state the philosophy of the shelter and what it can provide for battered women and children; 4) make a social statement, for instance your organization might advocate only heterosexual marriage and its benefits as a social statement.

Amnesty International uses the following ad to protest children soldiers and advocate for children's rights to be children.

FIGURE 9-1

Used with permission of the Designers: Woody Pirtle and Chris Dunn with Pentagram for Amnesty International.

House—An organization prepares an ad for use in its own publication or a publication over which it exerts control. No money changes hands. For example, a television station may run a house ad announcing its new fall programming. Because the public relations function usually controls publications, this type of advertising often falls under public relations advertising. See **Figure 9-5**.

Cooperative—This type of advertising allows a manufacturer to share costs with a retailer saving money because local advertising rates are less expensive than national rates. For example, Famous Footwear features Rockport sneakers in a co-op ad.

Often two national advertisers join together, e.g., in *The Penn Stater* magazine, the Penn State Alumni Association and MasterCard ran a cooperative ad featuring the Nittany Lion and Penn State Alumni Association logo on a MasterCard as a selling point.

Cooperative advertising also allows two organizations to "tie in" with one another. For example, Midas Muffler ran a co-op campaign with the Better Hearing Institute to promote good hearing. Midas benefited from positive public opinion and the Better Hearing Institute from lower advertising costs.

In the following ad (**Figure 9-2**), several Bucks County organizations co-op to promote the benefits of Bucks County, Pennslyvania.

Cause-related Marketing or Sponsorship offers an alternative to advertising in traditional media by allowing an organization to sponsor an event or programming. Sponsorship tends to reach a wide audience and can create brand or corporate name awareness. For example, Virginia Slims used to sponsor women's tennis—now Advanta (an insurance company) is seen as a better fit for a sport. Federal Express, among many others, sponsors a college bowl game.

Television sponsorship can have a powerful impact on viewers because of the control the advertiser exerts on not only the placement of commercials, but also on the content of the program. Often several advertisers sponsor a program together, for example, a sporting event.

Cause-related marketing comprises sponsorship, product placement and percentage of profits as techniques. Sponsorship is the most common, although **product placement** on television programming has become a phenomenon in the last few years. For example, Coke-branded cups appear in front of the judges of *American Idol* and James Bond movies feature Alpha Omega watches.

Paul Newman offers consumers the opportunity to preserve the rain forests by donating a **percentage of profits** from sales of his products to conservationists.

Many companies/organizations that make controversial products like cigarettes or products with possible unsafe byproducts like chemical companies use cause-related marketing to create a more positive image for their organization. Other companies simply want to ally with a cause they believe in. **Figure 9-7** shows a relationship between Eggland's eggs and Susan G. Koman's Race for the Cure to prevent breast cancer.

HAVE AN UNFORGETTABLE
BUCKS COUNTY
GETAWAY

VisitBucksCounty.com

Follow us on Twitter
**Twitter.com/VisitBucksPA
#VisitBucksCounty**

Visit Bucks County

3207 Street Road
Bensalem, PA 19020
215-639-0300
VisitBucksCounty.com

Experience Bucks County's fall foliage this year! It is truly one of the most breathtaking sights in the Delaware Valley. From themed festivals to larger-than-life scarecrows to haunted train rides, Philadelphia's northern countryside is full of fun and frights for the whole family this upcoming season. Share your Bucks County fall escape using the Twitter hashtag #VisitBucksCounty or post it to Facebook.com/VisitBucksPA.

(pictured: hayride at Shady Brook Farm)

New Hope Loves Kids!

New Hope & Ivy Land Railroad

32 West Bridge Street | New Hope, PA, 18938
215-862-2332 | **www.newhoperailroad.com**

All aboard! Fun Excursions for all ages! Special events, special seating options, and a variety of food and beverages are available. Trains depart daily from the New Hope station. With this ad receive $2.00 off each ticket (Up to $8.00 off!) Expires on 11/15/2012.

Bucks County Children's Museum

500 Union Square | New Hope, PA, 18938
215.693.1290 | **www.buckskids.org**

New Hope loves kids! The Bucks County Children's Museum is a great place where young learners explore, discover and play. Take advantage of a great deal: $1.00 Off General Admission with this ad (Limit 4, expires on 11/15/2012). Come explore with us!

Apron Chronicles:
A PATCHWORK OF AMERICAN RECOLLECTIONS

MERCER museum

Mercer Museum

Pine Street & Scout Way
Doylestown, PA 18901
www.mercermuseum.org

The Mercer Museum presents:
*The Apron Chronicles:
A Patchwork of American Recollections*
from October 6–January 13.

Exhibit features vintage aprons, stunning photography and personal narratives about aprons and those who wore them.

Organized by Grassroots Royalty, LLC
Sponsored by Visit Bucks County

James A. Michener Museum

138 South Pine Street Doylestown, PA 18901
215-340-9800 **www.MichenerArtMuseum.org**

Now through October 21, 2012
To Stir, Inform and Inflame: The Art of Tony Auth

FIGURE 9-2
Ad Courtesy of Visit Bucks County, official tourism promotion agency.

Institutional or Image—Corporate or institutional advertising concerns the image of an organization and thus focuses on public opinion formation or change. Commercials using the U.S. Army's "Be all that you can be" slogan feature the benefits you can derive from a career in the Army. For years, General Electric used the "We bring good things to life" campaign to enhance its image. Hallmark uses the image-building slogan, "When you care enough to send the very best."

According to Fraser Seitel, practitioner and author of public relations texts, corporate ads should strengthen the bottom line, be persuasive and appeal to what the public wants. According to *Public Relations Journal*, institutional ads should improve consumer relations, improve community and employee relations as well as enhance organizational image and reputation.

A survey by the Association of National Advertisers showed that the major purpose of institutional advertising was to build recognition.

Figure 9-3 shows an institutional ad for General Electric. Starting with the 2012 Olympics in London, GE introduced an institutional campaign to consumers. While GE makes technical medical devices, this campaign focuses on GE's healthy imagination rather than actual products. GE is trying to establish a corporate image using the Olympics as a setting to do so.

Public Service Announcements (PSAs)—If you remember Grunig's public information model, public service announcements provide the means to disseminate public information. These announcements require no fee to air or print. Many times agencies will produce PSAs on a pro bono (for the public good) basis, eliminating all charges for a nonprofit organization.

Bergh and Katz in *Advertising Principles* note that some highly successful PSA campaigns include: American Red Cross for blood donation; Federal Voting Assistance Program for getting out the vote; National Institute on Drug Abuse for drug abuse and AIDS prevention; and the U.S. Department of Transportation for drunk-driving prevention.

If a practitioner doesn't find a specific agency to produce an ad or an ad campaign, the Advertising Council, a private nonprofit organization, conducts public service advertising campaigns in the public interest. The council receives approximately 400 requests from private organizations and government agencies annually requesting campaign support. See **Figure 9-8**.

Writing Public Relations Advertising

Often in developing a campaign, an advertiser will design a plan. Similar to the situation analysis used by public relations practitioners, this evaluation of the circumstances surrounding the campaign helps advertisers to focus the messages in a targeted way. A situation analysis should include the advertising problem or challenge, a profile of the target audience, an analysis of the issue, a look at the competition, and a Strengths-Weaknesses-Opportunities-Threats (SWOT) analysis.

After the situation analysis is complete, advertisers formulate a creative plan. Creative people often develop a list of features and benefits to help stimulate creative thinking. When addressing

FIGURE 9-3
Used with permission of GE HealthyImagination.

a passive audience, **benefits** draw in those who may have only a latent interest. Conversely, if you face an active audience, this audience wants **features** to help it discriminate among the options.

As a PR practitioner, you may not have the time to formulate a full-fledged advertising campaign. It is important, no matter what the time/cost constraints, to develop a copy or **creative brief**—a document (or brief statement) that outlines the message/ strategy decisions behind an individual ad.

With your copy platform in place, you're ready to write. The following is a creative brief used to offer JC Penney new marketing/advertising ideas.

JC Penney Creative Brief
Why advertise in the first place?

The JC Penney brand does not resonate with young women and families. JCP needs to revamp its image to attract younger (age 25—34) female consumers. It lacks the trendier brands that specialty stores carry.

What is the advertising supposed to do?

- Rejuvenate and modernize the image of JC Penney in order to gain the trust of the younger, more fashion-conscious consumer while still maintaining the loyalty of the current consumer.
- Convince the target consumer that JCP is a sensible alternative to the competition because of its high quality products at reasonable prices.
- Build a long-term relationship with the target and remain their brand of choice as they grow older.

What is the advertising not supposed to do?

The advertising must not alienate the current loyal JCP consumers.

Who are we talking to?

Kimmy is a workaholic in her late twenties who tends to be a bit of a drama queen. She drives a Jetta and listens to DMB. She watches TMZ and reads Cosmo religiously. This pseudo-fashionista is budget conscious because she still has student loans. Her most prized possessions are her clothes, her iPhone and her credit cards. Despite her hectic lifestyle, she always makes time for family, friends and her pet dog, Roxy.

What do we know about the consumer that will help us?

The target consumer values reliable prices in this turbulent economy and is looking for good deals on brand name clothing, makeup and accessories. Seasonal sales, coupons and circulars trigger her purchases. She pays attention to social and interactive media and enjoys shopping online and picking up her purchase in the store.

What is the main thing we need to communicate?

JC Penney can help you save money while staying fabulous.

Source: Marisa Miloszewski, instructor, Rowan University

Basic Ad Components

When designing an ad, practitioners should keep in mind the following tips: keep the message simple, speak directly to your publics or audiences, and know the target market for your message.

Print ads—The following elements of a print ad will help you develop your creative approach. The **headline** should grab the reader's attention early and entice the reader into the body copy. According to advertisers, the headline, which usually appears in large type, has four seconds to catch the reader's attention. Common types of headlines include: 1) benefit; 2) news/informative; 3) provocative; 4) question; and 5) command.

Sometimes advertisers use an overline or an underline to entice the reader to get into the body copy of the ad. In a Taster's Choice ad the overline read, "The dilemma," while the headline stated, "Andrew or Michael?" The underline read, "It's your choice!" This print campaign refers to an ongoing soap-opera-like campaign where a woman who drinks Taster's Choice must pick between her estranged husband and her next-door neighbor.

The **overline** draws the reader into the headline and the **underline** draws the reader into the body copy. Advertisers use both direct and indirect headlines—the previous example was indirect. A **direct headline** is straightforward and informative, but may not lure the audience into the body copy. An **indirect headline** should compel the audience to read on, but provides less information than the direct head.

The **copy** or main textblock should be written for the target audience—at its level. It should build on the headline, promise, reward or benefit. The copy should heighten the reader's interest and desire and offer proof in the form of facts and testimony. Perhaps most importantly, the copy should encourage the reader to take action.

The **illustration** or artwork (or photo) should relate closely to the headline and copy, attract the reader's attention and appeal to the reader's emotions. Many creative directors recommend the use of two-thirds artwork to one-third copy for effectiveness.

The **logo** should convey the image of the sponsoring organization and should always include contact information. Often a slogan or tagline accompanies the logo. These devices are used for memorability. To differentiate, a **slogan** is repeated from ad to ad. A **tagline** wraps up the idea at the end of a particular ad.

In **Figure 9-4** on the following page, an ad for the Girl Scouts, callouts indicate the indirect headline, "Be There So She Can Be Here," the photo, copy block, logo and tagline.

According to Sandra Moriarty in her text *Creative Advertising*, practitioners can use this checklist to write effective copy.

- ▶ Use pictures and words together to create impact.
- ▶ Write to someone you know who represents the target audience.
- ▶ Make it conversational!
- ▶ Use short, succinct statements.
- ▶ Use short paragraphs to maintain reader interest.

FIGURE 9-4

"Be There So She Can Be Here" © 2012 Girl Scouts of the USA. Used by permission. All rights reserved.

▶ Personalize the copy by using the word "you."
▶ Avoid the word "we."
▶ Try not to sound preachy or pushy.

Research shows that the use of white space directs the eye of the reader, provides separation from adjoining messages and relieves a cluttered feeling that could make the ad difficult to read.

Commercial components—When preparing an electronic ad or commercial, most advertisers use **storyboards** or **thumbnail sketches** to design them. Practitioners should consider the time allocation of 10 seconds, 20 seconds, and 30 seconds or less commonly, 60 seconds.

In television commercials, advertisers consider the use of action and motion. The three-dimensional aspect of television advertising often makes it more compelling than print. The elements of television advertising include video, audio, talent, props, setting, lighting, graphics and pacing.
Video dominates the message in television and you as the copywriter can make use of the visuals to convey messages. The **audio** dimensions of television and radio are similar using music, voices and sound effects. **Talent** refers to the people in the commercials. They could be

PRactical TIP

Top Ad Mistakes to Avoid

According to Roy H. Williams on Entrepreneur.com, you should avoid these advertising mistakes:

1. Instant gratification—Don't establish only an immediate attraction—you need to gain long-term identity with the consumer.
2. Over-reaching the budget—Without placing an ad frequently, you won't gain retention. You can reach many, but not often enough.
3. Assume the client knows best—Remember, it's the audience, not client you'll ultimately please.
4. Unsubstantiated claims—Remember to offer evidence for claims your ads make.
5. Improper use of passive media—Use intrusive rather than non-intrusive media such as radio and TV to reach relational customers.
6. Create ads instead of campaigns—The most effective and memorable ads are those most like a rhinoceros. They make a single point, powerfully.
7. Using mostly late-week schedules—To avoid competition advertise on Sunday, Monday or Tuesday.
8. Great production without great copy—Go after believable, memorable and persuasive copy.

announcers, spokespeople, fictional characters or celebrities. **Props** refer to the product/idea and a setting where the action happens. **Lighting** can impact the setting by creating a romantic mood or a sterile environment. **Graphics** are generated on the screen by a computer. **Pacing** refers to the speed of the action.

In summary, the creative plan often makes or breaks the success of the advertising campaign. The strength of the creative effort affects the results of the persuasion. When a campaign causes behavioral change, most practitioners would consider it a success.

Writing Advocacy Ads

Advocacy ads should persuade the target audience to behave or to think in a certain way. They most often advocate the position of the organization on an issue. Let's say you're writing an ad for a national Greek organization advocating how to avoid date rape. 1) You should develop a copy platform or a series of ideas for the ad or ad campaign and then test it on a small number of your target population. 2) Using that research, you should design some direct and indirect headlines and see which work best. 3) Consider the use of an overline or underline to draw readers into the body copy. 4) Never make the first paragraph of body copy long—you'll lose your readers. 5) Write the ad in a non-preachy, conversational style. 6) Consider telling a story of a date rape to attract the readers. 7) Don't give the end of the story until you've made your point or advocated your position. 8) Close with an action for the reader to take as well as the end of the story. 9) Give appropriate contact information. 10) Make sure the sponsoring organization's logo is clear and readable. 11) Look over the ad for white space—did you use any? 12) Is your visual compelling?

In any type of persuasion, you deal with inert audience members. Convincing them to agree with you is easy compared to causing them to act. Don't expect miracles, but target your audience to receive maximum effect. See **Figure 9-1**.

Writing House Ads

As mentioned earlier, a house ad is prepared by an organization for use in its own publication. A danger in writing house ads is to assume that in-house audiences know as much as you do about your product, service or organization. Many house ads fail because audience members do not have the comprehensive overview that key managers or PR staff members do.

Because your audience knows you more so than an "outside advertiser," in-house ads must have a strong creative appeal to attract attention. Audience members may have a vested interest in owning or joining a related product/organization, for example the alumni association of their university. Always write in a conversational tone and avoid "pushy" language!

The following advertisement appeared in *Rowan Today* magazine promoting its continuing education programs, thus prepared by Rowan University to promote one of its colleges in this publication.

→ Your Life. Your Education.
{Your Terms.}

Get a Rowan University education on your terms with times, locations and modes of delivery to accommodate your busy schedule. Whether you prefer to take courses online, on-campus, or at a location near you, Rowan's College of Graduate & Continuing Education (CGCE) makes it convenient to acquire the education you need to advance your career.

Graduate level programs available in:
- Business Administration
- Communication
- Counseling/Behavioral Analysis
- Criminal Justice

- Nursing
- Education
- Engineering & Technology
- Mathematics
- Music

Undergraduate Degree Completion programs available in:
- Nursing
- Liberal Studies

**Visit www.rowan.edu/cgce
for more information.**

Rowan
University
College of Graduate &
Continuing Education

FIGURE 9-5
Courtesy of Rowan University.

Writing Cooperative Ads

The writing in this instance is complicated by having to serve two organizations. In a *Philadelphia* magazine ad, Nordstrom's and Sergio Ferragamo teamed up to produce a simple visual of a pair of men's dress shoes with the headline of Sergio Ferragamo and the Nordstrom's logo on the bottom of the photo. Several messages seemed evident—Nordstrom's sells quality men's shoes; Sergio Ferragamo makes top-quality men's shoes.

To write a cooperative ad, as any other ad, develop a copy platform; test your idea; design your headline and visual; and write the body copy. In this case, make sure each logo is displayed as well as contact information. See **Figure 9-2**.

Writing Cause-related Marketing Ads

For product placement, you don't have to write an ad, but rather determine where the use of a product placement would work most effectively. As mentioned in the sidebar, many organizations are integrating their advertising with programming to make it more invasive and persuasive.

For sponsorship advertising, one important consideration takes place well before writing the ad—what kind of organization do you want to sponsor/support? If you jump on the bandwagon like many post 9/11 organizations did and force your organization to look patriotic—it may not work. If, on the other hand, your organization can determine what values the target audience holds, you can appeal to those values. For example, many organizations whose primary audience is women choose to sponsor breast cancer research or treatment.

When writing sponsorship ads, adhere closely to the truth—beware of hyperbole/exaggeration. If you don't have a particularly positive image and wish to ally yourself with a cause or an organization with a more beneficial image, you don't want to exaggerate your claims. Avoid even the appearance of misleading your audience. So, to write sponsorship ads, do your homework. Find out more than demographics of your target audience. Appeal to deep-seated emotions. In a thesis conducted by Rowan University graduate student Ralph DeSimone, he noted that women seem more affected by cause-related marketing than do men. If you have an audience of primarily women, this is good news!

An example of cause-related marketing is Johnson & Johnson improving its image by partnering with UNICEF to provide medical care for women and babies in India.

Susan G. Komen has many national sponsors that ally with the cause of breast cancer research to benefit from this association. See **Figure 9-6**. One such sponsor is New Balance.

Race for the Cure® National Sponsors

The national sponsors of the Susan G. Komen Race for the Cure® series are among our most loyal supporters, with long-standing and highly integrated partnerships that generate more than $12 million annually.

National Sponsors

American Airlines

Susan G. Komen for the Cure® and AmericanAirlines have been partners in the fight against breast cancer since 1992. AmericanAirlines is the exclusive airline sponsor for the Komen Race for the Cure® Series and in 1994, AmericanAirlines was named the "official airline carrier" of the Series.

Ford Motor Company

Ford Motor Company serves as a National Series Sponsor of the Susan G. Komen Race for the Cure® for the seventeenth consecutive year. Ford is the exclusive automotive sponsor for the Komen Race for the Cure® Series.

New Balance Athletic Shoes, Inc.

For 23 years, Susan G. Komen for the Cure® has partnered with New Balance to work towards the common goal of finding a cure for breast cancer. New Balance has been a National Series Sponsor of the Komen Race for the Cure® Series since 1991 and in 2002 launched the Lace Up for the Cure® and Collection. From the retail sales of this collection, New Balance donates 5% of the manufactured suggested retail price to Komen for the Cure with an annual guaranteed minimum donation of $500,000. Together, step-by-step, New Balance and Komen are making excellence happen.

FIGURE 9-6

Used by permission of New Balance Athletic Shoes.

FIGURE 9-7 Example of a cause-related marketing ad for Eggland's Best.
Courtesy of Eggland's Best LLC.

Writing Institutional Ads

As mentioned earlier, a major purpose of institutional advertising is to build recognition. Most organizations need to enhance or maintain an image. First, a caution—don't take on a client with a poor identity—you can't change the identity with communication, but you can help change an image. In other words, make sure the organization does what it says it does and stands behind its ideas, products, etc.

Institutional ads are "big picture" ads—they don't detail product or service features—they convey an image or a perception of the organization. Many nonprofit organizations can shape their identity through institutional advertising. For example, many believe the American Red Cross does one thing—collect blood. If you have the American Red Cross as a client, consider stressing the emergency aid the organization offers worldwide and its first responder status.

So, to write institutional advertising, get a sense of what the organization offers to its publics. In the case of General Electric with the theme of "We bring good things to life," notice the general and overarching headline. The organization doesn't want you to think about missiles or washers and dryers, it wants you to think of the public good served by GE. Develop an overall theme for the organization.

A CIGNA company that offered worker's compensation insurance needed an institutional ad. It chose a Stradivarius violin being restored and the headline read, "The art of restoration." The ad stressed the association between a fine instrument and its restoration and workers and their rehabilitation.

Consider an analogy like the CIGNA advertisement used. Research is key here—you must understand enough about the organization to equate it to a commonly understood example.

Then use the principles we've discussed to complete your headline, body copy, logo and tagline. See **Figure 9-4**.

Writing Public Service Announcements (PSAs)

PSAs often lead to awards for the sponsoring agencies because nonpaying clients allow agencies creative freedom without the restrictions of budget approvals and many corporate lawyers. One of the most successful campaigns of all time, Smokey Bear and prevention of forest fires, is said to have saved lives and property by educating people on fire prevention. Likewise, the seat belt dummies have increased seat belt usage and thus have saved lives as well. Most people recognize these headlines: "Friends don't let friends drive drunk," and "This is your brain—this is your brain on drugs."

When creating PSAs, an organization has three choices: 1) design and produce the announcement in-house; 2) find an advertising agency to produce it on a pro bono basis; or 3) write a script (for electronic media) and allow the media outlet to produce it, for example, the on-air talent reads the script. Always prepare a variety of formats (10-second, 20-second, 30-second spots). The different formats will allow the media outlet the flexibility to use the spot at its convenience.

FIGURE 9-8
© Anna Hoychuk, 2013. Used under license
from Shutterstock, Inc.

Also, remember to send a script with an audio or videotape to make it easier for the broadcaster. Public service announcements should be for the good of the public and you should write them accordingly.

A particularly powerful PSA used a simple advertisement showing an egg in a frying pan, similar to the photo in **Figure 9-8**, suggesting that the effect of drugs on a brain was like a hot pan on an egg. Also, **Figure 9-9** depicts a television PSA script.

According to Chris Hampton in The Community Toolbox, use PSAs in the following circumstances:

When you work for a nonprofit.
When you have a specific announcement (upcoming event).
When your issue is clear and easy to understand.
When you have good contacts for airing your PSA.
When it's part of a larger media campaign.

Online Advertising

"Visit our website . . ." "Like us on Facebook . . ." "Download the latest coupons . . ."

For advertisers, the online environment presents a myriad of opportunities to reach consumers with instant information about products and services and facilitate equally instant purchase decisions.

The challenge, however, lies in the advertiser's ability to reach the *right* consumer with the *right* message at the *right* time, so in many ways the principles that guide effective online advertising differ little from those used in the print or broadcast media.

Online advertising campaign components must emanate from a single Unique Selling Proposition (USP), for example, that leads a consumer to choose that product from the multitude of competitors' products that line the virtual shelves. In this way, online advertising must contain even more focused language, appealing graphics, and direct selling propositions than

A Television PSA Against Drunk Driving

Scene—Home filled with men, women and children for a birthday party.

Cut to men sitting on the couch in front of the television.

Cut to close-up of another guy on the couch. He slaps Joe on the back.

Joe accept the drink and takes a sip.

Dissolve to outside the house as Joe's family, already in the car, prepares to leave the driveway. Joe fumbles the keys.

The car drives off and runs a stop sign, slamming into a truck. The video is out of focus, but you see a blurry image of the impact and you hear the plaintive wail of a horn. Fade to black. Graphic comes up—the noises from the scene still in the background.

Graphic reads: It's never okay to drink and drive.

Tagline on the bottom of the screen:

Mothers Against Drunk Driving

Frank: Hey Joe—want another? (He holds up a beer bottle)

Joe: I have to drive the family home. (He shows his keys.)

Frank: Aw, come on. One more won't kill you.

Joe: I don't know.

Ron: I've been driving a long time and nothing's happened to me. Go on, one more for the road.

Joe: Why not?

Karen (Joe's wife): Honey, do you want me to drive?

Joe: No, I'm okay.

Announcer: It's never okay to drink and drive. Never! If you care about yourself, think of what it can do to your family.

FIGURE 9-9

the ads of the past since consumers can easily "click" from one product to another without the hassle associated with physical attempts to comparison shop from store to store.

Tips to remember when advertising online:

▶ Prepare online advertisements with the same care and attention as you might prepare traditional print ads. Do not overwhelm the audience with text or leave out important details.

▶ Use graphics that sell and avoid graphics that add time to the download process but provide little information about your product. Consumers will not read ads that take "too long" to download or freeze up their computer or phone.

▶ Online advertisements comprise only *part* of your campaign and very rarely will serve as the exclusive form of advertising for any product or service. Online messages should reflect the content and character portrayed throughout the campaign so that consumers connect the online presence with other communications about the particular product or service. Traditional ads that direct consumers to a website, for example, can double the effectiveness of both tactics.

Source: Gina Audio, MA, instructor, Rowan University

Almost half of online advertising dollars are spent for search engine optimization. Google, Yahoo and Bing (MSN) are the major players. According to Nikesh Arora, SVP and Chief Business Officer of Google, the three online advertising trends of the future are: brand investment in the digital channel, the move to solution suites and the demand for cross-media measurement.

According to Arora, we're at the point where major brand advertisers look to digital media as a central part of their marketing efforts. For example, YouTube, previously an interesting ad buy has become a key ad buy. Companies now see the benefit of using the Web for brand recognition.

The second trend is the move to solution suites meaning that clients want complete solutions that work across all screens: desktop, mobile, tablet and for all types of formats—search, display or video ads.

Lastly, measurability is important to get brands to invest in new channels. Advertisers desire measurement tools that assess search across mobile and video as well as offline sales. According to Arora, businesses invest serious money only when they can measure the results.

Summary

As a PR writer, you'll face the decision of whether to use public relations, advertising or some combination. Because some types of advertising are closely related to public relations, you may be called upon to write the script or even the print ad yourself. If you have the luxury of supervising an agency, you should now know the basics of constructing an ad from a copy platform through the contact information. Writing advertising copy is somewhat different from academic or public relations writing. As a PR practitioner, you'll enjoy the flexibility of a different genre.

Chapter 10

Speech Writing

*"It usually takes more than three weeks
to prepare a good impromptu speech."*

Mark Twain

Despite the digital explosion, speeches continually serve as a viable communication resource for corporations, nonprofits and other organizations. One estimate puts the number of presentations in the United States at 8 billion per year. Public speaking is one of the most influential endeavors of a leader. Consider the oratory genius of President Abraham Lincoln's Gettysburg Address; Winston Churchill's "Never, never, never give up" admonition; or the Rev. Martin Luther King Jr.'s "I have a dream" speech.

A speech allows any organization to articulate its values and goals. It can inform and inspire internal and external audiences. Orations are powerful tools, not just for their original delivery, but for their subsequent replay through other online or traditional media outlets. A good public relations writer is caught up in the process on all fronts. She may give talks in front of others, she may train others in how to deliver effective speeches, and she may write them for executives and others in the workplace.

Just as Chapter 8 emphasized the role of storytelling in feature stories, it's even more pronounced (no pun intended) in verbally connecting with an audience. Many business leaders, unfortunately, are more tuned in to statistics and balance sheets. That's not exciting information for a majority of audiences to listen to, of course.

In the spring 2012 issue of *The Strategist*, PR veteran Jim Holtje produced a short article titled "Story Time: Bringing Business Speeches to Life." His three tips to executives wanting to connect with their audiences are:

1. **Tell your own stories first.**
2. **Be a reporter.**
3. **Consider borrowing.**

For his first point, Holtje points out personal stories are best known, of course, by the one who encounters them. Telling them with gusto will help make them memorable, more so than dry statistics. Perhaps Holtje should have added the word "investigative" before reporter in his second tips. Get stories and anecdotes from others in the office if yours don't quite fit this particular audience or occasion. Finally, reference relevant stories from well-known CEOs for your own presentations.

A public relations practitioner spends far more time writing speeches for others than delivering them. It's a valuable skill to develop. Workshops, conferences, newsletters and online sources assist those working in this field of communications. Experienced speech writers can command $10,000 or more for a 20-minute speech.

"One of the genuine surprises I've had in my career was learning how many great business leaders were bad public speakers," admits blogger Steve Farnsworth in "Ghostwriting Isn't Unethical (Most of the Time)" in a June 20, 2012, edition of *Ragan's PR Daily*. Training proved quite effective, however, in turning them into successful communicators in 99 percent of such cases, Farnsworth added.

"One of your major duties in public relations is speech ghostwriting, producing speeches for your chief executive officer or other key executives to deliver," Dr. Doug Starr, APR, Fellow PRSA, said. "You do most of the work; your speaker gets all of the credit. That is all right because the ghostwritten speech is a collaborative effort between you and your organization's speaker." Starr, a retired professor of agricultural journalism at Texas A&M University, has written his share of speeches for politicians and others over the years.

Following the actual delivery of a speech, the speechwriter will be charged with the task of creating additional promotional mileage from these verbal productions. Today's social media facilitate the spread of delivered speeches. They make the job easier and faster for a speechwriter or the PR staff given the job of creating more promotion for the original oratory.

The skills involved in all three areas above are crucial ones to master. Without effective oral presentations, a company can lose investors, sales and credibility. Personal interaction with a speaker puts a face on a company. An effective speech is also a way for the organization to be perceived as credible.

One of the more successful, yet somewhat controversial, speeches in 2012 was by an English teacher in the Boston area. He had the nerve to tell his high school commencement audience members that they were not so exceptional. His point was to have them be more realistic in today's self-esteem-obsessed society where all students perceive themselves to be way above average. "You see, if everyone is special, then no one is," David McCullough Jr. told the high school graduates. The address was an instant social media hit, and then became popular on traditional media.

This chapter will not attempt to cover Speech 101 topics. A great introduction to hook the audience, the body of the speech loaded with evidence and a strong conclusion should fit 99 percent of any speechwriter's duties. Suffice it to say, one of the bigger problems with delivering speeches is the anxiety factor. Numerous surveys have found speaking in public ranks as the number one fear among U.S. citizens. That prompted comedian Jerry Seinfeld to say that it's better, therefore, for you to be in the casket at a funeral than to give the eulogy.

Panic Attack

All kidding aside, it's comforting to know that such panic concern can actually become a positive experience when someone is delivering an address. Similar to what actors and athletes go through before a performance, such anxiety can help speakers focus and direct their energies in the proper direction. PR pros must be wary of any programs or workshops falsely promising they will eliminate speech anxiety. The achievable goal is simply to control it. What might help the company's spokeswoman accomplish such a feat? Below are the four R's for controlling speech anxiety, whether it's for the main speaker or for others the writer must coach in the workplace.

▶ Review—knowing the material thoroughly gives a speaker confidence. The orator should become the expert on this subject matter. Having proper notes handy can help guide the spokesman if needed.
▶ Rehearse—practicing aloud to yourself or a colleague will help avoid tongue twisters during the delivery. If possible, a speaker should try to get in the actual room for the speech so she can get comfortable with the lighting, microphone and lectern.
▶ Relax—walking and deep breathing exercises can minimize nervousness. Ideally, the speech deliverer should arrive early enough so he's not frantic about traffic, parking and getting to the exact location on time.
▶ Render—making frequent eye contact and gestures will help any speaker appear less nervous. Most audience members will not notice any anxiety. They're simply glad they are not speaking.

A related problem with nervousness is the overall body language of the speaker. Many studies conclude that more than half of communication is nonverbal. Writers may have to remind speakers to relax physically, look at the audience, act eager, use natural gestures and not white-knuckle grip the lectern.

Look Where?

Many inexperienced speakers look at their visual aids during their presentation instead of maintaining eye contact with their audience. Of course, you need to glance at visual aids as you present them—especially if you're referring to something specific on an aid. But this should be *only* a glance—not a gaze.

Speak Up! An Illustrated Guide to Public Speaking

Research Again?

Before beginning one word of the writing process for a speech, vital research is necessary. It's a big task on three fronts: situation, speaker and subject. As readers have noticed previously in this book, PR professionals shift automatically into research mode before tackling almost all other writing assignments. Speeches are no different. The more information that can be learned about the intended audience, the smoother the task will be. It's similar to the requirement of knowing the readers of a specific publication before you write and dispatch a news release or pitch letter.

If the occasion is a guest speaking gig for the CEO, the speechwriter must ask the program chairman about the purpose of the speech and those in attendance. She'll want to know how many, how much knowledge they may have about the intended subject and their disposition toward the topic. Are they supportive or suspicious? What's the seating arrangement? She needs to nail down as many specifics as she can. It will help the speechwriter use the right words, phrases and slant. It's necessary to learn as much as possible about the listeners, including their demographics. One public relations pro was asked to speak to about 60 business executives in North Carolina for a banquet meeting. Wanting to make his comments relevant, he inquired about the types of businesses represented at the event. Only after seeing the audience at the dinner, did he realize more than 90 percent of them were *retired, former* business executives.

It's also helpful to find out if there's a social function immediately following the speech. If the association's annual golf tournament starts as soon as the speaker says "thank you," the speech may need to stress excitement and entertainment more than facts and figures. It's necessary to keep the members' attention before they take off to do their PGA or LGPA impressions.

Another important related task to the situation research is for a writer to prepare a suitable introduction for the speaker. You must not take the chance an organization will research pertinent details to include in presenting the CEO to its audience. In fact, an overzealous program chairman might upstage the speaker by going overboard to prepare a 15-minute introduction for your speaker's 20-minute talk. Or the person may give a weak, lame introduction that will create no excitement for an organization's representative. A speechwriter needs to control what particulars she wants this audience to know about her speaker on this occasion.

This isn't the time to pull the bio from the online media kit and have someone simply read that in a nonchalant manner. Rather, the speaker introduction sets the stage for the presentation to this specific audience, and provides the representative's credentials for delivering that information. The public relations writer must let the audience know why the organization selected this speaker to talk to the members on this occasion. So he should write a one-page introduction using conversational terms, email it early to the contact person with instructions for its use, and bring a back-up copy along to the occasion in case the original document gets lost. Ideally, it should be about two minutes long, enough to build excitement about the speaker's personality and characteristics without giving away the gist of the comments. Rather, it serves as a brief teaser, to get the audience excited about the comments to follow. It's wise to conclude the introduction with a clue for audience applause as the CEO approaches the podium: "Let's please welcome . . ."

PRactical TIP

Do You Target Right Audience with Wrong Message?

"It's not you; it's me" may work for Seinfeld's George Costanza but not for company communications. Organizations that continuously deliver self-serving prose may confuse, anger or alienate their stakeholders.

Conversely, organizations that deliver timely, concise, honest, proactive and relevant communications will engage their audiences. Engaged audiences are many times more likely than their disconnected peers to buy your product, support your cause, attend your event, etc.

Here are warning signs of company-centric communications:

- ▶ "One-size-fits-all" messages sent to virtually all stakeholders
- ▶ Feedback is not considered important
- ▶ Communication vehicles are convenient for the company but not the intended audiences
- ▶ Content is jargon-laden or overly technical
- ▶ Benefits to the reader, viewer or listener are not apparent.

By focusing on your audience's needs, wants and constraints, you can develop communications that resonate with individuals who are essential to your organization's success.

By Rick Alcantara, Founder/Principal of Tara Communications, N.J.

And that brings up the second aspect of doing research. After knowing the situation about their audience, speechwriters must also thoroughly know their speaker. How can writers put words in someone's mouth if they're a stranger to that person's thinking? If PR writers have access to the CEO, as they should in a management function, they need to spend time knowing that person's style and mannerisms. So they will meet with that person to get her perspective on the topic. They'll want to take notes so they can capture the ideas as well as some of the exact words and phrases she uses. Ideally, the speech should sound as if the speaker wrote it. Does the CEO speak slowly or machine-gun fashion? Is the language formal or folksy? What about mannerisms and charm? Those are the types of things scribes must know before starting the writing process. Although colleagues might sometimes help in drafting a rough copy for a speech, it needs to have one voice, one speechwriter, for the most effective delivery.

Is the organization's speaker comfortable with humor? Do his jokes backfire and bomb? Or do they receive genuine laughter? Be careful with humor, of course. Material using sexism, racism and ageism—although unthinkable by any ethical ghostwriter—still appears frequently in online searches. The best and safest jokes are often the ones made by the speaker *about* the speaker. Is he a Robert De Niro fan or a Larry the Cable Guy fan? Humor can backfire and get an organization into global hot water as fast as you can say enter on a social media website.

If your speaker has no sense of humor, you can still get laughs from the audience by having her share appropriate funny quotations, wacky headlines (red tape holds up bridge) or personal anecdotes that are self-deprecating.

It's best to use conversational language with contractions when drafting the speech. Incomplete sentences are fine. PR writers should keep the wording simple since individuals in the auditorium don't have print document aids, such as subheads, or the ability to go back and read a paragraph slower a second time to understand it better. Jargon and elitist language build barriers between a speaker and the audience. A writer needs to eliminate exclusive terminology. Key words must be appropriate for the audience. A speaker can repeat them throughout the speech for maximum effect. But speech crafters should shy away from too many statistics. Saying *three out of four* is much better than *73.8 percent*. Ghostwriters write for the ear, not for the eye.

"Put the cookies on the lower shelf so that everyone can have some," advises speaker and leadership guru Dr. John C. Maxwell. In other words, common terminology will reach all members of the audience.

The opening of a speech is the time to make a great first impression. Don't let your speaker mumble into small talk—greeting certain members of the audience or head table, thanking the organization for this wonderful opportunity, talking about the weather, etc. Rather, a speaker wants to grab the listeners' attention from the start, or they may tune out quickly.

Brad Phillips, who specializes in media and presentation training, provides tips in his "5 Inviting Ways to Start a Speech" May 1, 2012, *PR Daily* piece:

1. The startling statistic is a terrific way to grab the audience's attention from your first word.
2. A story, case study or personal anecdote is perhaps the single most effective tool for transferring information from speaker to audience.

3. Ask the audience to imagine something by using a rhetorical question.
4. Ask a "show of hands" question, which can increase audience buy-in from the start as members are able to see how their answers compare to their peers.
5. Speak with your audience to create a climate of audience participation from the start.

Other Employees Can Serve as Company Mouthpieces

If the corporate CEO or designated spokesman is not a polished speaker, a PR task is to help train that person to be more comfortable in speaking situations. Other employees, of course, can fill in as company mouthpieces. In many countries, in fact, the most credible representatives might be someone other than corporate CEOs. Their high salaries and bonus packages made them especially unpopular in the USA starting a few years ago.

© Cherkas, 2013. Used under license from Shutterstock, Inc.

According to Edelman's annual international Trust Barometer both government and business leaders suffered credibility losses in its latest surveys.

A popular celebrity or athlete can backfire as a spokesperson, of course. Lindsay Lohan's constant crises rule her out for most celebrity gigs. Sean Payton, New Orleans Saints coach, lost endorsements when banned from the 2012–2013 NFL season for his link to "bountygate," an alleged system of rewarding players for hurting opponents. And Tour de France winner Lance Armstrong lost his sponsorships after a guilty finding was publicized regarding drug use. As Edelman's survey indicates, the most credible person in many nations could be the person wearing a lab coat with a clipboard. In other parts of the world, that individual might be viewed as a quack or a geek.

The point is that speechwriters should find such individuals in an organization who could be tapped to speak comfortably and confidently in front of cameras and crowds. They need to consider their body language and facial expressions when speaking, not just the words presented to them. Practice with these speakers so they are not glued to the lectern. A little movement on stage can keep audience members alert.

Writers need to know company representatives and listen to them so they can make these people appear in the words of the speech. Often ghostwriters have to conduct as much research about the chosen speaker as for the intended audience. PR practitioners have to understand the topic and what needs to be done with it. Do they in the speech explain it, sell it, condemn it or laugh at it? In other words, what do they want the speaker to accomplish when leaving the podium? What do they want the audience to do or remember as a result of the speech? What's the major overall purpose of the presentation? Once they know that point, it's time to dig up data. Web searches that can quickly deliver facts, stats and quotes enhance that type of research. Just typing in "memorable quotes" into Goodsearch produced over 100 pages of quotation reference. The same search on Google provided 10.8 million individual quotes.

When you have thoroughly researched the topic—as in other writing tasks—it makes the speech assembly process much smoother. You can select the two best quotes among the 12 appropriate ones that were found. You can choose the most gripping anecdote to grab the audience's attention at the start. And you can pick the most persuasive set of statistics to drive your point home.

Format Options

One of the easier parts of speechwriting is the format itself. Simply checking with your company speech giver can determine what the preference is. Or writers can develop their own style and make adjustments as requested, whether it's a full text, an expanded Roman numeral outline or simply a brief key-word system to follow. Rather than a news release appearance, a speech layout more closely resembles broadcast copy guidelines with wider outside margins as discussed in Chapter 6.

If a speech's budgeted time is about 20 minutes—long enough for any audience to endure—it's necessary to produce about 2,500 words in regular-size text. That would average about 10 or 11 double-spaced pages. This is a starting point for getting feedback, comments and final approval from the speaker. It may typically take more than one time to make additional revisions.

Perhaps an organization's spokeswoman wants her entire speech typed in 18-point type and triple-spaced on full sheets of paper. It's a good idea to go with

TOOLBOX TIP

General Guidelines for Special Occasions

A handful of generic guidelines can boost your chances of delivering an effective special-occasion speech, no matter what type you'll be giving. These suggestions include appealing to your audience's emotions, ensuring that your delivery suits the mood of the occasion, adapting your speech to your audience's expectations, evoking shared values, and respecting time constraints.

Speak Up! An Illustrated Guide to Public Speaking

a larger-than-necessary font (14-point minimum, double-spaced) because auditoriums can be rather dark. And the practice can eliminate one major distraction for the audience—a speaker constantly fumbling with putting on and taking off eyeglasses. Writers will probably want to have a maximum of about five inches of type across the page so they can adjust their margins accordingly. (As in broadcast copy, PR staffers don't want their speaker to lose her place jumping from one line to the next.) Another tip is not to center text; it should always be flush left with no hyphenations along the right margin. And veteran speechwriters never break from one page to the next in the middle of a paragraph.

It's wise for practitioners to always number the pages, just in case they slip from her grasp as she lifts them from her briefcase, but not to staple them together. Some speakers may prefer to use half sheets of paper so their notes do not appear as obvious to the audience. Others like 4 × 6 note cards rather than the standard 3 × 5 variety that's almost too small for writing much text.

Ghostwriters often provide delivery cues for the speaker. These clearly marked tips are inserted, for example, when there's a need for pausing, showing an audio-visual item or adjusting speaking volume.

A speechwriter should remember to bring two extra copies of the most recent version of the speech. If the company representative forgets her copy, asks for the backup copy, and then a server spills coffee all over it, a PR staffer can still be the hero when he pulls out one more at the last second to save the day. Another tip, of course, is to have a small flashlight or battery-operated lamp in case there's inadequate lighting to see even the 18-point speech.

Just Say No

Rather than accepting every speaking request that comes into an organization, a savvy public relations practitioner needs to select the ones most beneficial to the executive's agenda, and the company's bottom line and image. There must also be sufficient time for the speechwriter to prepare an appropriate manuscript. Just because external groups ask for the CEO to speak, it doesn't mean a public relations department has to always provide them that person to fulfill their needs. A survey by *prreporter* discovered more than half of the respondent executives spent at least 10 hours per month with external organizations, averaging 20 speeches annually.

Every CEO needs to address the public, but ideally it's to influential groups in the industry, not every social club in town. If an organization has created an extensive speaker's bureau at the workplace, it shouldn't have to say no when community groups or associations ask for a speaker. But the CEO can't possibly respond to every request. It's OK to just say no when groups constantly ask for the top individual. PR staffs must protect busy executives by having several other trained individuals make appearances when key management personnel can make better use of their time.

A short e-survey can determine which employees, retirees and volunteers have hobbies, skills and other interests they can share with outside groups. A quick lesson in presentations should get them ready to roll. Then PR practitioners must vigorously promote their speaker's bureau to outside clubs and organizations. They can distribute a brochure, post the speaker's bureau topics in the online media room and on social media sites, and send releases to organizations' program chairs and various media.

It's difficult for program directors to come up with exciting meetings month after month. So a company can let them know it can fill their speaking needs. Southwest Airlines, among many other corporations, created its own speaker's bureau for these same reasons. Utility companies typically are leaders in promoting their speakers for local organizations.

It's easier to tell the local program chairwoman of the Summit County Flower Society the CEO cannot be the keynote speaker at next month's luncheon *if* someone else more qualified has been lined up to tackle the assignment. An employee in accounting who grows orchids would love to talk to the society. And its members would enjoy the presentation much more. The best speech is always one that people will listen to. So the PR staff still created positive relations for its organization at the luncheon without expending the executive's valuable time and resources. Social media and word of mouth publicity about an active speaker's bureau are credible sources.

With much emphasis on return on investment within the public relations field, it's no wonder that speaker's bureaus now are also asked to prove their investment in time and resources. The Institute for Public Relations produced a white paper titled "Measuring the Effectiveness of Speakers Programs."

Speaking opportunities are often sought out by executives as a marketing opportunity to profile themselves and their company to a live audience for little cost. However, the investment in speaking opportunities can be quite significant. Time spent preparing a speech of presentation and traveling to the location can be considerable, for what is often a brief or shared opportunity at the podium.

The white paper suggests PR staffs should be thinking about the value of sending executives before the actual speaking event occurs. The authors gave five areas for consideration:

1. Set objectives—Before even thinking about evaluation, public relations practitioners must consider the attempted objectives.
2. Determine audience composition—It's crucial to know who will be in the audience.
3. Establish media opportunities—Interviews are ideal ways of expanding coverage.
4. Know how the event gets promoted—Organizations can benefit from such publicity.
5. Organize the talk centering on key messages—This communication needs to tie in with the objectives.

Handling Q-and-A Sessions

Speakers often allow time following their speeches for a few questions from audience members. Speech coaches need to ascertain if there will be such a question-and-answer session following the address. It can create a final opportunity to create positive relationships with the audience. To help speakers handle Q-and-A situations and interviews, it helps to prepare them as much as possible. This not only involves tone of voice and facial expressions, but it includes appropriate responses. Long before the speech delivery, public relations staff members typically come up with possible practice questions so the company representative will get a head start on those answers. This is not the time for slow-pitch softball questions. Speechwriters must think of the toughest inquiries coming from the most unpleasant members of the social or traditional media.

The public as well as the media have a legitimate concern about CEO performances, especially when they received skyscraper bonuses after steering their corporations' investments into the basement. So antagonism might be expected during the question-and-answer or interview sessions. Company speakers, however, always need to keep their composures. They should never engage in an argument with a journalist, who always has the last word.

Just in case there's a long pause for the start of such a Q-and-A session, some speechwriters have been known to give a sample question to a cooperative member of the sponsoring organization. Such a question allows the speaker to handle a nonthreatening inquiry and get at least one major point across. Often called sound bites from the broadcast industry, these are short statements or key words the speaker needs to reiterate during the interview or Q-and-A process.

This pre-speech practice should also include questions about major topics not mentioned in the speech. Every response should be a positive stand-alone quote that could become a sound bite. You must never lie to a journalist. A speaker shouldn't say, "As I mentioned earlier," since that portion of the Q-and-A may not make it on the air. The writer should remind presenters to politely avoid answering negative or loaded questions. And they should never repeat them since that portion of the interview will likely get into the news.

PRactical TIP

PowerPoint Problems

Although visuals have proven powerful in helping audiences recall a presentation, there are disadvantages as well. Is the medium more important than the message? PowerPoint is easy to use, which has become a problem. All speakers now think of themselves as experts in graphic design and color combinations, it seems. That means those in attendance will probably have to endure:

- ► 79 slides for a 20-minute speech
- ► 14-point type (or smaller) displayed in a large auditorium
- ► dark text (blue) on a dark background (maroon)
- ► dazzling and dizzying graphics overwhelming the verbal presentation
- ► host computer not finding the presentation
- ► projector or other equipment not working
- ► the audience reading the slides and ignoring the speaker
- ► the speaker facing the screen and ignoring the audience.

A few tips can help speakers get through a PowerPoint presentation without alienating an audience. Try to minimize the number of words per slide as well as the number of total slides. Avoid those fancy dissolves and spins for transitions.

Do not distribute handouts of your slides in advance. Notes are of little value without your comments, but they will keep your audience occupied squinting at the handout instead of listening to you. If you wish to leave handouts for the audience, let them know they will be available at the conclusion of your presentation. It's better to show the audience a few key words or an illustration, and have them anxiously await your comments or explanation.

Planning for responses in advance gives the speaker the opportunity to calmly consider issues relating to the main subject. Just voicing some key phrases during rehearsal will help with recall while being asked various questions in front of a live audience.

Speakers must use caution about attempting to go "off the record" with reporters. There's no such thing. If the statement is something the company doesn't want to appear in the media, then a speaker cannot say it. (It's wise to remember—as politicians seem to forget—microphones may be live before and after the official speech takes place.) Likewise, a speaker should avoid using the phrase "no comment" in response to any type of question. The overall interpretation by a majority of the public of those two words is, "You're guilty and trying to hide something." Options to say instead include:

▶ "I don't know, but I'll let you know when I do."
▶ "We can't release that information yet, but we will as soon as possible."
▶ "Those details are part of an investigation that is not yet complete."

In other words, just about any statement sounds less guilty than the declarative "no comment."

How to Get More Mileage from Speeches

As mentioned in the chapter's opening, speechwriters have another task after writing the speech. To obtain as much publicity as possible takes dedication and work. They want to get mileage from their well-written and researched speech by having many others who could not hear it read about it later.

Writing the speech involves hours, even days, gathering information, conducting online research, interviewing, reading, taking notes, writing, rewriting and polishing the speech. In contrast, the company representative might deliver that speech in 20 minutes to a conference gathering that's saddle sore and sleepy after devouring yet another big meal. To compound the problem, the next day only one local newspaper carries a five-inch article about the speech and the occasion, and much of that story is unnecessary information, such as including the exact time of the speech and where it was delivered.

Speechwriters can't settle for that. Their organization's speaker and the labor-intensive, speech-writing process demand far more than that. Every executive speech carries information wanted and needed by peers, by colleagues and competitors, by governmental and political leaders, by leaders in the business community, by employees and often by everyday citizens.

Leaving the task of securing publicity to the one or two reporters or bloggers who cover the speaking event is never enough. It's up to a speechwriter (and often only that individual) to provide the appropriate publicity. To accomplish that, public relations practitioners understand every presentation has three distinct receivers:

1. The primary audience—the smallest of the three—those listening to the actual speech as it is being delivered.
2. The secondary audience—the largest of the three—those who read or hear about the speech through traditional media—newspapers, news magazines, radio and television stations—social media and other Web outlets.
3. The tertiary audience—the most influential of the three—those who read about the speech in professional magazines and journals (both print and online). This audience—leaders in the business, industrial, governmental, political and professional communities—needs to know what CEOs say publicly because of their leadership positions in these fields.

The news media—print, online and broadcast—are always hungry for well-written, timely, information-laden stories about the various communities: business, education, medical, military, religion, scientific, etc. As mentioned earlier, media today do not have the staff to report on all of the news events they need to cover, so they have to depend upon public

PRactical TIP

Ghostwriters Can Strike Gold

Experienced speechwriters can easily pull in six-figure incomes. It's a valuable skill to put on any resume. Many work for one company, but others attempt the freelance route, picking up a variety of clients.

Speechwriter conferences, publications and organizations provide plenty of opportunities for networking and enhancing skills. Several newsletters are available that help put writers and clients together. Just a few of such blogs and publications, some free and some by subscription, are:

The Influential Executive: advice from speechwriters to help others.

On Speechwriting: free monthly e-newsletter.

Speechwriter's Newsletter: eight-pager from Ragan Communications.

The Speechwriter's Slant: blog by Hal Gordon.

The Speechwriters: Newsletter of the UK Speechwriters' Guild: a U.K.-based speechwriter's blog on the craft.

Vital Speeches of the Day: bringing excellent speeches to readers since 1934.

Washington Speechwriters Roundtable: great networking tool for D.C. writers.

relations professionals to provide them with news items. Bloggers, of course, can help spread quality news and speeches to their audiences. A plus for any speaking event story is having quality edited video for timely distribution.

Professional magazines and journals are even hungrier for news about activities in their fields. Like the newspaper, but with smaller staffs, they must depend upon public relations professionals to serve as their reporters. Thus, publication of the CEO's speech frequently appears in the professional magazines and journals that serve that organization's field. The story may be rewritten or shortened by editors, but it will get published among people of influence, nationally or internationally. Their online versions may not even edit the speechwriter's original submission, and they will usually have room for links to video and other tie-in features.

And, of course, your own company magazine, e-newsletter and online newsroom are prime outlets for news about busy executives' speaking engagements and the actual deliveries.

Doug Starr again provides helpful tips below on how to reach those audiences and maximize exposure for the CEO's speeches. These suggestions are neither difficult nor guaranteed, but they do put the odds in your favor for several reasons.

After your CEO has approved the final version of the speech, prepare a copy for every news medium in your organization's geographic area and for your company website.

At the speaking event, and before the speech delivery, distribute copies to all reporters and bloggers attending. Journalists will write their own stories, but you should be available for whatever help they need.

Obviously, only a few reporters will attend the speaking event. Therefore, you must serve as the on-site journalist for all publications and broadcast stations that do not send reporters. After the speech delivery, write the story, covering the speech and the speaking event as a reporter would, tersely, accurately and objectively. Include the name of the host organization and audience size, the frequency and length of applause, question-and-answer session, whatever.

Write two versions of the story: one for print and one for broadcast. Keep them short, no more than 250 words for newspapers, about 100 words for broadcast. And remember, broadcast news style differs from newspaper news style in that stories written for broadcast are written to appeal to the ear instead of to the eye.

It's worth the effort to provide a broadcast version because broadcasters appreciate having their needs taken into consideration. Getting valuable air time, in turn, makes your task seem worthwhile.

Email a copy of the story and a copy of the speech to every news medium in your geographic area. And post a copy of both your print and your broadcast story on your organization's online newsroom.

Write a longer story about the speech and the speaking event, providing greater detail than your newspaper version. Email and snail mail a copy of that story to every professional magazine and journal in your organization's field of interest and to the publication of the organization to which your CEO spoke.

After PR practitioners have done all that, they need to know how successful their publicity efforts were and they need to inform their CEO. They may not be able to determine how various broadcast media handled their CEO's speech, of course, but they can know how it fared among the daily newspapers, professional magazines, journals, social media and Web outlets. If their public relations office doesn't subscribe to a clipping service, someone in that department needs to thoroughly read and clip the papers and magazines, and surf the Web for other successful recycling efforts. (This often becomes an intern's major assignment.)

It's wise to make copies of each clipping, with the name and date of each publication or online source. The original can be safely filed and copies, with an appropriate notation, sent to their supervisor to document his or her success (as well as the speechwriter's own).

Christine Kent found new media suggestions for creating additional buzz from the original presentation in her "Recycle That Brilliant Speech" article in *Ragan's Daily Headlines* (Sept. 11, 2008):

▶ **Create an Online Freebie**
▶ **Make news on YouTube**
▶ **Create blog posts**
▶ **Build search-engine visibility:** Use speech video to add flavor to online campaigns, suggests Megan Schwartz, PR and marketing manager at Magnify360 in Los Angeles. "Adding the video to the landing pages of paid search campaigns provides you with greater credibility to potential clients, and also provides potential clients with more information on the company, its services and the executives behind the company," Schwartz says.

Providing whitepapers of the speech's main points can help spread its message. Clips on YouTube can get viewers' attention around the globe. Taking advantage of the blogosphere is one other tool Kent advises in her article. Finally, combining speech video with paid search engines can create credibility.

Best Speeches Don't Have to be Long Ones

Some speakers make the mistake of talking much longer than the ears of the audience can bear. That's why someone once said talk is cheap because supply exceeds demand. President Franklin D. Roosevelt provided three tips on the topic when he said, "Instructions for making a speech: Be sincere; be brief; be seated."

That may be why many seminaries now encourage their student preachers to keep their sermons to about 20 to 30 minutes, knowing today's attention spans in the pews have shrunk considerably.

President Abraham Lincoln's Gettysburg Address redefined the Civil War. Delivered on Nov. 19, 1863, in just over two minutes, it's fewer than 300 words:

"Four score and seven years ago our fathers brought forth on this continent, a new nation, conceived in Liberty, and dedicated to the proposition that all men are created equal.

"Now we are engaged in a great civil war, testing whether that nation, or any nation so conceived and so dedicated, can long endure. We are met on a great battle-field of that war. We have come to dedicate a portion of that field, as a final resting place for those who here gave their lives that that nation might live. It is altogether fitting and proper that we should do this.

"But, in a larger sense, we can not dedicate—we can not consecrate—we can not hallow—this ground. The brave men, living and dead, who struggled here, have consecrated it, far above our poor power to add or detract. The world will little note, nor long remember what we say here, but it can never forget what they did here. It is for us the living, rather, to be dedicated here to the unfinished work which they who fought here have thus far so nobly advanced. It is rather for us to be here dedicated to the great task remaining before us—that from these honored dead we take increased devotion to that cause for which they gave the last full measure of devotion—that we here highly resolve that these dead shall not have died in vain—that this nation, under God, shall have a new birth of freedom—and that government of the people, by the people, for the people, shall not perish from the earth."

Summary

Speeches provide organizations with an effective public relations tool, the ability to communicate with an audience in person with immediate feedback. The speechwriting process involves a tremendous amount of effort and research. The PR writer has to thoroughly understand the speaking situation (audience, venue, timing), the speaker (personality, word usage) and the topic of the talk. The task continues for a speechwriter in working to obtain extensive coverage following the speech.

Chapter 11

Law for PR Writing

"The first principle of a free society is an untrammeled flow of words in an open forum."

Adlai E. Stevenson

Sometimes the best way to avoid litigation is to make sure documents are properly drafted. Badly written business documents can be legally ineffectual. This can lead to problems with increased administration costs, as well as bad public relations because of misunderstandings. Clear communication and product information foster a sense of certainty for customers. For example, NALA/EBS research found that 89 percent of the public would change their financial institution if they believed the new institution's information was clearer.

With alarming frequency, electronic communication serves as the genesis in framing a case against a company. So the business writer in the 21st century needs to worry as much about internal memos as news releases sent to the media.

In fact, damaging internal communication can be mined from a host of sources in a company, even a CEO's hard drive, such as one used by Microsoft chief Bill Gates who found out the hard way that electronic communication leaves a long and lingering aftertaste. During the government's antitrust case against the computer software giant, prosecutors confronted Gates with copies of emails he had previously written that seemed to contradict what he said in sworn testimony. Time and time again, Gates found that email messages written years earlier contradicted his spoken testimony. This destroyed Gates' credibility in the eyes of the judge.

The dramatic growth of computer technology has redefined the way that business operates in today's information economy. However, the increased use of computer technology has also placed a daunting burden on corporations to control the production and dissemination of information. From the perspective of a plaintiff's attorney, it places a great advantage in the hands of the client who can capitalize on an embarrassing mistake or inadvertent communication produced by someone within the corporation.

Famed public relations expert Edward Bernays expanded on the narrow concept of press agentry, or working to influence government policy, into a far more ambitious—and controversial—realm of seeking to influence and change public opinion and behavior. Bernays recognized that formation of opinion required practitioners to shape methods of behavior on behalf of many business and industrial enterprises, welfare and civic groups, and governments at home and abroad. He favored surveys, releasing the results of experiments and polls to make a better case for his clients' positions and products.

Bernays famously wrote in 1971 that "Public relations, effectively used, helps validate an underlying principle of our society—competition in the market place of ideas and things." However, by 1991, when he turned 100, he said in an interview, "Public relations today is horrible. Any dope, any nitwit, any idiot can call him or herself a public relations practitioner." Unfortunately, Bernays' assessment of the state of the public relations profession—a view shared by other public relations leaders—cuts to the heart of the need for greater professionalism. As communicators we recognize the vital need that communication approaches have toward organizational success both internally and externally. However, many public relations professionals today remain rooted in the press agentry model of public relations and consequently lack grounding in the strategic approach to public relations. This invites disaster. Public relations professionals therefore must be well-versed in strategic business practices and communication outcomes. Perhaps one of the most important components to the strategic approach to public relations comes from an understanding of the law.

In business, image is everything. Public opinion of a company affects a consumer's views on that company's products and services, as well as its place in the marketplace of ideas. This, in turn, affects the company's profit, and essentially its standing.

Lawsuits or recalls have grave consequences and the cost of repairing a company's reputation could drive the company into bankruptcy. The need to communicate effectively and efficiently in written form may be the difference between reputation management or organizational collapse. Carefully reviewing documents before sending them to their intended readers should be the first rule in committing thoughts and ideas to writing. Also, writing ethically requires identifying those individuals who will gain or lose because of your message. Collectively, these *stakeholders* have a vested interest in your writing. When crafting your communication, think about the impact of the message and how best to communicate it. Facts must be free of ambiguity and purposes clearly stated. Also, writers must consider language issues such as race and gender roles, political correctness, generalizations, cultural awareness and religious sensitivity.

Under the law, most documents written by employees represent the position and commitments of the organization itself. You must always consider legal issues when writing a professional document, and this must be reflected in your writing style. Professional documents can serve as evidence in disputes over contracts and in product liability lawsuits.

PRactical TIP

A Quick Fix Toward Effective Prose

Somewhere around the third grade the typical student's writing took a turn for the worse. Third grade taught us the dreaded compound sentence, and this sowed the great misconception that good writing, *adult writing*, implies complex, convoluted sentence structure. Add to this a failure to adhere to sound grammatical structure, proper punctuation and spelling, and sloppy, rambling ideas and you have a recipe for disaster. Unfortunately, the only one enjoying this recipe may be a plaintiff's attorney who can take this flawed communication and build a lawsuit around it.

The quick fix for this ineffective prose employs returning to writing concise, crisp, clear sentences. Building straightforward and factual paragraphs void of frill and embellishment satisfies the purpose of most business communication—to communicate information effectively.

Poor writing skills can distort meaning and damage credibility. While writing mishaps and errors afflict credibility, they also, in severe cases, alter meaning. For example, improper word use can be construed to mean something completely different from what a writer intended it to communicate. This lack of clarity through ambiguous and error-filled writing requires subsequent communications to get the message across. From a business standpoint, poor writing skills prove wasteful and inefficient. From a legal standpoint, they give rise to litigation.

Among the most common writing maladies afflicting the writing process are using inflammatory language, spreading rumors, speculating on issues without factual grounds, expressing opinions outside of the employee's field of expertise and scribbling notes in the margins of printed material.

1. **Inflammatory language.** Inflammatory language often implies fault without first gathering all the facts. This type of writing often occurs when an employee exhibits the hero syndrome. Here the employee broadcasts that he has unearthed a major organizational problem without having proof to substantiate this assertion. Unsubstantiated assertions such as these provide fodder for a legal proceeding.

2. **Spreading rumors.** Passing a rumor in writing often creates havoc in an organization because it must defend itself against information that is often completely without merit. It often requires great efforts to disprove false information and casts a shadow of doubt over the organization's credibility.

3. **Speculating on issues without factual grounds.** Employees speculate when they communicate what they think they know rather than what they actually know. When they make statements without first getting valid details, the information can cast a cloud of uncertainty over the organization and create a need for substantial follow-up information to rectify the damage.

4. **Expressing opinions outside the field of expertise.** A plaintiff's attorney can weave a web of uncertainty and doubt about an organization's guilt when written information is attributed to someone in the organization who does not have the expertise in that particular area. For example, marketing personnel in the pharmaceutical industry can carry on an email discussion about the appropriate dosage of a drug. A defense attorney could present this information to a jury with the implication that in this organization dosage requirements come from marketing professionals rather than medical professionals. Too often these company insiders comment in writing on areas outside of their field of expertise.

5. **Scribbling notes in the margins.** Handwritten notes in the margins of printed internal documents often catch employees at their most unguarded moments. These notes, often penned without thought to clarity and appropriateness, have been deemed admissible in court.

Today, the average Fortunate 500 Company defends itself in hundreds of lawsuits at any given time. Often companies win their lawsuits, but the consequences of the damage in the court of public opinion transcend the wins and losses in a court of law. Lawsuits cost companies time and money that would be better spent improving business and products. Lawsuits also have consequences for a company's reputation. And often these lawsuits start because someone in the organization improperly communicated or failed to understand the power of the written word. Therefore, you must have an understanding of the law so you can deal with a spark before it becomes a fire.

Unclear messages and inappropriate comments often get companies involved in lawsuits. Companies should follow a simple rule: All communication should be understandable, clear and concise. Remember also that in a lawsuit, all documents may be subpoenaed. This means that any document from memos and emails to proposals and studies can be subject to revision by a court of law. Even handwritten notes on documents can become part of a lawsuit. While some documents may be privileged, that protection gets lost if senders and receivers abuse the privilege.

Strategic communication involves more than simply disseminating information. It involves knowing the rules for properly committing ideas to writing. That understanding begins first with an understanding of the legal rights, responsibilities and consequences of communication.

Understanding the First Amendment

Until 1694, English society had an elaborate system of licensing that required all attempts at publication to first get a government granted license. Famed English Jurist and Professor William Blackstone, in his commentary on the suppression of speech and of the press in English society, wrote, "[To] subject the press to the restrictive power of a licenser . . . is to subject all freedom of sentiment to the prejudices of one man, and make him the arbitrary and infallible judge of all controverted points in learning, religion, and government." In part, Blackstone's commentary served as the foundation behind the purpose of the First Amendment to the United States Constitution, and the framers' intent to abolish such prior restraints on publication. The founders were sensitive to restrictive speech, especially restrictions on seditious libel that made criticizing the government a crime under English rule. Simply, the framers wanted the First Amendment to empower expression rather than forbid punishment of seditious libel.

Inevitably, though, freedom of speech is not an absolute. The courts must decide what speech warrants protection by the First Amendment, and what speech the government can regulate. Although the framers wrote the First Amendment with absolute language that Congress *shall* make "no law" prohibiting speech, the Supreme Court of the United States has never accepted the view that the First Amendment prohibits all government regulation of expression.

The authors intended this book to help hone writers' technical skills. However, crafting effective prose cannot be accomplished without developing critical thinking skills, and understanding the freedoms and limitations of the laws of expression. Freedom of speech is crucial in a democracy, but all too powerful to go completely unchecked. Society works best when informed citizens make decisions. Professional communicators must be knowledgeable wordsmiths and protectors of free speech in order to serve both clients and society.

Ostensibly, the First Amendment offers more than a constitutional guarantee against government interference; it embodies one of the country's foremost normative and cultural symbols. Simply, it embodies the vital attributes of the American character. That character, of course, is rooted in the creation of sovereign power, or inalienable rights.

In using the phrase *inalienable rights,* the framers of the constitution made it clear that people cannot alienate—sell or trade—their rights because to do so would render the people less sovereign. Constitutional law scholar Erwin Chemerinsky writes that those who won our independence believed that the final end of the state was to make men free to develop their faculties, and that in its government the deliberative forces should prevail over the arbitrary. They believed indispensable to liberty was the freedom to think as you will and to speak as you think.

Professional communicators must concern themselves with a number of issues when crafting prose, placing messages or persuading publics. Today, communicators must embrace an integrated approach to communication that requires extensive knowledge of core free speech rights and trademark and copyright restrictions, as well as knowledge of the agencies and departments that regulate speech and the landmark court cases that have ruled on the constitutionality. Finally, communicators must distinguish between absolute protection of speech and the necessity to regulate certain types of speech.

Content Neutral vs. Content Specific

The Supreme Court of the United States frequently has declared that the very core of the First Amendment is that government cannot regulate speech based on its content. The distinction between content neutral and content specific speech is the first step in understanding restrictions on language. When the Court is determining the constitutionality of a restriction that is not based on content, it uses some form of a balancing test. That test employs three distinct levels—ordinary scrutiny, intermediate scrutiny, and strict scrutiny. Ordinary scrutiny requires the government to show that its restriction *reasonably* relates to a *legitimate* governmental interest. This type of restriction generally refers to economic and social restrictions. Intermediate scrutiny, sometime referred to as heightened scrutiny, requires the government to show that the restriction is *substantially* related to an *important* government interest. Intermediate scrutiny applies to classifications based on gender and illegitimacy.

However, the test for regulation of speech, a fundamental right expressed in the Bill of Rights, requires adherence to a much higher standard. The most rigorous of the three levels of scrutiny, strict scrutiny requires that for a restriction to pass constitutional muster the challenged government action must be *closely* related to a *compelling* government interest.

The Distinction Between Content-Based and Content-Neutral Laws

Perhaps the most central feature of First Amendment law is the distinction between restrictions based on the content of expression and restrictions not based on content. When the Court attempts to determine the constitutionality of a restriction not based on content it uses some form of balancing test. We judge content-based restrictions by a more strict categorical approach: if a content-based measure does not fall within one of several relatively narrow categories—such as obscenity, fighting words, defamation, commercial speech, or incitement—there is a nearly conclusive presumption against its constitutionality. For example, the Court declared in *Police Department of Chicago v. Mosely* that above all else, the First Amendment means that government has no power to restrict speech because of its message, its ideas, its subject matter or its content. Once a forum is opened up to assembly or speaking by some groups, government may not prohibit others from assembling or speaking on the basis of what they intend to say. Selective exclusions from a public forum may not be based on content alone, and may not be justified by reference to content alone. The Court relies on an equal protection perspective in framing its distinction between content-based and content-neutral.

Mosley involved a Chicago ordinance that prohibited picketing or demonstrations within 150 feet of a school building while the school was in session, except for peaceful picketing in connection with a labor dispute. Earl Mosley frequently picketed the school, usually by himself, to protest what he perceived as race discrimination by the school. The protests were conceded by the city always to be peaceful, orderly and quiet. The Supreme Court expressly used equal protection for analyzing the Chicago ordinance. Justice Marshall, writing for the Court, concluded that the law was unconstitutional because it was an impermissible subject-matter restriction on speech. Peaceful picketing on the subject of the school's labor-management dispute is permitted, but all other peaceful picketing is prohibited, Marshall concluded. The operative distinction is the message appeared on a picket sign.

In a subsequent decision, the Court further established its position. In *R.A.V. v. City of St. Paul,* the court declared that "content-based regulations are presumptively invalid." *In Turner Broadcasting System v. Federal Communication Commission,* the Court reasoned that content-based restrictions on speech must meet strict scrutiny, while content-neutral regulation only needs to meet intermediate scrutiny. Writing for the Court, Justice Kennedy concluded that the level of scrutiny applicable to content-neutral restrictions that impose an incidental burden on speech is the intermediate level of scrutiny. The justice added, "Government action that stifles speech on account of its message, or that requires the utterance of a particular message favored by the Government, contravenes this essential First Amendment right."

As a general rule, laws that by their terms distinguish speech on the basis of the ideas or views expressed are content-based. By contrast, laws that confer benefits or impose burdens on speech without reference to the ideas or views expressed are in most instances content-neutral.

The First Amendment prohibits content-based restrictions that censor particular points of view, and content-neutral restrictions that unduly constrict the opportunities for free expression. The government must demonstrate an inability to achieve the infringement of speech by less restrictive means. The government cannot merely suppress unpopular ideas or information or to manipulate the public debated without sound reason.

Editor in chief Kermit L. Hall, writing in *The Oxford Companion to the Supreme Court of the United States,* states that the Court has fashioned free speech doctrine around a principle that has two fundamental tenets: (1) free speech serves special and significant constitutional purposes, and (2) the First Amendment should not protect all speech but only speech of a certain quality. The free speech principle reflects a tension between two cardinal values in our constitutional system, liberalism and democracy. Liberal values stress individual liberty and beckon the Court to protect expression that does not constitute substantial direct harm to society, while democratic norms endorse the right of the majority to enact value judgments that limit liberty. The Court has seemed to balance the two values by applying liberal standards to protected speech but tolerant controls to unprotected expressions.

The Court has relied extensively on the rationale developed in *Chaplinsky v. New Hampshire.* The state of New Hampshire convicted Chaplinsky under a New Hampshire statute for using offensive language toward another person in public. He contended that the statute was invalid under the United States Constitution because it placed an unreasonable restraint on freedom of speech and because it was vague and indefinite. The Court upheld Chaplinsky's conviction. In doing so, Justice Frank Murphy put forth a two-tier theory of the First Amendment. Justice Murphy concluded that certain well-defined and narrowly limited categories of speech fall outside the bounds of constitutional protection. Justice Murphy stated that lewd, obscene, profane and libelous speech, along with insulting or fighting words failed to contribute to the expression of ideas and possessed no social value in search of truth. However, subsequent cases have altered the broad-based opinion expressed in *Chaplinsky*.

The Court repeatedly has held that speech about judicial proceedings is political speech protected by the First Amendment. The Courts have held that speech that reports on judicial proceedings or criticizes the Court serves an essential public purpose. For example, in *Bridges v. California,* the Court held a publisher in contempt for an out-of-court statement that presented a clear and present danger of harm to the legal system. A newspaper was held in contempt for a series of editorials concerning the pending sentencing of two members of a labor union who had been convicted of assaulting nonunion truck drivers. The editorial described the assailants as "thugs" and advocated prison sentences for them. The Supreme Court overturned the contempt conviction and, in an opinion by Justice Black, forcefully declared that the assumption that respect for the judiciary can be won by shielding judges from published criticism wrongly appraises the character of American public opinion. To enforce silence, however limited, solely in the name of preserving the dignity of the bench, would probably engender resentment, suspicion and contempt much more than it would enhance respect. The Court concluded that speech concerning the judicial process only could be punished if there was a clear and present danger of harm.

Whether analyzed under equal protection or solely under the First Amendment, the government cannot regulate speech in a public forum based on the viewpoint or subject matter of the speech unless the restriction meets the standard of strict scrutiny.

Commercial Speech

As early as 1942, the Supreme Court of the United States held that commercial speech was not protected by the First Amendment. In *Valentine v. Chrestensen* (1942), the Court first articulated its commercial speech doctrine. The justices in *Valentine* upheld as constitutional a city ordinance prohibiting the distribution of "any handbill or other advertising matter in or upon any street." Without analysis or explanation, the Court stated, "We are equally clear that the Constitution imposes no such restraint on government as respects purely commercial advertising."

In 1951 the Court further stressed the commercial feature of a transaction when it upheld the constitutionality of a law that prohibited sellers of goods from going door-to-door. In *Bread v. City of Alexandria,* the Court clearly distinguished between what it deemed unprotected commercial speech from the circumstances of an earlier case, *Martin v. City of Struthers* (1943), which dealt with noncommercial speech. In *Martin* the Court declared unconstitutional a city ordinance, which was used to punish a religious group that went door-to-door to solicit for religion. Here the Court emphasized that religious speech was not commercial.

Commercial speech remained unprotected in American jurisprudence until 1975. Then, in *Bigelow v. Virginia* (1975), the Court held protected under the First Amendment advertisements for abortion services in newspapers. The Court stated, "speech is not stripped of its First Amendment protection merely because it appears as a commercial advertisement." Furthermore, the Court expressly held that speech that "does no more than propose a commercial transaction" is protected by the First Amendment. This proved a dramatic shift in the Court's interpretation of commercial speech.

The ruling in *Bigelow* set the stage for the landmark case on commercial speech, *Virginia State Board of Pharmacy v. Virginia Citizens Consumer Council* (1976). Here the Court declared unconstitutional a statute banning the advertisement of prescription drug prices. The Court further reasoned that in a free enterprise economy consumers depend on the free flow of commercial information as a means of conveying vital information. However, the Court suggested that deceptive or misleading advertising, even if not false, did not serve any social interests and could be regulated.

In recent years the Court has demonstrated a willingness to protect only speech that furthered the social interests in the free flow of information. Consequently, under the commercial speech doctrine, audience interest has taken priority over speakers' interests.

Once the Court decided that the First Amendment protected commercial speech, it needed to then tackle a seemingly more difficult task, defining commercial speech. Clearly, advertising the price and availability for a product is a form of commercial speech. However, advertising can also be purely political in nature. In *New York Times v. Sullivan* (1964), the Court extended the commercial speech doctrine to include political speech. This landmark case also signaled a critical shift in First Amendment jurisprudence by embracing a more speech protective analysis that focused on the danger that actions for libel might deter expressions that rest at the heart of the amendment.

Of course, the foundation for any discussion of commercial speech begins with the language contained in the First Amendment. At its very core, the First Amendment advances the idea that government may not tell you to shut up just because it doesn't like the content of your message. It may, however, put reasonable restrictions on the time, place and manner of your speech, and it can also balance your rights of free speech against other important rights.

The Supreme Court also ruled that free speech cannot be restricted merely because the speaker is a corporation rather than a natural person; nor is the corporation's right of free speech limited to matters that affect the company's business. In *First National Bank of Boston v. Bellotti* (1980), the court struck down a law forbidding spending for corporate advocacy.

In *Central Hudson Gas & Electric Corp. v. Public Service Commission of New York* (1980), the Court addressed the issue of the constitutionality of a state law prohibiting promotional advertising by an electrical utility. Again the Court reaffirmed its stance that commercial speech is protected by the First Amendment but said that it nonetheless "recognized the commonsense distinction between speech proposing a commercial transaction, which occurs in an area traditionally subject to government regulation, and other varieties of speech." In *Central Hudson,* the Court introduced a four-part test to help lower courts and business communities determine what commercial speech would be protected.

1. Does the commercial speech concern lawful activity, and,
2. Is the government interest in restricting the speech a truly important interest?
   If yes to these two, then the court asks,
3. Does the proposed governmental regulation directly advance the interest asserted?
4. Is the regulation more extensive than necessary to serve that interest?

In *Board of Trustees of the State University of New York v. Fox* (1989), the Court modified the fourth part of its four-part test. In this case, dealing with state regulation that prohibited commercial solicitations on campus, the Court stated that government regulation of commercial speech need not use the least restrictive alternative. However, in place of the least restrictive means requirement, the Court said that government must use a means narrowly tailored to achieve the desired objective.

False and Deceptive Advertising

The Sherman Antitrust Act provided the primary statutory basis for American antitrust enforcement. The Act targets activities restricting marketplace activities. The Court's landmark decision in *Standard Oil Co. v. United States* (1911) and *United States v. American Tobacco Co.* (1911) paved the way for extended political debate and prompted Congress to pass the Clayton and Federal Trade Commission Acts in 1914 to supplement the Sherman Act. Today, the Federal Trade Commission is the most active agency controlling and regulating advertising. During the 1970s the FTC set its sights on regulating unfair or deceptive advertising.

Section 5 of the FTC Act (1914) gave the Commission the authority to regulate "unfair methods of competition." Congress later changed the Act by the Wheeler-Lea Amendment to give the FTC authority over both unfair methods of competition and unfair or deceptive acts or practices. The Wheeler-Lea Amendment gave the FTC authority to regulate deceptive advertising.

In its 1993 Policy Statement on Deception, the FTC articulates that it considers a marketing effort to be deceptive if:

1. there is a representation, omission, act or practice, that
2. is likely to mislead consumers acting reasonably under the circumstances, and
3. that representation, omission, or practice is "material."

The term "material" refers to the fact that some deceptive claims are trivial, and that the FTC will only regulate deceptions that are important to consumers.

To prove a claim of deceptive advertising, the FTC concerns itself with what the ad conveys to consumers. The FTC considers an ad deceptive if its conveyed message differs from the reality of the product's attributes. This standard requires the Commission to look at two types of evidence: (1) evidence concerning what message is conveyed to consumers, and (2) evidence concerning the product attribute's true qualities. Among the methods the Commission employs are surveys to consumers to discover what message is conveyed in an advertisement, and laboratory tests of products to check the validity of claims such as automobiles' fuel efficiency. However, the FTC does require advertisers to conduct testing prior to making the advertising claim.

If an advertising claim is deemed deceptive, the advertiser will face one of three possible remedies.

1. A Cease and Desist Order, which requires the advertiser to stop making the claim; or
2. An Affirmative Disclosure Order, which forces the advertiser to provide consumers with more information; or
3. Corrective Advertising, which is a form of affirmative disclosure that is intended to correct lingering deception that results from a long history of deceiving the consumer.

PRactical TIP

Federal Agencies and Departments that Regulate Advertising

The consumer movement propelled the notion of consumerism to the forefront of marketing communication. Starting in the 1960s, advertisers began to concern themselves more and more with the power of consumerism and its social actions to dramatize their buying power. Consequently, marketers today pay more attention to product claims and concerns of consumers in preliminary research in order to cement a bond between consumers and the companies they patronize.

Organizations like the Consumer Federation of America, the National Council of Senior Citizens, the National Consumer League, and the National Stigma Clearinghouse exchange and disseminate information among members. This creates an intricate network of consumer information groups continually investigating advertising complaints and conducting campaigns to halt objectionable advertising. This politically active network works to investigate complaints made against marketers. With precise use of government intervention, media support and an occasional court-ordered cease-and-desist, these consumer information networks possess the power to derail any advertising campaign directed toward consumers. Consequently, marketers pay careful attention to these groups and attempt to cultivate relationships through self-regulation and open communication.

With such a competitive consumer market and an active and mobile consumer movement, advertisers police themselves to gain consumer confidence in the industry as well as the products and services they market. In addition to self-regulation among advertising agencies, the industry as a whole has established a network of professional affiliations to monitor itself. This network includes advertising publications that report issues and court actions to educate advertisers about current issues and legislation and professional trade associations that scan the industry for abuses. Three of the most active and prominent member agencies are the American Association of Advertising Agencies (AAAA), the American Advertising Federation (AAF) and the Association of National Advertisers (ANA).

AAAA comprises the largest advertising agencies in the United States. It controls agency practice and oversees the ethical standards agreed upon by the industry. AAAA Standards of Practice and Creative code established the principles for membership. The organization readily denies membership to agencies deemed unethical.

Founding members of the AAF helped establish the Federal Trade Commission. Also, its early vigilance committees were the forerunners of the Better Business Bureau. AAF's Advertising Principles of American Business defined the standard for truthful and responsible advertising and articulated them in eight standards ranging from truthfulness to taste and decency.

AAF maintains a network of local advertising clubs and also sponsors an annual College World Series of Advertising for college students interested in the field. This helps the organization establish the principles of ethical and truthful advertising in the minds of young professionals.

The strength of the consumer movement, the increased use of media as a source of information, and the importance of legislation to protect the buying public established a relationship between business and consumers that continues to grow. Fostered by a sustained commitment by the business community to provide good products, at fair prices, and disseminated with truth and accuracy, consumers clearly enter the information age with the realization that their voice truly matters. The consumer movement, which took root prior to the 20th century and grew to become a driving force behind improved products, services and legislation, established the standards for the truthful and ethical behavior of business and protected the individual by respecting the demands of the activist groups. Consequently, advertisers developed higher standards of ethical responsibility toward the dissemination of information and increased understanding of social responsibility through the establishment of trade associations.

Puffery, Unfairness and Subliminal Appeals

The FTC considers puffery, a form of opinion statement, beyond its ability to regulate. Critics, however, claim the puffery defense creates a loophole for many deceptive claims. The FTC has defined puffery as claims that (1) reasonable people do not believe to be true product qualities and (2) are incapable of being proved either true or false.

In addition to its power to regulate deceptiveness, the FTC also regulates unfair marketing practices. After nearly 14 years of debate, the FTC incorporated a definition of unfairness into the Commission's Enabling Act. The new definition limits the application of the FTC's unfairness power to an act or practice that (1) causes or is likely to cause substantial injury to consumers, (2) which is not reasonably avoidable by consumers themselves, and (3) is not outweighed by countervailing benefits to consumers or to competition.

Perhaps the most overanalyzed topic in persuasive communication concerns subliminal perceptions. Subliminal advertising by definition means "below the limen" or below the threshold of consciousness. Critics advance the argument that advertisers hide images within advertisements, and that these images manipulate our behavior without our even realizing we have seen them. While a fun topic to debate, no evidence exists that marketers embed hidden images in advertisements.

TOOLBOX TIP

Beware of Email Abuse

Email, unlike any other technological innovation, has altered the business communication landscape. Lawyers can mine the recesses of a hard drive and unearth a treasure trove of documents that may help an attorney create a "smoking gun" in a legal case.

Abuse involving rash statements by writers often results when scribes forget that they just produced a permanent recorded communication. Unfortunately, the simplicity of email lulls emailers into treating the medium like a telephone rather than a printing press.

Reforming email abusers and developing policies that safeguard the organization helps avoid legal consequences and public relations nightmares. PR professionals must work with legal counsel proactively to develop inexpensive training programs and develop policies to safeguard against severe legal consequences.

Copyright and Trademark

Copyright affects things we communicators deal with all the time—writings, pictures, graphics materials and audiovisual works. You need to be concerned with two issues: using other people's copyrighted material, and preventing others from using your material.

The exception to the first is Fair Use. It says you may copy copyrighted material in certain circumstances:

1. the purpose of the use, commercial vs. non-commercial
2. the nature of the copyrighted work
3. how much you copy
4. the effect your copying may have on the potential market for the copyrighted material.

You should put a copyright notice on all proposals. Register copyrighted material with the copyright office in Washington.

Who owns work produced by a freelancer? The copyright statue by itself seems to say that the employer owns it. The Supreme Court ruled in 1989 that in the case of independently produced work, the freelancers own the copyright, unless there is an express agreement to the contrary. Copyright law appears in Section 17 of the United States Code, separated into 13 chapters. Each chapter deals with a distinct aspect of copyright.

Trademark gives you exclusive use of a particular word, name, symbol or slogan to identify your company's products. A trademark is any word, name, symbol, device or combination adopted and used by a person or entity to identify goods made or sold and to distinguish them from the goods made or sold by another person or entity. If you sell products or goods, think trademark. Examples of trademarks include Kleenex (facial tissues), Coca-Cola (soft drink beverage, Microsoft (computer software). Trade name differs from trademark in that a trade name identifies the owner of the business, while a trademark identifies a good or service a business provides.

A company that sells a service rather than products can have something analogous to a trademark, called a service mark. A service mark gets the same protection as a trademark. Business owners or entities use service marks to identify services rendered or offered and to distinguish them from the services rendered or offered from competitors. Examples of service marks include McDonald's Restaurant Services, Wal-Mart Retail Business Services. Service marks may often be slogans such as the American Airlines slogan, "Something Special in the Air," or a plumber using "The Leak Fixers." The United States Army's "star" is a registered trademark, while the slogan "An Army of One" is a registered service mark used by the Army from 2001 to 2006. Currently the United States Army uses "Army Strong," a registered service mark for its recruiting purposes.

Registering a trademark with the U.S. Patent and Trademark Office in Washington, D.C., notifies the public that the owner of the mark claims exclusive rights to use the mark in association with products and services identical or substantially similar to those of the mark's owner. The owner of the mark does not need to register it in order to protect its rights. Use automatically provides trademark right in the geographic area of use. However, registration is necessary to protect the use of the mark nationally.

Another important term in trademark law is *secondary meaning*. The term *secondary meaning* refers to the use and consumer awareness of a mark that makes it become distinctive. The key element of secondary meaning is a mental association in a buyer's mind between the mark and a single source of the product, even if the source is anonymous. For a mark to be protected as a trademark, it must be distinctive. If the mark is not inherently distinctive, it can acquire the necessary distinctiveness through the development of secondary meaning. Secondary meaning shows that the mark has some meaning to the public beyond the obvious meaning of the terms or images of the mark itself. In other words, if the primary significance of the mark in the consuming public's mind has become the *source* of the goods or services, rather than the product itself, it has acquired secondary meaning.

However, it should be understood that when discussing whether a mark has acquired secondary meaning, the focus is not on what things the owner has *done,* but on how *effective* those things were—thus, surveys are very important because they show the impact of the mark's owner's actions on the consuming public. That is, surveys can show whether a spectrum of the consuming public recognizes the mark as being distinctive.

Examples of marks that were not originally protectable but which have since been found to have acquired the necessary secondary meaning including KOOL (for menthol cigarettes), CHAP STICK (for lip balm) and Blockbuster (for a chain of video rental stores). The seminal case on secondary meaning was *Zatarian's, Inc. v. Oak Grove Smokehouse, Inc.* The Court determined that Zatarian's "fish-fri" gained secondary meaning and competitors use of it infringed on its use.

Trademark protection lasts 10 years with renewable options for 10-year periods thereafter. However, an Affidavit of Continuing Use must be filed with the Patent and Trademark Office between the fifth and sixth years following registration, or cancellation will occur or registration will be lost.

Self-Regulation and Consumer Advocacy

Corporate attorneys scrutinize messages to help the company avoid legal pitfalls and the embarrassment and adverse publicity as a result of high profile lawsuits. Agencies also help regulate the process by maintaining a watchful eye concerning the legality of advertisers' claims as well as insisting on adequate documentation to support any claims made by the company in commercial messages. The business community itself has established its own regulatory bodies to control advertising practices. The Better Business Bureau (BBB), the largest and best known, handles consumer complaints about local business practices and advertising misuse. The BBB's parent organization, the Council of Better Business Bureaus, deals with consumer complaints at the national level. The National Advertising Division (NAD) and the Children's Advertising Review Unit (CARU) work closely with the National Advertising Review Board (NARB) with respect to maintaining accuracy, decency and truth in national advertising.

In addition to the control and self-regulation at the corporate and agency level, and the advertising industry's own system of self-regulation, many advertising professionals adhere to advertising guidelines developed through local, state and national organizations.

The American Medical Association (AMA) and the American Bar Association (ABA) remain the most active of these professional organizations regulating member use of advertising. Both the AMA and the ABA maintain strict guidelines on advertising as a way of preserving professionalism and for safeguarding against unethical and fraudulent claims by members.

Laws Prohibiting Professionals from Soliciting Prospective Clients

All 50 states have enacted legislation that prohibits unfair competition and unfair acts, and allows people to sue over deceptive messages. In most instances consumers can recover monetary damages and attorney fees as well as put a halt to deceptive advertising. Furthermore, the Supreme Court of the United States has held the First Amendment does not protect even true commercial messages that inherently risk being deceptive. The Court has advanced its protection in two forms—laws prohibiting professionals from advertising or practicing under a trade name and laws restricting professionals from soliciting prospective clients.

In *Friedman v. Rogers* (1979) the Supreme Court upheld a state law that prohibited optometrists from advertising and practicing under trade names. The Court reasoned that trade names are a form of commercial speech and nothing more and that states can regulate their use because of their inherent risk of deception. The significance of Friedman is that even truthful advertising by professionals can be regulated if it is the type that can be used to mislead the public.

In *Bates v. State Bar of Arizona* (1977) the Court ruled that the government may not prohibit attorneys from engaging in truthful, non-deceptive advertising of their services. However, the Court also held permissible state laws that prohibit attorney in-person solicitation of prospective clients for profit. The Court's rationale is that face-to-face solicitation risks becoming deceptive, and clients will become deceived and pressured because no one is there to monitor the situation. However, the Court stated in *In re Primus* (1978) that personal solicitations are permissible if the lawyer offers to represent the client free of charge.

When the communication is done in written form, the Court has a slightly different view. In *Shapero v. Kentucky Bar Association* (1988) the Court declared unconstitutional a state law that prohibited targeted, direct mail solicitation by lawyers for pecuniary gain. However, seven years later in *Florida Bar v. Went for It, Inc.* (1995) the Court carved out an exception when it prohibited attorneys from soliciting personal injury or wrongful death clients for 30 days after an accident. The Court said "the purpose of the 30-day targeted direct-mail ban is to forestall the outrage and irritation with the state-licensed legal profession that the practice of direct solicitation only days after accidents has engendered."

The battle cry with agency clients who seem bothered by any restrictions placed on their commercial messages is always the same: *What about our First Amendment right to free speech?*

Simply, free speech is not an absolute. Rather, the government has always placed reasonable restrictions on speech.

Summary

Professional communicators must have a working knowledge of the law in order to properly do their job. However, they just also recognize the need to forge strategic relationships with legal counsel so they can work together to protect the institution and the public it serves.

Chapter 12

PR Campaign Writing

"What do you want to achieve or avoid?
The answers to this question are objectives.
How will you go about achieving your desired results?
The answer to this you can call strategy."

William E. Rothschild

Good plans shape good decisions. Planners must sift through mounds of research and consider a host of ideas in order to create a viable roadmap for success. A good plan helps shape dreams and creates a blueprint that will lead to achieving the overarching goal. In essence, professional planners combine the logical analysis associated with left-brain thinking with the creative execution associated with right-brain thinking. The plan weaves science and art into a workable document that assesses the Real State and maps out the steps necessary to reach the Ideal State. Simply, professional planners engage in strategic thinking by first identifying problems, researching the situation, separating the problems into components, and fashioning workable solutions.

No two public relations plans are the same. Taking a *cookie-cutter* approach to public relations planning dooms the plan to failure. Therefore, research and problem identification must be the first step in creating the plan. However, the framework for writing the plan can follow a logical order. While the research, analysis and ideas differ based on the problems identified, the planner can craft the final document using the following elements.

- ▶ Executive Summary
- ▶ Situation Analysis
- ▶ Research Summary
- ▶ Goals/Objectives/Strategies
- ▶ Target Audience
- ▶ Key Messages
- ▶ Tactics

Let's face it, the look of the document impresses clients and bosses—they're only human. All other things being equal, a well-organized and attractively prepared plan communicates competency and creates a sense of trust in the mind of the client that your ideas will work. So, what can you do to help ensure success? We'll address a number of elements in an effective public relations plan and focus on how to properly craft a plan for optimal success.

Keep in mind that strategic thinking involves assessing problems and devising ideas based on an analysis of the research. Strategic planners schedule practical activities to achieve the ambition. They provide the blueprint for solving problems. We'll focus primarily on the technical process of being a strategic planner in the following pages. But, an effective public relations campaign requires both strategic thinking and strategic planning. Public relations planners must combine science and art to create and communicate a tapestry of ideas and solutions.

Professor Anthony Fulginiti of Rowan University, a member of the College of Fellows with the Public Relations Society of America, writes that a public relations plan combines three activities—*learn, think* and *plan*.

Learning begins with a Situation Analysis where the strategic planner crafts a Real State assessment. The situation analysis is a methodical checklist that provides foundation for the problem at hand. The situation analysis must be rooted in research and written in a clear, concise manner that focuses on the issues, problems and challenges.

The situation analysis provides a professional, thought provoking critique. It must be research based and focused on audiences. Objectivity reigns supreme so strategic planners must use statistics and facts and avoid rhetoric. Often a SWOT analysis—Strengths, Weaknesses, Opportunities and Threats—provides a detailed, analytical method to identify important issues. The situation analysis or Real State Analysis offers the most authoritative, fact-based part of the plan. Its persuasive power comes from its research based content.

The learning phase of the plan must also include the research analysis. The research analysis contains all of the information and data you collected about the internal and external environments. The length of this section depends on the amount of research conducted and the complexity of the problems. The situation analysis provides details about internal and external contexts and includes any relevant secondary literature review.

Writers may include the following in crafting the situation analysis.

Internal Factors

▶ Statements of the organization's mission, charter, bylaws, history and structure.
▶ Biographical sketches and photos of key individuals.
▶ Detailed descriptions of programs, products, services, and ideas.
▶ Statistics about resources, budget, staffing and programs.
▶ Summaries of interviews with key personnel about the problem situation.
▶ Copies of policy statements and procedures related to the problem.
▶ Complete descriptions of how the organization currently handles the problem.

External Factors

▶ Clippings from secondary research sources.
▶ Reports from external vendors.
▶ Content analyses of media coverage.
▶ Lists and descriptions of individuals, groups and organizations that share similar problems.
▶ Lists of groups opposed to your position.
▶ Survey results.
▶ Lists of government agencies with the power to affect the problem.
▶ Copies of published research on topics related to the problem situation.

Despite our best efforts we often miss something in the data collection stage. So, planners often need to report assumptions. Writers must be careful to properly label these assumptions. If you must make assumptions, list them in detail.

The preliminary research should isolate the overriding problem, and determine consequences if you fail to act on the problem. The problem statement itself should be concise and very specific. Try to use 25 words or less and use standard subject-verb-object order. This will focus on the active voice and provide a forceful, crisp problem statement, critical to the plan's success. Mess up here and your plan goes off course. Identifying the wrong problems, or communicating these problems ineffectively, also dooms the plan for failure. So, get to the root of the problem and boldly state the problem in concrete language. Remember also to distinguish between attitudes and opinions in formulating your plan.

Attitudes, internal predisposition to act, arise from peoples' backgrounds, education and socialization. *Opinions,* outward expressions of attitudes, reflect our current state on an issue and can be more easily affected by communication. Your job is to distinguish between attitudes and objectives so you can later address realistic short- and long-term strategies to achieve objectives. Remember that clients may recognize that a problem exists, but unless they see a consequence with inaction or improper action, the client will find little value in the plan. Explain in one concise, declarative sentence the consequences and avoid any ambiguity.

PRactical TIP

Sample Situation Analysis

Overview

The Medford Christian School first opened its doors in 1950. MCS experienced steady enrollment increases, at a comfortable level, for most of its existence. Recently, though, MCS purchased a new elementary campus adding to its well-established upper campus.

Over the last eight years, MCS's total enrollment has decreased from more than 1,000 students at its upper campus in 2012 to 815 students currently enrolled in both its elementary and upper campuses. MCS hopes to increase enrollment at both campuses to 1,000 students. Currently, MCS relies on word-of-mouth marketing activities to attract students. In addition, MCS gets limited local media coverage for its athletic teams and school programs.

Of its 815 students, MCS reports only 285 students at its elementary campus—which houses pre-kindergarten through fifth grade. MCS's dwindling enrollment for its upper campus—grades six through 12, represents a dramatic decrease from years past.

MCS administration hopes to increase enrollment by 23 percent while maintaining its student-faculty ratio of 11-to-1.

Thinking refers to describing an Ideal State analysis. At this phase the writer must identify audiences, write messages and select channels. The Ideal State describes the purpose of the campaign. The writing in this phase differs from that in the learning phase because of its persuasive intent. Audience identification, vital to the campaign, insures that you have directed your message to the right people. Without identifying audiences you run the risk of crafting messages that miss the mark.

When crafting the plan, you must distinguish among publics, stakeholders and audiences. Publics, groups of people with similar interests, differ from stakeholders. Stakeholders are specific publics with a vested interest in the organization or individual. An audience is a public with whom you direct your communication toward.

Once you identify audiences, you need to craft messages that will achieve the desired result. You need to consider the following.

▶ Determining whom your message will affect.
▶ Identifying who you need to persuade.

▶ Enlisting the services of those whose cooperation is vital to your campaign's success.

▶ Reaching opinion leaders who will help deliver credible messages to your audiences.

▶ Selecting appropriate channels to reach identified audiences.

After identifying audiences you must then analyze how each segment acts or is likely to act toward the issue. This behavioral analysis takes the guessing out of the plan. It blends the artistic expression of the message with the psychological analysis of the audience. The purpose of the writing, therefore, is to persuade and this requires a different audience analysis. Writers should consider these tips when writing persuasive copy.

▶ Anticipate audience objections. By thoroughly researching audiences you can draft copy that addresses objections before the audience can express them.

▶ Stress rewards. Opinion formation results when the audience recognizes a reward for the behavioral change.

▶ Control the tone. Use the first person when you want to signal ownership. Use the second person when you want to signal familiarity. Use the third person when you want to signal objectivity.

▶ Be clear. Vague writing tends to alienate audiences and pushes them away from the message.

▶ Clinch your argument. Effective arguments have three phases: Purpose, Evidence, Clincher. The tighter the clincher, the stronger the argument.

 PRactical TIP

Sample Ideal State Analysis

Families who currently send their children to MCS must recognize that the school appreciates their support and needs their continued cooperation to increase enrollment. MCS must enlist their support as key communicators to reinforce their commitment to the school and to serve as agents to attract new families. MCS must communicate its standing as a premier private school that enjoys a reputation for academic and athletic excellence that reinforces Christian values. Enrollment will increase when families share their successes and feelings about the learning environment with prospective families.

Planning takes place after you have identified issues, audiences, messages, and channels. In drafting the plan you'll state a goal, fashion objectives, design strategies, select tactics, and evaluate effectiveness. The plan contains four action steps—Goals, Objectives, Strategies, and Tactics. Each part requires a variation of the writing process.

The Goal. The overarching ambition of the plan, the goal ambitiously states what you hope to accomplish. The goal must be stated in measurable terms.

> *Example:* Within three years increase enrollment at MCS by 23 percent by implementing a positive, social media based campaign.

Objectives. Objectives contain portions of your goal and tell readers "What" you have to accomplish. You need to logically divide your goal into carefully crafted, measurable objectives. Objectives represent the specific knowledge, opinion and behavioral outcomes to be achieved.

Effective objectives should be realistic, short and simple. They should support the organizational goals. They should specify a public and a time of accomplishment. And, they must specify task achievement in a measurable way.

> *Example:* Increase media coverage of MCS's athletic program by 35 percent over a one-year period.
>
> Increase public awareness of MCS's academic excellence by 40 percent within six months of implementing the social media campaign.

Strategies. Strategies provide the approach to achieve the objective. A strategy is partially "what" you need to do combined with a "how" you plan to do it. Imbedded in a strategy is a message. Strategies creatively connect audiences to messages.

> *Example:* Create a Twitter account among current MCS family members that will strengthen their school bond and compel them to share their association with like-minded members of the target audience.

Tactics. Tactics fulfill the ambition of the strategy. They connect audiences, messages and strategies in a specific way. When drafting tactics you should keep in mind ACT—Agent, Cost and Time. Who will do it? That's the agent. What will it Cost? When will it happen and how long will it take? That's the time.

> *Example:* Create an interactive Facebook page to promote upcoming events at MCS.

Creating Issues

Crafting issue statements affords the planner the opportunity to communicate the organization or situational real state. Planners must carefully develop an issue statement to reflect the current situation and avoid the tendency for purposive statements (to solve the problem). Issues should include audiences and, if correctly written, should lead to corresponding objectives.

Example

Real State
Bongo Athletic Attire Company, Inc. seeks a link between improved internal communication and decreased worker apathy.

Issues
- ▶ Unions encourage worker apathy.
- ▶ Upper management seeks to downside print communication employees find useful.
- ▶ Limited IT access creates a challenge for sales personnel.
- ▶ Upper management lacks understanding about the benefits of an employee recognition program.

From an analysis of the issues, the planner then develops a goal statement.

Goal
Increase worker motivation by improving internal communication to strengthen the relationship between management and employees.

Plan Components Checklist

The following plan components must be included in a comprehensive public relations plan.

- ▶ Situation analysis
- ▶ Research questions and actions
- ▶ Goal statement
- ▶ Plan outline
- ▶ Objective and objective copy
- ▶ Strategy and strategy/tactic copy
- ▶ Examples of tactics as they appear in text (sample blog, Facebook page, etc.)
- ▶ Gantt chart (graphic of time and tactics)

Sample Objective, Strategies and Tactics

The following example of elements of a plan pertains to the fictitious Battleship Columbia Museum and Memorial.

Example Objective Outline

Objective 3.0

Raise involvement among local residents and college students by 25 percent by the end of the plan about the Battleship Columbia Museum and Memorial services.

Strategy 3.1:   Develop an "Adopt the Battleship" advertising campaign to increase awareness by highlighting the BCMM's services.

    Tactic 3.1.1: Place newspaper advertisements.

    Tactic 3.1.2: Place billboard advertisements along highways leading to colleges and universities.

    Tactic 3.1.3: Place television advertisements on local stations and college stations.

    Tactic 3.1.4: Build a BCMM car to drive around local towns.

Strategy 3.2:   Create an electronic media campaign to increase college students' awareness of the BCMM.

Toolbox Tip

Brainstorming Can Bring a Deluge of Ideas

One of the best ways to gather tactics to accomplish the measurable objectives of a public relations campaign is to conduct a brainstorming session. This process involves the PR team to gather in an informal setting with a recorder. Ideas are given by members (and typed for overhead projection or printed on a whiteboard) without any evaluation or comments.

The goal is listing as many ideas as possible. Individuals may see a lousy idea but can build on it to create a more effective way of achieving objectives. In fact, brainstorming studies confirm that the best ideas often come near the end of a session. So those bad ideas initially proposed can get the creative juices flowing in others to tweak them into productive plans for a campaign's success.

Sample Objective Copy

Objective 1.0

Increase corporate sponsorship by 30 sponsors by the end of the plan.

Statement: The BCMM currently lacks an organized, dedicated sponsorship program for corporations, student organizations and classroom sponsors. By creating a dedicated sponsorship program, BCMM will improve the museum's visibility in the community while allowing social and service organizations to help those less fortunate and fulfill their service responsibilities.

Justification: Preliminary research identified several weaknesses in the current sponsorship program. The BCMM lacks a dedicated corporate sponsorship program to enhance its presence in the community. The BCMM needs sponsors to help raise its awareness among the target market and increase visibility in the community.

Behavior: Sponsors will see the benefit of the program and recognize that it will yield a return on investment for their organizations. Corporate sponsors will see that BCMM sponsorship benefits them by increasing their community exposure. Student and auxiliary groups will benefit by fulfilling their organizations' charter to do community service and satisfy their desire to positively impact the community.

Technique: BCMM will provide opportunities for sponsors to fulfill their philanthropic desires and contribute to community growth. By offering several levels of sponsorship, BCMM will provide a sponsorship program that meets the needs of a host of organizations.

Benefits: Establishing sponsorship opportunities will encourage prospective sponsors to take an active role in the BCMM and its mission. Furthermore, the sponsorship program will benefit both BCMM and the sponsor by strengthening the ties to the community.

Evaluation: BCMM will evaluate its success by conducting a quantitative study of community members, after full implementation of the plan, to measure their current level of awareness of BCMM. Furthermore, BCMM will conduct a qualitative study of sponsorships, through personal interviews, to assess their level of satisfaction with BCMM and their sponsorship.

Sample Strategy Copy

Issue: Local residents and college students appear unaware of BCMM's activities.

Objective 3.0: Raise involvement among local residents and college students by 25 percent by the end of the plan about the Battleship Columbia Museum and Memorial services.

Statement: According to research the BCMM's current advertising campaign fails to reach the target market, college students. By developing a target specific electronic media advertising campaign, BCMM will reach college students with a target specific message about its services.

▶ **Update website weekly:** BCMM will hire graphic designers to update and refresh its website. The website will provide a forum to highlight community and campus events. By designating someone with sole responsibility for updating the website, BCMM will insure its target market gets current, relevant information.

▶ **Create BCMM MySpace and Facebook pages:** Research shows that the target market frequently uses, and trusts, MySpace and Facebook for information. By creating a presence on these two credible sites, BCMM maximizes communication with the target market.

▶ **Produce and post live streaming video of events on the BCMM:** BCMM will create interest in daily events and special events by affording visitors to its website an opportunity to interact with it from a remote site.

Justification: Research shows that college students have limited knowledge of BCMM's activities; however, research indicates that these same college students have an interest in the type of activities hosted by BCMM. Consequently, BCMM currently uses no electronic media in its advertising campaign. In order to increase overall awareness by 25 percent, BCMM must develop target specific messages discriminated through a credible medium.

Benefits: BCMM benefits from this strategy by creating a strong, recognizable name among members of the college community. College students will want to take part in BCMM activities and help it accomplish its goals because they will feel a greater connection to the museum.

Proof: BCMM will conduct a survey at the conclusion of the implementation of the full plan to assess the anticipated increase in the level of awareness. An analysis of these responses will determine if BCMM reached its proposed 25 percent increase in involvement among the target market.

Summary

Writing the public relations plan is vital to the success of any campaign. It takes a specific formula to cover all the necessary ingredients. Carefully followed, a seemingly impossible campaign can be effectively pulled off.

Index

A

Abbreviations, 28
Abstract, 54
Active voice, 5, 6
Active *vs.* passive voice, 5
Ad components, 147–150
   audio, 149
   commercial, 149
   copy, 147
   headline, 147
   print ads, 147
   video, 149
Addresses, 28
Advertising copywriting, 139–158
   ad components, 147–150
   advocacy ads, 150
   cause-related marketing ads, 152, 153,
      154
   cooperative ads, 152
   house ads, 150
   institutional ads, 155
   mistakes to avoid, 149
   online advertising, 156–158
   public relations advertising, 141–146
   public relations *vs.* advertising, 140
   public service announcements (PSAs),
      155–156
Advertising Principles (Bergh and Katz),
   117, 144
Advocacy ads, 150
Advocacy/issue, 141

Agencies, and regulations, 185–186
Alcantara, Rick, 163
The American Dairy Council, 36
American Bar Association (ABA), 189
American Medical Association (AMA),
   189
The American Press Institute, 121
American Society of Newspaper Editors,
   120
Anecdote, 132, 133
Annual report writing, 52–53
AOL Instant Messenger, 77
Appendix, 54
AP style, 5, 26, 27–28, 70, 82
Arendt, Hannah, 87
Arora, Nikesh, 158
The Art and Craft of Feature Writing:
   Based on the Wall Street Journal
   Guide (Blundell), 130
Associated Press (AP), 13, 27, 119
The Associated Press Stylebook, 27
Association of Business Communicators
   (IABC), 102
Audience, 36–38, 171
   knowing, 36, 194
   targeting, 163
   types of, 36–38
Audience analysis, and persuasion,
   103–104
Audio, 87, 133
Audio, Gina, 158

B

Babbitt, Natalie, 119
Bae, Keunmin, 120
Baltimore Sun, 13
Bates v. State Bar of Arizona, 190
Bernays, Edward, 101, 176
Bernstein, Theodore, 42
Better Business Bureau (BBB), 189
Bigelow v. Virginia, 183
Bit.ly, 80
Blackstone, William, 179
Blank-screen syndrome, 129
Blogging/blogs, 63, 70, 87, 136, 137, 172
Blogosphere, 70
Blundell, William E., 130
*Board of Trustees of the State University of
    New York v. Fox*, 184
Boilerplate, 24
Brainstorming, 123, 198
Bread v. City of Alexandria, 182
Breaking news, rules for writing, 89–90
Bridges v. California, 182
Broadcast lead, characteristics, 90–92
Broadcast news, 88–95
    features *vs.* straight news, 93–94
    history of, 88
    news judgment, 93
    radio, 96–100
    story components, 92–93
    story organization, 92–93
    video news releases, 94–96
Brochures, 112
Buffet, Warren, 12
Bulwer-Lytton, Edward, 1
Burkley, Linda, 26
Business Week, 75
Business writing, 2, 6, 35–55
    audience, 36–38
    intranet copy, 66–67
    letters/emails, 46–52
    newsletter, 59–62
    readability, 39–43
    reports, 52–55
    structure, 43
    websites, 63
Buzz, creating, 171–173

C

Campaign writing, 8, 191–201
    brainstorming, 198
    creating issues, 196
    external factors, 193
    ideal state analysis, 195
    internal factors, 193
    plan components, 197
    plan elements, 192
    research, 191
    situation analysis, 194
Caps, 43
The Careful Writer, 42
Cause-related marketing, 142, 152
*Central Hudson Gas & Electric Corp. v.
    Public Service Commission of
    New York*, 183
Chaplinsky v. New Hampshire, 181
Chemerinsky, Erwin, 179
Children's Advertising Review Unit
    (CARU), 189
Chouteau, Garth, 75
Churchill, Winston, 159
Clarity, 3, 4, 39, 40, 41, 90
Clark, Roy Peter, 121
Clichés, 41, 42, 98
CNN, 12
Coherence, 2
Commercial speech, 182–183
Communication Briefings, 39, 59
Complex, as audience, 37
Concrete words, 3
Content-based laws, 180–182
Content-neutral laws, 180–182

Content neutral *vs.* content specific, 180
Cooperative ads, 152
Copyright, 187–189
Copywriting, 7
Council of Better Business Bureau, 189
Cover page, 53
Creative Advertising (Moriarty), 147
Creative brief, 146
Credibility, 107, 139, 140
Crescenzo, Steve, 14
Cross-trained writer, 13
Cuellar, Jesus Hernandez, 120
Curley, Tom, 27
Cutshaw, Lise, 30

D

The Daily Beast, 12
Design, 58–59
Dietrich, Gini, 134
Dillard, James Price, 120
Direct Mail and Mail Order Handbook
    (Hodgson), 115
Direct mail letters, 115–117
Direct request email, 46, 47
Direct request letter, 46, 47
Discussion boards, 63
Dorsey, Jack, 77
DuBay, William, 26
Dusenberry, Philip, 139

E

Economy of words, 39, 40, 41
Editorial letters, 108–110
Electronic media, 87–100
Electronic press kit (EPK), 89
Elsasser, John, 140
Email abuse, 187
Email format, 44, 46
    direct request, 46
    good news, 50

informative, 47, 48
persuasive, 48
E-newsletter, 62–65
Exaggeration, 131
Executive, as audience, 37
Executive summary, 54
Expert, as audience, 36
Expert/executive, 37
Experts *vs.* bottom liners, 36
Expert/user, 37

F

Facebook, 70, 73, 74, 74–76
    branding on, 74, 75
    mistakes to avoid, 76
    tips for writing posts, 75
The Facebook PR Handbook, 74
*The Face-to-Face Book: Why Real
    Relationships Rule in a Digital
    Marketplace* (Keller & Fay), 74
Fact sheet, 32–33
False and deceptive advertising, 184–185
Farnsworth, Steve, 160
Fay, Brad, 74
Features, elements of, 94
Feature stories *vs.* straight news, 93–94
Feature writing, 7, 119–138
    brainstorming, 123
    ideas for, 126–127
    mat release, 124
    and nut graphs, 132–133
    research for, 129–132
    sidebars, 127
    tips for pitching ideas, 134–138
    types of features, 123
    and writer's block, 128–129
Federal Communication Commission
    (FCC), 97
First Amendment, 179, 182, 190
First degree writing, 3

First National Bank of Boston v. Bellotti,
   183
Fleming, Grace, 109
Florida Bar v. Went for It, Inc., 190
Format, speech, 166–167
Formula writing, 14
Frauenfelder, Mark, 75
Free-flow writing, 129
Free speech. *See* First Amendment
Friedman v. Rogers, 190
Fulginiti, Anthony, 192

G

Gates, Bill, 175
Gavin, Martin, 75, 76
Gettysburg Address, 159, 174
Ghostwriter, 160, 167, 171
Gillespie, Jack, 2, 63, 139
Global communication, 69
Good news email, 50
Good newsletter, 50
Google+, 70, 73, 81–82
   tips for business page, 81–82
Google Alerts, 74
Graphics, 150

H

Hall, Kermit L., 181
Hall, Steve, 75
Hampton, Chris, 156
Hard news leads, 91
Hauge, Michael, 122
Henry, Rene, 140
Hindes, Andrew, 120
Hines, Stephanie, 69
Hodgson, Richard S., 115
Holtje, Jim, 160

Holtjie, Jim, 160
House ads, 150
HTML, 62
Huffington Post, 75

I

Iacocca, Lee, 57
Ideal state analysis, 194, 195
   sample, 195
Illustration, 147
Imagery, 131
Inalienable rights, 179
Inflammatory language, 177
Informative email, 48
Informative letter, 47–48
Instagram, 73
Institutional ads, 155
Internet, 63–67, 69. *See also* Electronic
      media; Social media
   E-newsletters, 59–63
   and newspapers, 12
   three PR rules to follow, 73–74
Intranet copy, 66–67
   actionable content, 67
   comprehensive coverage (data), 66
   fragments, 66, 67
   nonlinear, 66
   pursuit of actionable content, 66
   reader-driven, 66
Investigative journalism, 93
Italics, 42, 43

J

Jargon, 41, 42, 98
Jefferson, Thomas, 11
Journalistic mindset, 24–25, 29
   eight basic steps in, 4–5

K

Keller, Ed, 74
Kent, Christine, 173
Kiley, David, 75, 76
King, Martin Luther, Jr., 159
Kuraoka, John, 115
Kurtz, Howard, 12

L

Lauterborn, Dave, 136
Law, and PR writing, 8
Law for PR writing, 175–190
    commercial speech, 182–184
    content neutral *vs.* content specific, 180
    copyright, 187–189
    and electronic communication, 175–176
    Email abuse, 187
    false and deceptive advertising, 184–186
    and the First Amendment, 179
    inflammatory language, 177
    and lack of expertise, 178
    and lawsuits, 178
    puffery, 187
    and rumors, 177
    and solicitation of clients, 190
    and speculation, 178
Lawsuits, 176, 178
Layout and design, 59
Layperson, as audience, 36
Layperson/executive, 37
Layperson/user, 38
Lead, characteristics of, 90–92
Lee, Ivy, 11, 101
Letter, 44–52
    direct request, 46, 47
    example of, 45

format, 44
good news, 50
heading, 44
informative, 47–48
negative message, 50–51
persuasive, 48–49
Lighting, 150
Lincoln, Abraham, 101, 159
LinkedIn, 70, 73, 82–83
List of works cited, 54
Logo, 147

M

MAC triad, 139
Manners, electronic, 66, 73
Martin v. City of Struthers, 182
"Maximizing the Value of Your News: From Twitter to Google," 12
Maxwell, John C., 164
McDonald's, 7, 69, 70
McIntyre, John, 13
McLuhan, Marshall, 70
McNeill, Christi Day, 75
"Me" attitude, 43
Media advisory, or alert, 18–19
Media kits, 30–33
    contents, 31–32
Media relations, 29–30
MediaStudios.ca, 119
Media writing, 4–6
    identifying newsworthy information in, 4–5
Mendelson, B.J., 70
Message, five levels for successful, 4
Metaphor, 131
Misspellings, 25
Mixed audience, 38
Moriarty, Sandra, 147

N

Nader, Ralph, 36
National Advertising Division (NAD), 189
National Advertising review Board
    (NARB), 189
Negative message letter, 50–52
Negative writing, 42
Netiquette, 66, 73
Newman, Paul, 142
News features, rules for writing, 89–90
News judgment, 93
Newsletter
    components, 60, 61
    design issues with, 58–59
    steps for writing, 62
    writing copy for, 59–62
Newson, Earl, 102
Newson's theory of persuasion, 102
Newspaper Association of America, 12
News release disaster, 15–18
News story construction, 5
The New York Times, 110
New York Times v. Sullivan, 183
Nielsen, Jack, 66
Noun and adjective stacks, 42, 42–43
Numbers, 28
Nut graph, 132

O

*Obit: Inspiring Stories of Ordinary People
    Who Led Extraordinary Lives*
    (Sheeler), 124
Objective copy, 199
Objective outline, 198
Odell, Rebecca, 83
Ogilvy, David, 117, 122
Oliver, Mary Beth, 120
Online advertising, 156
Online Journalism Review, 63
Op-eds, 108–110, 112

P

Pachter, Barbara, 66
Pacing, 150
Passive voice, 5, 6, 42
Perloff, Susan, 66
Personification, 131
Persuasion theory, 102
Persuasive email, 48
Persuasive letter, 48–49
Persuasive writing, 2, 7, 101–117
    audience analysis, 103–104
    brochure copy, 114–115
    brochures, 112–114
    credibility in, 107
    direct-mail letters, 115–117
    editorial letters, 108–109
    Newson's theory of persuasion, 102
    op-ed pieces, 109–110
    persuasion theory, 102
    pitch letters, 104, 105
Petersen, Deborah, 125
Philadelphia Business Journal, 66
Phillips, Brad, 164
Phrases to avoid, 41
Pink ribbon (breast cancer campaign),
    70, 71
Pinterest, 70, 83–84
Pitching, 134–138
Pitch letters, 104, 105
Plan/planner, 191
elements of plan, 192, 197
Pluth, Lisa, 83
Police Department of Chicago v. Mosely,
    180
Political Communication, 110
Poor writing, 14
Porter, Jeremy, 70
Position papers, 106–107
Postscripts, 43
PowerPoint problems, 169
The Practice of Public Relations (Seitel), 11

Print ads, 147
Print media, 5, 11–34
    common problems in releases, 16–17
    magazines, 12
    newspapers, 12
    and PR writing, 11, 12–13
    websites and, 12
Print *vs.* web writing, 66
Problem/issue, 107
ProCopyTips, 62
Product placement, 142
Proofreading, 25–26
Props, 150
Public relations, *vs.* advertising, 140
Publicity, 170–171
Public relations (PR)
    advertising, 141
    campaign writing in, 8
    importance of writing in, 11
    law, 8
    persuasive writing in, 7
    and print media, 11
    and social media, 7
Public Relations Society of America
       Member Code of Ethics, 101
Public Relations Society of America
       (PRSA), 14, 102
Public Relations Tactics, 31
Public Service Announcements (PSAs), 7,
    97, 157
Puffery, 187
Punctuation, 28

Q

Q & A sessions, 168–170

R

Radio, 87, 96–100, 136–137
    sample news release, 100
    script, 97

    writing for, 96–97
    writing guidelines, 97–99
Radio Advertising Bureau, 136
Ramirez, Courtney, 70, 72
R.A.V. v. City of St. Paul, 181
Readability, 39–43
    tips for, 41–43
Recalls, 176
Regulation agencies, 185–186
Release
    effective, 19–21
    poorly written, 15–17
    regulations for, 19–21
    sample of effective, 22
    writing leads in, 21
Report writing, 52–55
    abstract, 54
    annual, 52–53
    appendix, 54
    cover page, 53
    executive summary, 54
    letter of transmittal, 53
    list of works cited, 54
    table of charts and graphs, 54
    table of contents, 54
    technical, 54–55
    title page, 53
Research, 129–132, 162–166, 192, 193, 198
Robbins, Jenna Rose, 73, 74
Roosevelt, Franklin D., 173
Rothschild, William E., 191

S

Salisbury, Harrison, 110
Sandberg, Sheryl, 74
Schwartzman, Eric, 31
Search Engine Optimization (SEO), 81,
    158
Secondary meaning, in trademark law,
    188–189
Second degree writing, 3

The Secretary's Letter, 41
Securities and Exchange Commission
   (SEC), 52
Seitel, Fraser P., 11, 144
Self-regulation, and consumer
   advocacy, 189
Serialization, 58
Service mark, 188
Shankman, Peter, 88, 89
Shapero v. Kentucky Bar Association, 190
Sheeler, Jim, 124, 125
Sidebars, 127
Simile, 131
Simmons, Annette, 122
Sims, Elizabeth, 119
Situation analysis, 192, 194
   crafting, 193
   sample, 194
Skills, in writing, 3–4
Sklar, Rachel, 75
Social media, 7, 69–85
   and boring content, 72
   Facebook, 74–76
   Google+, 81–82
   and lack of planning, 72
   LinkedIn, 82–83
   most popular, 70–72
   and over-selling, 70, 72
   Pinterest, 83–84
   and print media, 12
   and PR writing, 7
   six "C's" tips, 72
   Twitter, 77–80
Social Media is B.S. (Mendelson), 70
Soft news leads, 92
Speech writing, 8, 159–174
   3 distinct presentation receivers,
      170–171
   5 ways to begin a speech, 164–165

   format, 166–167
   length of speech, 173–174
   PowerPoint problems, 169
   Q & A sessions, 168–170
Spellchecker, 25, 27
Spokesperson, 165
Srategy. *See also* Strategic writing
Standard Oil Co. v. United States, 184
Starr, Doug, 160, 172
Stevenson, Adlai E., 175
Stone, Biz, 77
Storyboards, 149
Straightforwardness, 39, 40–41
Strategic *vs.* creative process, 4
Strategic writing, 1–4
Strategic writing process, 4
Strategy, 1–4
Strategy copy, 200
Structure, 43–44
Subject, 6
Subject lines, 43
Subject-verb-object (S-V-O), 40–41
Subliminal appeals, 187
Summary leads, 91
Suspended interest leads, 92
SWOT (Strengths, Weaknesses,
   Opportunities and Threats)
   analysis, 192

T

Table of charts and graphs, 54
Table of contents, 54
Tagline, 147
Tamul, Daniel, 120
Technical report writing, 54–55
Television, 87
Television journalist, 88
Tennant, Kyle, 70

Text message services, 77
Third-degree writing, 3
"Three Cardinal Sins of Social Media
    Writing" (Ramirez), 70, 72
Thumbnail sketches, 149
Title page, 53
Tools, 1
Trademark, 187–189
Traditional letter form, 44
    sample of, 45
Traditional media, 13. *See also* Print
    media
Transition, 3
Transmittal letter, 53
Traphagen, Mark, 81
Turner, Jamie, 114
Twain, Mark, 35, 159
Twitter, 70, 73, 76, 77–80, 137
    bio, 77–78
    gaining followers, 78–80
    retweets, 79–80
    targeted audience, 77
    tweet tips, 78
Twitterholics, 77

U

*Unfriend Yourself: Three Days to Detox,
    Discern and Decide About Social
    Media* (Tennant), 70
United States v. American Tobacco Co., 184
Unity, 2
USA Today, 83, 133
User, as audience, 37

V

Valentine v. Chrestensen, 182
Vatican, 11
Verb, 6
Video, 87, 133
Video news release (VNR), 88–89, 94–96
    sample, 95–96
*Virginia State Board of Pharmacy v.
    Virginia Citizens Consumer
    Council*, 183

W

Washington Examiner, 75
The Washington Post, 110
The Weather Channel, 12
Web. *See* Internet
White papers, 106–107
Wiki, Wikipedia, 63, 129
Williams, Evan, 77
Williams, Roy H., 149
Writer's block, 128–129
Writer's Digest, 119
The Writer's Market, 137
On Writing Well, 42

Y

YouTube, 89, 158
You *vs.* me attitude, 38

Z

Zinsser, William, 42
Zuk, Ryan, 137